TOP `10`
ROME

REID BRAMBLETT &
JEFFREY KENNEDY

EYEWITNESS TRAVEL

Left **Palatine Hill** Right **Piazza Navona**

LONDON, NEW YORK,
MELBOURNE, MUNICH AND DELHI
www.dk.com

Produced by Sargasso Media Ltd, London

Reproduced by Colourscan, Singapore
Printed and bound in China by
Leo Paper Products Ltd

First American Edition 2002
08 09 10 9 8 7 6 8 4 3 2 1

Published in the United States by DK
Publishing, Inc., 375 Hudson Street, New
York, New York 10014

**Copyright 2002, 2008 © Dorling
Kindersley Limited, London**

**Reprinted with revisions 2003, 2004,
2006, 2007, 2008**

ISSN: 1479-344X
ISBN: 978-0-75662-398-2

Within each Top 10 list in this book, no
hierarchy of quality or popularity is implied.
All 10 are, in the editor's opinion, of
roughly equal merit.

Floors are referred to throughout in
accordance with British usage; ie the "first
floor" is the floor above ground level.

Contents

Rome's Top 10

Vatican City	8
The Pantheon	14
Roman Forum	16
Galleria Borghese	20
The Colosseum & Imperial Fora	22
Musei Capitolini	24
Museo Nazionale Romano	28
Santa Maria del Popolo	32
San Clemente	34
Ostia Antica	36
Moments in History	38
Ancient Sights	40
Museums & Galleries	42
Churches	44
Squares & Fountains	46
Masterpieces	48
Palazzi	50

The information in this DK Eyewitness Top 10 Travel Guide is checked regularly.
Every effort has been made to ensure that this book is as up-to-date as possible at the time of
going to press. Some details, however, such as telephone numbers, opening hours, prices,
gallery hanging arrangements and travel information are liable to change. The publishers
cannot accept responsibility for any consequences arising from the use of this book, nor for
any material on third party websites, and cannot guarantee that any website address in this
book will be a suitable source of travel information. We value the views and suggestions of
our readers very highly. Please write to: Publisher, DK Eyewitness Travel Guides,
Dorling Kindersley, 80 Strand, London, Great Britain WC2R 0RL.

Cover: Front **DK Images** Mike Dunning clb; **Hemispheres Images** Pawel Wysocki main. Spine **DK Images** John
Heseltine b. Back **DK Images** cr; Mike Dunning c, cl.

Left **Rome rooftops** Right **Campidoglio at night**

Underground Sights	52
Hidden Rome	54
Writers in Rome	56
Cinecittà Films	58
Romantic Spots	60
Green Spaces	62
Rome for Children	64
Festivals	66
Shopping Streets	68
Cafés & Gelaterie	70
Pizzerias	72
Restaurants	74
Roman Dishes	76
Pubs and Bars	78

Around Town

Around Piazza Navona	82
Around the Pantheon	90
Campo de' Fiori to the Capitoline	98
The Spanish Steps & Villa Borghese	110
Ancient Rome	118
The Esquiline & Lateran	126
The Quirinal & Via Veneto	132
Trastevere & Prati	138
Beyond the City Walls	150

Streetsmart

Practical Information	158
Places to Stay	172
General Index	180

Left **Interior, the Pantheon** Right **Trinità dei Monti church**

As a guide to abbreviations in visitor information blocks: Adm = admission charge; DA = disabled access; D = dinner; L = lunch

ROME'S TOP 10

Rome's Highlights
6–7

Vatican City
8–13

The Pantheon
14–15

Roman Forum
16–19

Galleria Borghese
20–21

The Colosseum and
Imperial Fora
22–23

Musei Capitolini
24–27

Museo Nazionale
Romano
28–31

Santa Maria del Popolo
32–33

San Clemente
34–35

Ostia Antica
36–37

Top Ten of Everything
38–79

🔟 Rome Highlights

Although functioning as a vibrant, modern capital akin to any in Europe, the unique appeal of Rome is that the entire city is a vast, 3,000-year-old, indoor-outdoor museum. In every quarter you'll find ancient monuments, art treasures and timeless architecture in churches, galleries and protected ruins. Home to the world's smallest city, the Vatican, Rome has religion at its heart and history in its soul – a city that dazzles and inspires visitors time and time again.

Vatican City
This tiny city-state is home to the Pope, the world's greatest museum, largest church, and the most astounding work of art ever created – Michelangelo's Sistine Chapel ceiling *(see pp8–13).*

2 The Pantheon
The most perfectly preserved of all ancient temples, this marvel of architectural engineering has a giant oculus forever open to the sky *(see pp14–15).*

3 Roman Forum
At the once-bustling heart of ancient political, judicial and commercial power, there's now an evocative emptiness, punctuated by grandiose arches, solitary columns and carved rubble *(see pp16–19).*

Galleria Borghese 4
A stunningly beautiful pleasure-palace, this was the vision of an immensely rich, hedonistic papal nephew, who filled it with Graeco-Roman, Renaissance and Baroque works by the greatest masters *(see pp20–21).*

Map labels: Prati, Città del Vaticano, Giardini Vaticani, PIAZZA S. PIETRO, Borgo, VIA D. CONCILIAZIONE, VIA LEONE IV, VIA COLA DI RIENZO, VIA CRESCENZIO, Ponte, Parione, Gianicolo, Trastevere, LUNGOT. TOR DI NONA, CORSO VITTORIO, VIA GIULIA, LUNGOT. DEI TEBALDI, VIA D. PORTA CAVALLEGGERI, GALLERIA PRINCIPE AMEDEO SAVOIA AOSTA, LUNGOT. GIANICOLENSE, VIA DI SANGALLO, LUNGOTEVERE D. FARNESINA, VIA G. CARDUCCI, Fiume Tevere, LUNGOT MICHELANGELO, CAMPO DE' FIO

600 — yards ┐0┌ metres — 600

20km
🔟

7 Museo Nazionale Romano

These collections, housed at two sites, feature some of the world's finest ancient art, including Classical sculpture and stunning mosaics (see pp28–31).

5 Colosseum and Imperial Fora

Imperial Rome constructed many impressive monuments, including the spectacular amphitheatre (see pp22–3).

8 Santa Maria del Popolo

Built over emperors' tombs, this church offers one of Rome's richest displays of Renaissance and Baroque art, including masterpieces by Pinturicchio, Raphael, Caravaggio and Bernini (see pp32–3).

9 San Clemente

With its mysterious passages and legends, this fascinating church provides first-hand experience of the layers that comprise Rome; here you can descend to a depth of 18m (60 ft) and go back over 2,000 years (see pp34–5).

Musei Capitolini 6

At the ancient centre of religious Rome are found some of the world's greatest masterpieces, from 4th-century BC Greek sculptures to Caravaggio's revolutionary – even scandalous – paintings (see pp24–7).

10 Ostia Antica

Extending over several square kilometres, the remarkable ruins of ancient Rome's main port city hold many surprises and convey a powerful sense of everyday Imperial life (see pp36–7).

🔟 Vatican City

The Vatican is the world's smallest nation, covering just 50 ha (120 acres), and is a theocracy of just over 550 citizens, headed by the Pope, but its sightseeing complex is beyond compare. Within its wall are the ornate St Peter's Basilica (see pp12–13), the astonishing Sistine Chapel (see pp10–11), lush gardens, apartments frescoed by Fra' Angelico, Raphael and Pinturicchio, and some 10 museums. The latter, detailed on these pages, include collections of Egyptian, Greek, Etruscan and Roman antiquities; Paleochristian, Renaissance and modern art; and a world-class ethnographic collection.

Vatican courtyard

🍴 There is a café inside the Vatican Museums although it is often crowded.

🕊 When in town, the Pope gives a mass audience on Wednesday mornings. You must book the free tickets in advance through the Prefecture of the Papal Household (Fax 06 6988 5863).

• Map B2
• www.vaticano.va
• Museums and Sistine Chapel: Viale Vaticano, 06 6988 3333; Open 8:45am–12:20pm, 1-4:45pm Mon-Fri, 8:45am-12:20pm Sat and last Sun of month, closed 8 & 25 Dec, 1 & 6 Jan, 11 Feb; Adm €12.00 (€8.00 students under 26); DA (partial).
• St Peter's Basilica: Piazza S Pietro; 06 6988 1662; Open Jan–Mar & Nov–Dec: 7am-7pm daily, Apr–Oct: 7am-6pm daily; Free (basilica); Adm €5.00 (treasury) & €7.00 (dome).

Top 10 Features

1. Sistine Chapel
2. Raphael Rooms
3. Apollo Belvedere
4. Raphael's *Transfiguration*
5. Chapel of Nicholas V
6. Laocoön
7. Caravaggio's *Deposition*
8. Borgia Apartments
9. Belvedere Torso
10. Leonardo da Vinci's *St Jerome*

Sistine Chapel
Michelangelo's ceiling *(right)* is one of the most spectacular works of art in the world *(see pp10–11)*.

Raphael Rooms
Raphael decorated Julius II's apartments between 1508 and 1520. The Stanza della Segnatura features the School of Athens, a convention of ancient philosophers bearing portraits of Renaissance artists such as Leonardo da Vinci as bearded Plato in the centre.

Apollo Belvedere
This Roman copy of a 4th-century BC Greek statue *(left)* is considered a model of physical beauty. It inspired Bernini's *Apollo* in Galleria Borghese *(see pp20–21)*.

Raphael's Transfiguration

Raphael was labouring on this gargantuan masterpiece (1517–20) when he died at 37, leaving students to finish the base. It depicts Christ appearing to the Apostles in divine glory *(below)*.

Chapel of Nicholas V

The Vatican's hidden gem is this closet-sized chapel colourfully frescoed (1447–50) with early martyrs by Fra' Angelico.

Plan of Vatican City

Caravaggio's Deposition

Caravaggio's *chiaroscuro* technique accentuates a diagonal composition (1604) filled with peasant figures and grisly realism.

Belvedere Torso

The highly crafted, bulging muscles of this 1st-century BC torso of the god Hercules were regularly used as a prime sketching model for Michelangelo and many other Renaissance masters.

Borgia Apartments

Pope Alexander VI had these beautiful rooms frescoed by Pinturicchio (Raphael was once his junior collaborator) between 1492 and 1495. The walls are now hung with lesser pieces from the Modern Art collection.

Leonardo da Vinci's St Jerome

Sketchy and unfinished – Leonardo was often a distracted genius – this 1482 painting is nevertheless an anatomical masterpiece.

Museum Guide

The Vatican Museums (a 15-minute walk around the Vatican walls from St Peter's) are made up of 10 collections plus the Sistine Chapel and papal apartments. To see highlights only, first visit the Pinacoteca, to the right of the entrance turnstile. The Sistine and other collections are to the left.

Laocoön

One of antiquity's most famous sculptures *(right)* is this 1st-century AD Trojan prophet and his sons being strangled by serpents as they try to warn against the besieging Greeks' sneaky gift horse.

Left **Adam and Eve** Right **Ezekiel, Prophets**

Sistine Chapel Works

Adam and Eve
God imparts the spark of life to Adam in one of western art's most famous scenes, then pulls Eve from Adam's rib.

Creation
God separates darkness from light, water from land and creates the Sun and Moon. Michelangelo veers towards blasphemy by depicting God's dirty feet.

The Sacrifice, Flood, and Drunkenness of Noah
After disassembling his scaffolding and gazing from floor level, Michelangelo noticed that these three tumultuous scenes were too minutely drawn.

Last Judgment
This vast work identifies saints by their medieval icons: Catharine with her wheel, Bartholomew with the knife which flayed him.

Sibyls and Prophets
Hebrew prophets, including Jonah shying away from the whale, mingle with the Sibyls who foretold Christ's coming.

Old Testament Salvation Scenes and Ancestors of Christ
Portraits from Jesus's family tree are above the windows, and bloody Salvation scenes, including David and Goliath, are on corner spandrels.

Plan of the Sistine Chapel

Life of Christ Scenes
The chapel's right wall stars Botticelli's *Cleansing of the Leper*, Ghirlandaio's *Calling of Peter and Andrew*, as well as Perugino's work below.

Giving the Keys to St Peter
Classical buildings form the backdrop to this pivotal scene of transferring power from Christ to the popes. Each scene is divided into three parts.

Life of Moses Scenes
Left wall highlights include Botticelli's *Burning Bush* and Signorelli and della Gatta's *Moses Giving his Rod to Joshua*.

Botticelli's Punishment of the Rebels
Schismatics question Aaron's priestly prerogative to burn incense. A vengeful Moses opens the earth to swallow them.

For more Roman masterpieces **See pp48–9**

Top 10 Painters of the Sistine Chapel

1 Michelangelo (1475–1564)

2 Perugino (1450–1523)

3 Sandro Botticelli (1445–1510)

4 Domenico Ghirlandaio (c.1449–94)

5 Luca Signorelli (c.1450–1523)

6 Rosselli (1439–1507)

7 Fra Diamante (1430–98)

8 Pinturicchio (1454–1513)

9 Piero di Cosimo (1462–1521)

10 Bartolomeo della Gatta (1448–1502)

Understanding the Sistine Chapel Art

The Sistine's frescoes are not merely decorations by some of the greatest Renaissance artists – the images tell a story and make a complex theological argument. Pope Sixtus IV commissioned wall frescoes for the Pope's Chapel in 1481–83. They were intended to underscore papal authority, in question at the time, by drawing a line of power from God to the pope. In the Life of Moses cycle, Moses' and Aaron's undisputed roles as God's chosen representatives are affirmed by the fate of those who oppose Aaron – significantly and anachronistically wearing a papal hat – in the Punishment of the Rebels. *Directly across from this work, Perugino's* Giving the Keys to St Peter *bridges the Old Testament with the New as Christ hands control of the church to St Peter – and therefore to his successors, the popes (who are pictured between the Sistine windows). Michelangelo's ceiling (1508–12) later added Genesis, Redemption and Salvation to the story.*

Original Sin
Part of Michelangelo's Genesis cycle shows Adam and Eve being expelled from Paradise for eating the forbidden fruit from the Tree of Knowledge.

The Life of Moses, Sandro Botticelli

Left **The Dome** Right **Baldacchino**

Rome's Top 10

🔟 Features of St Peter's Basilica

1 Pietà
Michelangelo carved this masterpiece *(see p48)* in 1499 at the age of 25. It is at once graceful and mournful, stately and ethereal. It has been protected by glass since 1972, when a man screaming "I am Jesus Christ!" attacked it with a hammer, damaging the Virgin's nose and fingers.

2 The Dome
When Michelangelo designed a dome to span St Peter's massive transept, he made it 42 m (138 ft) in diameter, in deference to the Pantheon's 43.3-m (142-ft) dome. You can ride an elevator much of the way, but must still navigate the final 330 stairs between the dome's inner and outer shell to the 132-m-high (435-ft) lantern and sweeping vistas across the city.

3 Piazza San Pietro
Bernini's remarkable semi-elliptical colonnades transformed the basilica's approach into a pair of welcoming arms embracing the faithful *(see p46)*. Sadly, the full effect of entering the square from a warren of medieval streets was spoiled when Mussolini razed the neighbourhood to lay down pompous Via della Conciliazione. The obelisk came from Alexandria.

4 Baldacchino
Whether you view it as ostentatious or glorious, Bernini's huge altar canopy is at least impressive. Its spiralling bronze columns are claimed to have been made from the revetments (portico ceiling decorations) of the Pantheon *(see p14)*, taken by Pope Urban VIII. For his desecration of the ancient temple the Barberini pope and his family *(see p51)* were castigated with the waggish quip: "What even the barbarians wouldn't do, Barberini did."

5 Statue of St Peter
A holdover from the medieval St Peter's, this 13th-century bronze statue by the sculptor Arnolfo di Cambio has achieved holy status. The faithful can be seen lining up to rub (or kiss) Peter's well-worn foot for luck.

Michelangelo's Pietà

Treasury

Among the ecclesiastical treasures here is a 6th-century, jewel-encrusted bronze cross (the Crux Vaticana), various fragments of the medieval basilica including a ciborium by Donatello (1432), and Antonio Pollaiuolo's masterful bronze slab tomb (1493) for Sixtus IV, the pope's effigy surrounded by representations of theological virtues and liberal arts.

Alexander VII's Monument

Apse

Bernini's exuberantly Baroque stained-glass window (1666) centres on a dove representing the Holy Ghost, surrounded by rays of the sun and a riot of sculptural details. Beneath the window sits the Chair of St Peter (1665), another Bernini concoction; inside is a wood and ivory chair said to be the actual throne of St Peter. Bernini also crafted the multicoloured marble *Monument to Urban VIII* (1644) to the right, based on Michelangelo's Medici tombs in Florence. It is of far better artistic quality than Giuglielmo della Porta's similar one for Pope Paul III (1549) to the left.

Plan of St Peter's Basilica

Crypt

Many of the medieval basilica's monuments are housed beneath the basilica's floor. During excavations in the 1940s workers discovered in the Necropolis the legendary Red Wall behind which St Peter was supposedly buried. The wall was covered with early medieval graffiti invoking the saint, and a box of bones was found behind it. The late Pope John Paul II is buried in the crypt.

Alexander VII's Monument

One of Bernini's last works (1678) shows figures of Justice, Truth, Chastity and Prudence gazing up at the pontiff seated in the deep shadows of the niche. A skeleton crawls from under the flowing marble drapery to hold aloft an hourglass as a reminder of mortality.

Central Piers

Until modern times, a church was measured by its relics. St Peter's Basilica houses the spear of St Longinius, which jabbed Jesus's side on the Cross, St Veronica's handkerchief bearing Christ's face, and a fragment of the True Cross.

🔟 The Pantheon

When Emperor Phocas donated this pagan temple to Pope Boniface IV in 608, he unwittingly ensured that one of the marvels of ancient Rome would be preserved, virtually unaltered, in its new guise as the Christian church Santa Maria ad Martyres. Emperor Hadrian, an amateur architect, designed this lovely structure in AD 118–125. It has been lightly sacked over the ages – barbarians took portable pieces, Constans II stole its gilded roof tiles and, in 1625, Urban VIII melted down the portico's bronze ceiling panels to make cannon for Castel Sant' Angelo. Yet the airy interior and perfect proportions remain, a wonder of the world even in its own time.

Agrippa inscription, Pantheon façade

🍴 There's a good gelateria, Cremeria Monforte, on the Pantheon's right flank, and an excellent coffee shop, La Tazza d'Oro, just off the square *(see p71)*.

🌂 Rather than bemoan a rainy day in Rome, scurry to the Pantheon to watch the water fall gracefully though the oculus and spatter against the marble floor and down a drain. Snowfalls are even better.

- Piazza della Rotonda
- Map M3
- Open 8:30am–7:30pm Mon–Sat, 9am–6pm Sun (9am–1pm during hols); Mass: 5pm Sat & 10:30am Sun
- Free

Top 10 Features

1. Dome
2. Oculus
3. Portico
4. Doors
5. Walls
6. Royal Tombs
7. Raphael's Tomb
8. Fountain
9. Marble Decorations
10. Basilica of Neptune Remains

Dome
The widest masonry dome in Europe *(above)* is precisely as high as it is wide: 43.3 m (142 ft). Its airy, coffered space, cleverly shot through with a shaft of sunlight from the oculus, is what lends the Pantheon an ethereal air.

Oculus
The bold, 8.3 m-diameter (27-ft) hole at the dome's centre provides light and structural support: the tension around its ring helps hold the weight of the dome.

Portico
The triangular pediment *(below)* is supported by 16 pink and grey granite columns, all original save the three on the left (17th-century copies).

Doors
The massive bronze doors *(right)* are technically original, but were so extensively renovated under Pius IV (1653) they have been practically recast.

Walls
The 6.2-m (20-ft) thick walls incorporate built-in brick arches to help distribute the weight downwards, relieving the stress of the heavy roof.

Royal Tombs
Two of Italy's kings are honoured by simple tombs. Vittorio Emanuele II (1861–78) unified Italy and became its first king. His son, Umberto I, was assassinated in 1900.

Raphael's Tomb
Raphael, darling of the Roman Renaissance art world but dead at 37, rests in a plain, ancient stone sarcophagus. Poet Bembo's Latin epitaph translates as: "Here lies Raphael, whom Nature feared would outdo her while alive, but now that he is gone fears she, too, will die." Other artists buried here include Baldassare Peruzzi.

Fountain
Giacomo della Porta designed this stoop *(below)* Leonardo Sormani carved it in 1575. The Egyptian obelisk of Rameses II was added in 1711.

Marble Decorations
Red porphyry, giallo antico, and other ancient marbles grace the interior. More than half the polychrome panels cladding the walls are original, the rest careful reproductions, as is the floor *(below)*.

Basilica of Neptune Remains
Of the Pantheon's old neighbour, all that remains are an elaborate cornice and fluted columns against the Pantheon's rear wall.

The First Pantheon
Emperor Augustus's son-in-law, Marcus Agrippa, built the first Pantheon in 27 BC, replaced in AD 118–125 by Hadrian's rotunda. The pediment's inscription "*M. Agrippa cos tertium fecit*" ("M. Agrippa made this") was Hadrian's modest way of honouring Agrippa. The pediment also provided the illusion of a smaller temple, making the massive space inside even more of a surprise (the Pantheon was originally raised and you couldn't see the dome behind). Bernini's "ass ears", tiny towers he added to the pediment, were removed in 1883.

🔟 Roman Forum

Gazing on it today, a picturesque shambles of ruins and weeds, you would hardly guess that the Forum was the symbol of civic pride for 1,000 years. Its humble beginning, more than 3,000 years ago, was as a swampy cemetery for the original village on Palatine Hill. Gradually it rose, ever more glorified, as Rome's power grew. After the marsh was finally drained off in the 6th century BC, it took on its central role in the life of the Republic. The Forum showed its most elegant face starting with the reign of Augustus, the first Roman emperor, who is said to have turned the city from brick to marble.

The Curia

🍴 The only option in the immediate area for drinks and snacks is one of the mobile refreshment vendors. For something more substantial, there are plenty of cafés and restaurants on Via Cavour.

⏱ In summer, it's best to visit the Forum either early or late in the day, to avoid the intense heat.

- Via dei Fori Imperiali
- Map Q5
- 06 3996 7700
- Open 9am–1hr before sunset daily, closed 1 Jan, 25 Dec
- Forum: Free; Palatine and Museum: Adm €9.00 (includes Colosseum)

Top 10 Features

1. Arch of Septimius Severus
2. Temple of Vesta and House of the Vestal Virgins
3. Curia
4. Temple of Castor and Pollux
5. Arch of Titus
6. Basilica of Maxentius and Constantine
7. Temple of Vespasian
8. Via Sacra
9. Temple of Saturn
10. Temple of Antoninus and Faustina

Arch of Septimius Severus
This well-preserved triumphal arch *(below)* celebrates the emperor's Middle Eastern victories. It was erected in AD 203 by his sons, Geta and Caracalla, then co-emperors.

Temple of Vesta and House of the Vestal Virgins
A graceful round temple and its adjacent palace *(right)* were the centre for one of Rome's most revered cults. Noble priestesses tended the sacred flame and enjoyed the greatest privileges.

Curia
The 3rd-century-AD Senate retains its original polychrome inlaid floor, its risers, where the 300 senators sat in deliberation, and the speaker's platform. For 2nd-century views of the Forum, examine the large marble reliefs, showing Emperor Trajan's good works.

For more ancient sights in Rome See pp40–41

4 Temple of Castor and Pollux

Three Corinthian columns remain of this temple to the *Dioscuri* – twin brothers of Helen of Troy and sons of Jupiter and Leda. The shrine marked the spot where they miraculously appeared in 499 BC to announce a crucial Roman victory.

IMPERIAL FORA
see page 23

VIA DEI FORI IMPERIALI

6 Basilica of Maxentius and Constantine

Three vast, coffered barrel vaults *(below)* proclaim the Forum's largest structure, built around AD 315 and used as the legal and financial centre of the Empire.

7 Temple of Vespasian

Until 18th-century excavations were undertaken, these graceful corner columns (AD 79) of the temple to a former emperor stood mostly buried beneath centuries of detritus.

Original Plan of the Roman Forum

9 Temple of Saturn

Eight grey-and-red Ionic columns constitute what's left of this temple (also the state treasury) to the ruler of agriculture and of a mythic "Golden Age." Saturnalia, celebrated each December, was very similar to modern-day Christmas.

10 Temple of Antoninus and Faustina

Dedicated by Antoninus Pius in AD 41 to his deified wife Faustina, this is one of the best preserved temples *(centre)*. With its Baroque-style top-knot, it is also one of the oddest. Note the carvings of griffins along the side frieze.

Forum Guide

You can access the Forum from Via Dei Fori Imperiali. However, for a great view of the whole site, enter from one of the high points at either end. From the northwest end, begin on the Capitoline (to the right and behind the huge, white Victor Emmanuel Monument) and take the stairs down from Largo Romolo e Remo. From the southeast end, start at the Colosseum *(see p22)* and climb the small hill just to the northwest. Enter by the Arch of Titus, which is also near the main entry gate to the Palatine.

5 Arch of Titus

The oldest extant arch in Rome *(above)* was erected in AD 81 by Emperor Domitian to honour his brother, Titus, and his father, Vespasian, for putting down the Jewish Revolt. Reliefs show soldiers sacking Jerusalem's Holy of Holies and taking sacred objects, such as a golden menorah.

8 Via Sacra

Paved with broad, flat, black basalt stones, Rome's oldest road wound from the Arch of Titus through the Forum and up to the Capitoline. Republican heroes staged triumphal processions here, but it degenerated into a hangout for gossips, pickpockets and other idlers.

Left **Farnese Gardens** Centre **Stucco relief, Cryptoporticus** Right **Domus Flavia**

🔟 Palatine Hill Features

Domus Flavia
Marked today mainly by the remains of two fountains, this imposing edifice was the official wing of a vast emperors' palace, built by Domitian in AD 81.

Livia's House
This 1st-century BC structure, now below ground level, formed part of the residence of Augustus and his second wife. Here you can examine a number of mosaic pavements and wall frescoes.

Palatine Museum and Antiquarium
This former convent houses a wealth of artifacts unearthed here, including pottery, statuary, ancient graffiti and very fine mosaics. You can also study a model of the Iron Age Palatine.

Romulus's Iron-Age Huts
Traces of the three 9th-century BC huts were uncovered in the 1940s. Legend says that this tiny village was founded by Romulus, who gave Rome its name *(see p38)*.

Stadium
Possibly a racetrack, or just a large garden, this sunken rectangle formed part of Domitian's palatial 1st-century abode.

Domus Augustana
All that remains of the private wing of Domitian's imperial extravaganza are the massive substructure vaults.

Plan of Palatine Hill

Temple of Cybele
The orgiastic Cult of the Great Mother was the first of the Oriental religions to come to Rome, in 191 BC. Still here is a decapitated statue of the goddess. Priests worshipping Cybele ritually castrated themselves.

Farnese Gardens
Plants and elegant pavilions grace part of what was once an extensive pleasure-garden, designed by Vignola and built in the 16th century over the ruins of Tiberius's palace.

Cryptoporticus
This series of underground corridors, their vaults decorated with delicate stucco reliefs, stretches 130 m (425 ft). It connected the Palatine to Nero's fabulous Golden House *(see p41)*.

Domus Septimius Severus
Huge arches and broken walls are all that remain of this emperor's 2nd-century AD extension to the Domus Augustana.

Top 10 Ancient Roman Belief Systems

1 State Religion of Graeco-Roman Gods (especially the Capitol Triad: Jupiter, Juno, Minerva)
2 Household Gods: Ancestors and Genii
3 Cult of Cybele, the Great Mother
4 Deification of Emperors, Empresses and Favourites
5 Orgiastic Fertility Cults
6 Mithraism
7 Cult of Attis
8 Cult of Isis
9 Cult of Serapis
10 Judeo-Christianity

Roman Bathhouses
As the centre of Roman social life, bathhouses were grandiose affairs, as seen in the remains *(below)* in the Baths of Caracalla *(see p119)*.

A Day in the Life of a Roman Household

Most Romans lived in insulae, *apartment buildings of perhaps six floors, with the poorest residents occupying the cheaper upper floors. An average Roman male citizen arose before dawn, arranged his toga, and breakfasted on a glass of water. Then out into the alleys, reverberating with noise. First, a stop at a public latrine, where he chatted with neighbours. Next a visit to his honoured patron, who paid him his daily stipend. Lunch might be a piece of bread washed down with wine. Bathing waited until late afternoon, when he met his friends at a public bathhouse. There he lingered – conversing, exercising, reading, or admiring the artwork – until dinnertime. The main meal of the day was taken lying on couches, with his slaves in attendance. Then it was bedtime. Roman matrons, apart from their time at the baths, spent the entire day at home, running the household.*

Roman toga

10 Galleria Borghese

The Borghese Gallery is one of the world's greatest small museums. A half dozen of Bernini's best sculptures and Caravaggio paintings casually occupy the same rooms as Classical, Renaissance and Neo-Classical works. The setting is the beautiful frescoed 17th-century villa set in the greenery of Villa Borghese park, all of which once belonged to the great art-lover of the early Baroque, Cardinal Scipione Borghese. Scipione patronized the young Bernini and Caravaggio, in the process amassing one of Rome's richest private collections.

Bernini's David
Young Bernini's *David* (1623–4) *(above)* was the Baroque answer to Michelangelo's Renaissance version. The frowning face is a self-portrait.

Façade, Galleria Borghese

🍴 There's a decent café in the museum basement, although the Caffè delle Arti (06 3265 1236) at the nearby Galleria Nazionale d'Arte Moderna is better, with a park view.

✪ Entrance to the gallery is strictly by reservation. Book well ahead of time – entries are timed and tickets often sell out days, even weeks, in advance, especially if an exhibition is on.

• Villa Borghese, off Via Pinciana
• Map E1
• Tel. 06 328 101
• www.galleria borghese.it
• www.ticketeria.it (for reservations)
• Open 9am–7pm Tue–Sun
• Adm €6.50, €5.25 EU citizens 18–25 (free under 18 and over 65)
• Max. viewing time 2 hours

Top 10 Exhibits
1. Bernini's Apollo and Daphne
2. Bernini's Rape of Persephone
3. Bernini's David
4. Caravaggio's Madonna of the Serpent
5. Canova's Pauline Bonaparte
6. Caravaggio's Self-Portrait as a Sick Bacchus
7. Raphael's Deposition
8. Bernini's Aeneas and Anchises
9. Titian's Sacred and Profane Love
10. Correggio's Danae

Bernini's Apollo and Daphne
A climactic moment frozen in marble (1622–5). As Apollo is inches from grabbing Daphne, the pitying gods transform her into a laurel *(right)*.

Bernini's Rape of Persephone
Bernini carved this masterpiece at age 23 (1621–2). Muscular Hades throws his head back with laughter, his strong fingers pressing into the maiden's soft flesh as she struggles to break free of his grasp.

Caravaggio's Madonna of the Serpent
Baroque tastes disliked this altarpiece's lack of ornamentation (1605). It spent only weeks on St Peter's altar before being moved to a lesser church then sold to Borghese.

For more masterpieces in Rome See pp48–9

5 Canova's Pauline Bonaparte

Napoleon's sister caused a scandal with this half-naked portrait (1805–8), lounging like a Classical goddess on a carved marble cushion.

6 Caravaggio's Self-Portrait as a Sick Bacchus

This early self-portrait (1593) as the wine god was painted with painstaking detail, supposedly when the artist was ill. It shows finer brushwork than later works.

7 Raphael's Deposition

The Borghese's most famous painting (1507), although neither the gallery's nor Raphael's best *(right)*. The Perugian matriarch Atalante Baglioni commissioned the work to honour her assassinated son (perhaps the red-shirted pall-bearer).

8 Bernini's Aeneas and Anchises

Pietro Bernini was still guiding his 15-year-old son in this 1613 work. The carving is more timid and static than in later works, but the genius is already evident.

10 Correggio's Danae

A sensual masterpiece (1531) based on Ovid's *Metamorphoses*. Cupid pulls back the sheets as Jupiter, the golden shower above her head, rains his love over Danae *(below)*.

Key

First floor

Ground floor

9 Titian's Sacred and Profane Love

Titian's allegorical scene (1514), painted for a wedding, exhorts the young bride that worldly love is part of the divine, and that sex is an extension of holy matrimony *(below)*.

The Borghese Collectors

Scipione used this 17th-century villa as a show-place for a stupendous antiquities collection given to him by his uncle, Pope Paul V, to which he added sculptures by the young Bernini. When Camillo Borghese married Pauline Bonaparte, he donated the bulk of the Classical sculpture collection to his brother-in-law Napoleon in 1809. They now form the core of the Louvre's antiquities wing in Paris.

7

2

1

3

Rome's Top 10

🔟 The Colosseum and Imperial Fora

This rich archaeological zone, rudely intruded upon by Mussolini's Via dei Fori Imperiali, contains some of the most grandiose and noteworthy of Rome's ancient remains. Dominating the area is the mighty shell of the Colosseum, constructed in AD 72–80 under the Flavian emperors and originally known as the Flavian Amphitheatre. The quarter also holds other imperial wonders, such as the Arch of Constantine, the gigantic fora of various emperors, most notably Trajan's, and the 1st century AD folly of Nero's Golden House, now a subterranean revelation of Roman interior design. Plans are under way to turn the area into one great archaeological park, and the broad thoroughfare crossing the zone is more and more frequently closed to traffic, as those aims are gradually realized.

Loggia, House of the Knights of Rhodes

🔵 One of the friendliest places for a light meal is Caffè Valorani, at Largo Corrado Ricci 30.

✴ At the Colosseum, use one of the student guides – they work for tips and really bring the place to life.

• 06 3996 7700 (reservations for all archaeological sites)
• Colosseum: Piazza del Colosseo, Map R6, Open 9am–1 hr before sunset daily, Adm €9.00 (includes the Palatine)
• Trajan's Markets: Via IV Novembre, Map P4, 06 6978 0532, Access to site limited - call for opening times, Adm €3.20
• Nero's Golden House: Viale della Domus Aurea, Map E4, Currently closed for restoration, Adm €5.00
• Mamertine Prison: Clivo Argentario 1, Map P5, Open 9am–5pm (winter), 9am–7pm (summer) daily, Donation

Top 10 Sights

1. Colosseum
2. Trajan's Markets
3. Nero's Golden House
4. Trajan's Forum and Column
5. Arch of Constantine
6. Mamertine Prison
7. House of the Knights of Rhodes
8. Forum of Nerva
9. Forum of Julius Caesar
10. Forum of Augustus

① Colosseum
Here the imperial passion for bloody spectacle reached its peak of excess. When Emperor Titus inaugurated the amphitheatre *(right)* in AD 80, he declared 100 days of celebratory games, some involving the massacre of 5,000 wild beasts. All such slaughter-as-sport was legal until AD 523 (see p40).

② Trajan's Markets

The emperor and his visionary architect, Apollodorus of Damascus, built this attractive, very modern looking shopping and office mall *(left)* in the early 2nd century AD. There were 150 spaces in all, the top floor utilized by welfare offices, the lower levels by shops of all kinds.

For more sights in Ancient Rome **See pp118–21**

Nero's Golden House (Domus Aurea)

This mad emperor's self-indulgence resulted in the largest, most sumptuous palace Rome ever saw, yet it was meant only for amusement. In its heyday it covered several acres and boasted every luxury, including its own forest (see p41).

Original Plan of the Imperial Fora

VIA DEI FORI IMPERIALI

ROMAN FORUM
see page 17

Trajan's Forum and Column

Trajan's Forum was so splendid that it left all who beheld it awed by its nobility. Now cut off by modern streets, all that stands out is the magnificent column (right), commemorating in fine graphic detail the emperor's victories in what is now Romania. Access to part of it is through Trajan's Market.

Mamertine Prison

Legend holds that St Peter was imprisoned here. Prisoners were originally dropped down through a hole in the floor and the only exit was death.

Forum of Nerva

If Pope Paul V hadn't stripped it to build the Acqua Paola fountain in the 17th century, the main attraction here would have been the Temple of Minerva. Two Corinthian columns remain, and a frieze above, depicting the myth of Arachne.

Forum of Julius Caesar

The first of Rome's Imperial Forums, Caesar's line, the Julians, traced their ancestry back to Venus herself, so he erected the Temple of Venus Genetrix (46 BC) and placed there statues of himself and Cleopatra, his great love.

Forum of Augustus

Julius Caesar's successor (see p38) made the focus of his forum the Temple of Mars the Avenger, identified by the broad staircase and four Corinthian columns.

Arch of Constantine

This arch (right) marks the victory of the first Christian emperor over his rival emperor Maxentius (see p38). Yet it is mostly a pastiche of pagan elements taken from several earlier monuments, but the beautiful hunt-scene roundels come from a temple dedicated to Emperor Hadrian's male lover, Antinous.

House of the Knights of Rhodes

This 12th-century priory was owned by the crusading order of the Knights of Rhodes. Inside are the original portico, three shops and the Chapel of St John.

Area Guide

Expect to take three hours to see everything. There are likely to be queues for the Colosseum and for Nero's Golden House; a guided tour is mandatory, with only 30 people at a time, so booking is advised. Use the Via IV Novembre entrance to Trajan's Markets. The other fora are viewed from Via dei Fori Imperiali.

🔟 Musei Capitolini

Capitoline Hill was ancient Rome's religious heart, and is now home to a magnificent museum. A gently stepped grade, the Cordonata leads you up the hill and provides an unforgettably theatrical experience, just as Michelangelo planned it in the 16th century. At the top you notice the outstretched hand of Emperor Marcus Aurelius, as he dispenses peace from astride his horse. The sides of the star-shaped piazza are graced by twin palaces that contain some of Rome's greatest treasures. The collections in the Palazzo Nuovo, detailed below, and in the Palazzo dei Conservatori (see pp26–7) were inaugurated in 1471 with a donation of bronzes by Pope Sixtus IV, and have been judiciously added to ever since.

Façade, Palazzo dei Conservatori

☕ **The café behind the Palazzo dei Conservatori has a wonderful terrace with a spectacular panorama of the city.**

🔄 **Part of the underground passage between the museums is the Tabularium, ancient Rome's Hall of Records, from which you can get unusual views of the Forum.**

- Piazza del Campidoglio
- Map N5
- 06 8205 9127
- Open 9am–8pm Tue–Sun
- Adm €8.00 (free EU citizens under 18 and over 65).
- The Capitolini Card costs €10.00 and is valid for 7 days. The card also gives admission to the Montemartini Art Centre (see p152).

Top 10 Features

1. Hall of the Emperors
2. Dying Gaul
3. The Capitoline Venus
4. Mosaic of the Doves
5. Marforio
6. Resting Satyr
7. Hall of the Philosophers
8. Cupid and Psyche
9. Mosaic of the Masks
10. Drunken Old Woman

Key

◼ First floor

◻ Ground floor

1 Hall of the Emperors

The hall contains several portraits of the emperors and empresses of the Imperial Age. Among them is a bust of the brutal ruler Caracalla *(right)* from the 3rd-century AD.

2 Dying Gaul

The collection's most renowned piece *(below)* conveys great pathos. It is probably a 1st-century AD Roman copy of a Hellenistic bronze from the 3rd century BC.

3 Capitoline Venus

The shimmering goddess of love gets a room of her own. This fine 1st-century BC copy of a Praxiteles' Aphrodite from the 4th century BC shows her risen voluptuously from her bath, attempting to cover herself, as if reacting to someone's arrival.

4 Mosaic of the Doves
Originally the centre-piece of a floor decoration in Hadrian's Villa *(see p154)*, this jewel-like composition *(right)* uses tiny marble and glass chips *(tesserae)* to achieve a sense of texture and volume.

5 Marforio
This hirsute reclining giant *(below right)* was originally a river god, and is believed to come from the Forum of Augustus *(see p23)*. A Renaissance sculptor added the attributes of the god Ocean and placed him here, as overseer of this courtyard fountain.

8 Cupid and Psyche
The god of love embracing the personification of the soul, the two lovers are eternally united. This Roman copy of a Hellenistic original has inspired many sentimental variations.

9 Mosaic of the Masks
This floor decoration of two Greek theatre masks is probably from the 2nd century AD. The use of perspective, light and shadow is highly skilled, employing small squares of coloured marble to create dramatic effects.

6 Resting Satyr
Used to adorn an ancient grove or fountain, this young mythological creature is a copy of a 4th-century BC original by Praxiteles. His pointed ears, panther-skin cape and flute are attributes of the nature-god Pan. The statue inspired Nathaniel Hawthorne's novel *The Marble Faun (see p56)*.

10 Drunken Old Woman
This copy of a Hellenistic original from the 3rd century BC is from a series of sculptures depicting the wages of vice.

Museum Guide
The Palazzo Nuovo, on the left as you enter the piazza, contains mostly restored ancient sculpture. The finest pieces are on the upper floor. Then take the stairs down to the underpass that leads to the Palazzo dei Conservatori *(see pp26–7)*. The courtyard displays ancient marble fragments. The next floor up has 16th- and 17th-century decorations and Classical statuary. On the top floor are Renaissance and Baroque paintings.

7 Hall of the Philosophers
Roman copies of idealized Greek portrait busts of the greatest Hellenic poets and thinkers fill this room, including the blind epic poet Homer *(right)*.

Left **Lo Spinario** Right **Bronze She-Wolf**

🔟 Palazzo dei Conservatori Exhibits

1 Colossal Statue of Constantine Fragments

Found in the ruins of the Basilica of Maxentius and Constantine, these surreal outsized body parts (c.AD 313–24) formed the unclothed segments of an overwhelming seated effigy of the first Christian emperor, recognizable by his protuberant eyes. The rest of the sculpture was made of carved wood dressed in sheets of bronze.

2 Lo Spinario

One of the precious bronzes that comprised Sixtus IV's donation to the people of Rome, this charming sculpture dates from the 1st century BC. Hellenistic in its everyday subject matter, the head recalls more archaic models. The boy's unusual and graceful pose inspired many works during the Renaissance.

3 Caravaggio's St John the Baptist

Shocking in its sensuality, the boy's erotic pose, his arm around the ram, created an iconographic revolution when it was unveiled around 1600. Masterful *chiaroscuro* brought the holy image even more down to earth.

4 Bronze She-Wolf

The most ancient symbol of Rome, from the 5th century BC, of Etruscan or Greek workmanship. The she-wolf stands guard, at once a protectress and a nurturer, as the twins Romulus

Key to Palazzo dei Conservatori

■ Second floor

■ First floor

■ Ground floor

and Remus *(see p38)* feed on her milk. This was also part of the 1471 donation of Pope Sixtus IV.

5 Guercino's Burial of St Petronilla

The influence of Caravaggio is clearly evident in this huge altarpiece, executed for St Peter's Basilica between 1621 and 1623. Powerful effects of light and dark combined with pronounced musculature and individuality of the figures bring the work directly into the viewer's physical world.

6 Caravaggio's Gypsy Fortune-Teller

An earlier work by Caravaggio, but just as revolutionary as his St John the Baptist. This subject is taken from everyday street life in

Caravaggio's Gypsy Fortune-Teller

late 16th-century Rome, which the painter knew intimately. Notice that the gypsy is slyly slipping the ring from the unsuspecting young dandy's finger.

Bust of L. Junius Brutus
Dating from between the 4th and 3rd centuries BC, this bronze bust is possibly the rarest object in the museum. Its identification as the first Roman consul is uncertain, because it also resembles Greek models of poets and philosophers. Its intense, inlaid glass eyes make it one of the most gripping portraits.

Pietro da Cortona's Rape of the Sabines
Baroque painting is said to have begun with this work (c.1630), where symmetry is abandoned and all is twisting, dynamic movement. It depicts an early episode in Roman history:

the new city had been founded but the population lacked women, so they stole those of the neighbouring Sabine tribe *(see p38).*

Bust of Commodus as Hercules
The 2nd-century emperor, who loved to fight wild animals in the Colosseum, had himself represented as the demigod Hercules, to promote his own divinity. The club in his right hand, the lion's mantle and the apples of the Hesperides in his left hand are all symbols of Hercules' labours.

Equestrian Statue of Marcus Aurelius
A copy of this 2nd-century AD bronze masterpiece *(left)* stands in the centre of the Capitoline star; the original is displayed on the first floor of the Palazzo dei Conservatori.

Marcus Aurelius on horseback

⁙10 Museo Nazionale Romano

The National Museum of Rome, with its excellent Classical art collection, grew too vast for its home in the Baths of Diocletian, which closed in 1981. In 1998 the collection was split between various sites, becoming a truly modern, 21st-century museum. The Ludovisi, Mattei and Altemps collections of sculpture moved into the gorgeous 16th-century Palazzo Altemps near Piazza Navona (see pp30–31). The 19th-century Palazzo Massimo alle Terme, a former Jesuit College near Termini, received some of the best individual sculptures, as well as ancient mosaics and fantastic frescoes, some never previously displayed, as detailed below. The ancient Aula Ottagona inherited the oversized bathhouse sculptures; the Baths of Diocletian re-opened in 2000 with an important epigraphic collection and exhibition space (see p133).

Façade, Palazzo Massimo alle Terme

🍴 From Palazzo Altemps, pop into Piazza Navona for refreshments at Tre Scalini *(see p88)*.

🎫 Call ahead for Palazzo Massimo tickets, as the frescoes and mosaics on the top floor are timed entry-only.

• Palazzo Massimo alle Terme: Largo di Villa Peretti 1, Map F3, 06 3996 7700, Open 9am–7:45pm Tue–Sun, Adm €7.00
• Palazzo Altemps: Piazza Sant'Apollinare 44, Map L2, 06 3996 7700, Open 9am–7:45pm Tue–Sun, Adm €7.00
• A €20 ticket (valid for 7 days) gives admission to all Museo Nazionale Romano sites and many archaeological areas, the €7.00 Museo Nazionale Romano card gives entry to all museums and is valid for 3 days

Top 10 Exhibits

1. Statue of Augustus
2. Triclinium Frescoes
3. Four Charioteers Mosaic
4. Wounded Niobid
5. Leucotea Nursing Dionysus
6. Bronze Dionysus
7. Discus Thrower
8. Ostia Altar
9. Scenes from the Basilica of Giunio Basso
10. Numismatic Collection

1 Statue of Augustus

This statue of Rome's first emperor *(below right)* once stood on Via Labicana. It shows Augustus wearing his toga draped over his head – a sign that, in AD 12, he added the title *Pontifex Maximus* (high priest) to the list of honours he assigned himself.

2 Triclinium Frescoes

These frescoes (20–10 BC) depicting a lush garden came from the villa of Augustus's wife, Livia. They were in the *triclinium*, a dining pavilion half-buried to keep it cool in summer.

3 Four Charioteers Mosaic

The imperial Severi family must have been passionate about sports to have decorated a bedroom of their 3rd-century AD villa with these charioteers *(above)*. They are dressed in the traditional colours of the Roman circus's four factions.

For more museums in Rome See pp42–3

4 Wounded Niobid

This hauntingly beautiful figure of Niobid (daughter of Queen Niobe), reaching for the fatal arrow that killed her siblings *(right)*, was sculpted around 440 BC for a Greek temple, and was later acquired by Julius Caesar.

6 Bronze Dionysus

Few large Classical bronzes survive today, making this 2nd-century AD statue special beyond its obvious grace, skill and preserved decoration. You can still see the yellow eyes, red lips and a comb band in the grape-festooned hair.

9 Scenes from the Basilica of Giunio Basso

Colourful marble inlays represent paganism's dying grasp among prominent Roman families *(below)*. The empire had converted to Christianity by AD 331 when consul Giunio Basso (pictured as a charioteer in one panel) commissioned the scenes for his meeting hall.

7 Discus Thrower

This 2nd-century AD marble copy *(below)* of the famous 450 BC Greek original by Myron is faithful to the point of imitating the original bronze's imperfect dimensions.

10 Numismatic Collection

Italian coinage and currency is on display here, from the Roman Republic and Empire coins through to the medieval and Renaissance principalities, to the lira and the euro.

Gallery Guide

The Palazzo Massimo exhibits all its statuary relating to Republican and Early Imperial Rome (up to Emperor Augustus) on the ground floor, along with a few precious earlier, Greek pieces. The first floor exhibits detail art in the political, cultural and economic spheres of Imperial Rome up to the 4th century. The second floor, which must be visited on a timed-entry ticket, preserves ancient mosaics and frescoes. The numismatic collection is in the basement, alongside some gold jewellery and a mummified eight-year-old girl.

5 Leucotea Nursing Dionysus

A luxuriously frescoed villa, discovered in 1879, included this bedroom scene of the nymph nursing the wine god *(below)* with additional scenes in the niches.

8 Ostia Altar

This Trajan-era altar connects the foundation of Rome to the divine consorts Mars and Venus. Mars is shown as father to Rome's legendary founder Romulus *(see p38)*; Venus bears the hero Aeneas, who fled Troy for Rome and consequently founded the Iulia dynasty (Julius Caesar's own, invented family tree).

Left **Grande Ludovisi sarcophagus** Right **Relief, Ludovisi throne**

🔟 Palazzo Altemps Collection

1 Garden of Delights Loggia
The loggia frescoes (c.1595) are a catalogue of the exotic fruits, plants and animals then being imported from the New World.

2 Athena Parthenos
The 1st-century BC Greek sculptor Antioco carved this statue to match the most famed sculpture in antiquity, the long-lost Athena in Athens' Parthenon.

3 "Grande Ludovisi" Sarcophagus
This mid-3rd century AD sarcophagus, deeply carved and remarkably well-preserved, shows the Romans victorious over the barbarian Ostrogoth hordes.

4 Orestes and Electra
This 1st-century AD statue was carved by Menelaus, an imitator of the great Greek artist Praxiteles. The scraps of 15th-century fresco nearby depict some wedding gifts from the marriage of Girolamo Riario and Caterina Sforza.

Colossal Head of Ludovisi Hera

5 Ludovisi Throne
This set of 5th-century BC reliefs depicting the birth of Aphrodite came to Rome from a Calabrian Greek colony and were discovered in the 19th century.

6 Dionysus with Satyr
Imperial Rome was in love with Greek sculpture, producing copies such as this grouping of Dionysus, a satyr and a panther.

7 Apollo Playing the Lute
There are two 1st-century AD Apollos in the museum, both restored in the 17th century.

8 Suicidal Gaul
This suicidal figure supporting his dead wife's arm was part of a trio, including the Capitoline's Dying Gaul *(see p24)* commissioned by Julius Caesar to celebrate a Gaulish victory.

9 Egyptian Statuary
The Egyptian collections are divided into three sections related to that culture's influence on Rome: political theological, popular worship and places of worship. The showpiece is the impressive granite *Bull Api*, or *Brancaccio Bull* (2nd century BC).

10 Colossal Head of Ludovisi Hera
German writer Goethe called this his "first love in Rome". It is believed to be a portrait of Claudius's mother, Antonia.

Top 10 Ancient Art Collections

1. Museo Nazionale Romano *(see pp28–31)*
2. Vatican Museums *(see pp8–9)*
3. Musei Capitolini *(see pp24–7)*
4. Montemartini *(see p152)*
5. Ara Pacis *(see p91)*
6. Villa Giulia *(see p112)*
7. Trajan's Column *(see p23)*
8. Column of Marcus Aurelius *(see p92)*
9. Palatine Antiquarium *(see p18)*
10. Museo Barracco *(see p104)*

Ancient Roman Art

Ancient Rome's art was as conservative as its culture. Sculpture, the most durable art form, was also the least original. From the middle Republican period through to the Imperial age, Romans shunned original pieces for copies of famous Greek works. The Caesars imported shiploads of Golden Age statuary from Greece and its old colonies in southern Italy; Roman workshops churned out headless, toga-wearing figures in a variety of stock poses to which any bust could be affixed. It was at bust portraiture that Romans truly excelled, especially up to the early Imperial age when naturalism was still in vogue. Roman painting is divided into styles based on Pompeii examples. The First Style imitated marble panels; the Second Style imitated architecture, often set within the small painted scenes that became a hallmark of the Third Style. The Fourth Style was trompe-l'oeil decoration. Mosaic, initially developed as a floor-strengthening technique, could be simple black-on-white or intricate wall-mounted scenes using tiny marble chips to create shading and contour. Opus sectile (inlaid marble) was a style that was imported from the East.

Roman Goddess
Marble carving, such as this sitting figure of a goddess, was one of the most popular and enduring of Roman art forms. The fluidity of the woman's robes is particularly impressive.

Mosaic of Virgil and the Muses

TOP 10 Santa Maria del Popolo

Few churches are such perfect primers on Roman art and architecture. Masters from the Early Renaissance (Pinturicchio, Bramante), High Renaissance (Raphael) and Baroque (Caravaggio, Bernini) exercised their genius in all disciplines here: painting, sculpture, architecture and decoration. It's also one of the few churches with major chapels still intact, preserving the artworks that together tell a complete story (most Italian chapels have been dismantled, their paintings now in museums). In the Cerasi Chapel, Caravaggio and Caracci collaborated with a frescoist to create a depiction of Peter, Paul and Mary and, on the vault, their connections to Heaven. Bernini altered Raphael's Chigi Chapel to help clarify the interplay of its art across the small space.

Façade, Santa Maria del Popolo

🍴 Canova and Rosati cafés *(see p116)* are both on Piazza del Popolo.

🔦 Some of the church's treasures are behind the High Altar in the choir and apse. When mass is not in session, you are allowed to go behind the curtain to the left of the altar and switch on the lights in the fuse box to see them.

• Piazza del Popolo 12
• Map D2
• Open 7am–noon, 4–7pm Mon–Sat, 8am–1:30pm, 4:30–7pm Sun
• Free

Top 10 Features

1. Crucifixion of St Peter
2. Conversion of St Paul
3. Raphael's Chigi Chapel
4. Bernini's Chigi Chapel
5. Pinturricchio's Adoration
6. Sansovino Tombs
7. Marcillat's Stained-Glass Window
8. Bramante's Apse
9. Cybo Chapel
10. Sebastiano del Piombo's Nativity of the Virgin

1 Crucifixion of St Peter

Caravaggio has avoided the melodrama and goriness of his earlier works and packed drama into this *chiaroscuro* work (1601). The naturalistic figures quietly go about their business, the tired workers hauling the cross into place, Peter looking sad and contemplative *(below)*.

2 Conversion of St Paul

Again, Caravaggio leaves all drama to the effects of light, depicting an awe-struck Paul transfixed by blinding light (1601).

3 Raphael's Chigi Chapel

Raphael designed this exquisite chapel for papal banker Agostini Chigi, including the frescoes and niche statues (1519–23).

For more Roman churches **See pp44–5**

4 Bernini's Chigi Chapel

Cardinal Fabio Chigi hired Bernini to finish the job begun by Raphael 130 years earlier. The artist only deviated from the original plan in two Biblical niche statues *(above)*.

5 Pinturicchio's Adoration

Raphael's elder contemporary retained more of their teacher Perugino's limpid Umbrian style in this 1490 work in the della Rovere chapel. Also in the chapel is Cardinal Cristoforo's tomb sculpted by Francesco da Sangallo (1478), while Domenico's tomb (1477) features a *Madonna with Child* by Mino da Fiesole.

6 Sansovino Tombs

Under triumphal arch tombs, Tuscan Andrea Sansovino gave a Renaissance/Etruscan twist to the traditional lying-in-state look (1505–07). These effigies of Cardinal Girolamo Basso della Rovere and Cardinal Asciano Sforza recline on cushions as if merely asleep *(below)*.

7 Marcillat's Stained-Glass Window

The only Roman work by Guillaume de Marcillat (1509), the undisputed French master of stained glass, depicts the Infancy of Christ and Life of the Virgin *(below)*.

8 Bramante's Apse

The Renaissance architect's first work in Rome, commissioned by Julius II around 1500, was this beautiful light-filled choir and scallop shell-shaped apse.

Plan of Santa Maria del Popolo

9 Cybo Chapel

Carlo Fontana managed to make this Baroque confection of multicoloured marbles and a Carlo Maratta *Immaculate Conception* altarpiece blend together in his 1682–7 design.

10 Sebastiano del Piombo's Nativity of the Virgin

This altarpiece in the Chigi Chapel (1530–34) is in contrast to the dome's Neo-pagan themes, the Eternal Father blessing Chigi's horoscope of planets symbolized by pagan gods.

The People's Church

The ghost of Nero, buried in the Domitia family crypt on the Pincio *(see p62)*, terrorized this neighbourhood in the form of demon crows that lived in a cursed tree. Pope Paschal II reassured the locals in 1099 by replacing the tree with a chapel paid for by the people *(il popolo)*. It was enlarged in 1227 and rebuilt in Lombard style in 1472–7. Andrea Bregno may have added the Renaissance façade, and Bernini a Baroque touch to the interior.

🔟 San Clemente

Nowhere else in Rome can give such a clear idea of the city's layering and millennia of cultural riches than this wonderful church. The very lowest level remains largely unexplored, dating back to Republican Rome, probably the 2nd century BC. At the deepest excavated level there are 1st-century AD buildings, including an early house of Christian worship and a temple dedicated to the Persian god, Mithras. Above that is a partially intact 4th-century AD basilica. When that edifice was burned in the Norman sacking of 1084, the space was filled in and a new church was built, using some of the original architectural elements. In 1857, the Irish Dominican prior, Father Mullooly, accidentally discovered the lower church and began the long process of emptying out the rubble.

Façade, San Clemente

🍽 Cafés and restaurants abound in the area. Try Cannavota *(see p131)* for a traditional Roman meal.

🔦 Bring a small torch, so that you can make out the ancient decorations in the shadowy Mithraeum. But no photos or videos are allowed, and they mean it!

• Via di S Giovanni in Laterano
• Map F4
• 06 774 0021
• Open 9am–12:30pm, 3–6pm daily (from 10am Sun)
• Adm €3.00 to lower levels

Top 10 Features

1. Apse Mosaic
2. Legend of Sisinius Frescoes
3. Mithraeum
4. St Catherine's Chapel
5. Miracle of San Clemente Frescoes
6. Schola Cantorum
7. 1st-century BC Domus
8. Cosmatesque Pavement
9. Paschal Candlestick
10. Courtyard and Façade

Apse Mosaic

Few images are more joyous than this 12th-century variation on the tree-of-life, in the Upper Church *(below)*. Plump cupids, winsome animals and lush foliage evoke a new-found Paradise. The stone and glass squares were taken from a similar work in the destroyed 4th-century church below it.

Legend of Sisinius Frescoes

These frescoes in the Lower Church relate how a wealthy pagan, Sisinius, was struck deaf and blind for suspecting his Christian wife of infidelity. St Clement cures him but incurs his wrath and Sisinius's furious commands are the first known inscriptions in Italian.

Mithraeum
3 The triclinium, with its platforms along both sides, was used for ritual banqueting, where the male-only congregation imitated the gods' last meal before they re-ascended to heaven. The altar painting shows Mithras slaying the Cosmic Bull to bring about Creation.

St Catherine's Chapel
4 The restored frescoes (above) in the Upper Church by the 15th-century Florentine artist Masolino show vibrant scenes from the life of St Catherine of Alexandria. These provide one of the few opportunities in Rome to appreciate the painting of the early Florentine Renaissance.

Miracle of San Clemente Frescoes
5 These frescoes in the Lower Church show how St Clement saved a boy from drowning.

Schola Cantorum
6 The enclosure for the choir in the Upper Church (above right), a gift from Pope John II (AD 535–55), was retained when a new choir was built. It is walled with panels of white marble inlaid with colourful mosaics and carved with early Christian symbols.

1st-century BC Domus
7 This mansion belonged to a man named Clemens, perhaps a relative of an early Christian martyr and of St Clement, perhaps a freed man of Jewish birth. The 4th-century church was built precisely over the 1st-century site.

Cosmatesque Pavement
8 This technique (below), developed by the Cosmati family in the 12th century, involved using fragments of stone from Roman ruins, to create intricate, geometric patterns.

Paschal Candlestick
9 This 12th-century spiral-ling motif (left), striped with glittering mosaics of ancient glass, is another magnificent example of work by Cosmati artisans in the Upper Church.

Courtyard and Façade
10 The original entrance was through the quadro-porticus, the medieval colonnaded square forecourt. The fountain and the scrolled façade were added in the early 18th century.

Church Guide
You can usually enter both through the balconied front gate or by a side door, off the small piazza on Via di San Giovanni in Laterano. The entrance to the Lower Church and archaeological areas is through the sacristy vestibule, where you'll also find books, slides and attractive postcards of the two churches and the Mithraic temple's works of art. The 1st-century alleyways beneath are no place for claustrophobics, but the refreshing sound of the underground spring down below may provide some relief.

🔟 Ostia Antica

*Some 2,000 years ago, ancient Rome's lively international port city was right on the beach and at the mouth of the Tiber (*ostium *means "river mouth"). In the ensuing millennia the sea has retreated several kilometres and the river has changed course dramatically. Ostia was founded in the 4th century BC, first as a simple fort, but as Rome grew, the town became ever more important, as the distribution point for imports from around the Mediterranean. Grain was the most vital commodity, to feed Rome's one million inhabitants, and so huge storage bins (*horrea*) were built here. Goods were sent up to Rome on river barges. Ostia's heyday ended in the 4th century AD, and it died completely as an inhabited area about 1,000 years ago.*

Forum

🍴 There's a snack bar behind the museum, which is a great place to refuel and refresh on a hot day.

🎧 The ruined walls can look confusingly similar, so rent one of the audioguides where you buy your entrance ticket.

• Viale dei Romagnoli 717
• Metro B, trams 3 & 30, or buses 23, 95, 75, 280 to Piramide, then local train from Porta San Paolo station to Ostia Antica
• 06 5635 8099
• Open 8:30am–6pm Tue–Sat, 8:30am–12:30pm Sun
• Adm €4.00 (free under 18 and over 65)
• The port area (Trajan's Port) can be visited on request, 06 6501 0089

Top 10 Features

1. Decumanus Maximus
2. Theatre
3. Casa di Diana and Thermopolium
4. Museum
5. Forum
6. Capitolium
7. Terme dei Sette Sapienti
8. House of Cupid and Psyche
9. Terme di Nettuno
10. Mithraeum of the Serpents

1 Decumanus Maximus

You enter the park by way of the ancient Via Ostiensis. The white marble goddess on the left marks the beginning of city's main street, the Decumanus Maximus *(above)*.

2 Theatre

The original theatre was twice as tall as it now stands *(centre)*. Behind the stage was a temple, of either Ceres (goddess of grain) or Dionysus (god of theatre). Around the square, mosaics *(right)* advertise various import businesses: grain, wild animals, ivory and shipping.

3 Casa di Diana and Thermopolium

You can climb up to the top of this *insula* (apartment block) for a great view. Across the street is the Thermopolium, a tavern with a wall-painting of menu items.

Museum
Beautifully organized, the displays include precious sculptures, sarcophagi and mosaics found among the ruins. One of the highlights is a marble statue of the god Mithras about to sacrifice the Cosmic Bull.

Forum
The rectangular heart of officialdom was originally surrounded by columns. In the centre was a shrine to the Imperial Lares (household gods).

Ostia Antica

Terme di Nettuno
Built in the 2nd century, this bath complex *(left)* was enhanced with fine mosaics of sea-gods and sea-monsters, which you can view from a small terrace. You can also go down along to the left to study close-up the baths' ingenious heating system.

Mithraeum of the Serpents
This was one of 18 Ostian temples to Mithras. The cult was very popular with Roman soldiers, and flourished especially well in port towns. The frescoes of snakes invoked the earth's fertility, while the platforms were for lying on during mystic banquets.

Capitolium
Dominating the city was the monumental temple to the Capitoline Triad – Jupiter, Juno and Minerva. Climb the staircase *(above)* to examine the threshold stone of rare Lucullan marble.

Terme dei Sette Sapienti
This elaborate bath complex contains a painting of Venus, floor mosaics of hunters and animals and nude athletes and marine scenes.

House of Cupid and Psyche
The wealthy had villas like this refined example of a 3rd-century AD *domus*. You can still admire the Doric columns, the fountain *(nymphaeum)* and the inlaid marble decorations.

Park Guide
Arrival by local train is very easy, and takes about 20 minutes from Porta San Paolo station, next to the Piramide underground stop. The cost of the trip is one regular bus ticket. From the Ostia Antica train station, walk straight out to the footbridge that goes over the highway. Continue straight on past the restaurant until you get to the ticket booth. The park is very extensive and a decent visit will take at least three hours. Wear sturdy shoes, and bring sunscreen and a bottle of water on hot days.

Left **Rome burns** Right **Mussolini and Fascists march on Rome, 1922**

Moments in History

1 Romulus and Remus
The foundation of Rome is said to have occurred in 753 BC. Twins Romulus and Remus, sons of Mars and a Vestal Virgin, were set adrift by their evil uncle and suckled by a she-wolf. They then founded rival Bronze Age villages on the Palatine, but Romulus killed Remus during an argument, and his "Rome" went on to greatness.

2 Rape of the Sabine Women
To boost the female population in the 750s BC Romulus's men kidnapped women from the neighbouring Sabine kingdom. As Rome began to expand, however, the kingdoms were united. Rome was later conquered by the Etruscan Tarquin dynasty. In 510 BC, a patrician-ruled Republic was formed that lasted more than 450 years.

3 Assassination of Caesar
A series of military victories, adding Gaul (France) to Rome, increased General Julius Caesar's popularity. He marched his army to Rome and declared himself Dictator for Life, but on 15 March 44 BC he was assassinated. Caesar's adopted son Octavian changed his name to Augustus and declared himself emperor in 27 BC.

Bust, Julius Caesar

4 Rome Burns
In AD 64 fire destroyed much of Rome. Emperor Nero rebuilt many public works, but also appropriated vast tracts of land to build his Golden House. Hounded from office, he committed suicide in AD 68 *(see p41)*.

5 Battle at Milvian Bridge
In 312 Emperor Constantine, whose mother was a Christian, had a vision of victory under the sign of the Cross and defeated co-emperor Maxentius at Milvian Bridge. He declared Christianity the state religion.

6 Fall of the Empire
By the late 4th century Rome was in decline, as Barbarians from across the Rhine and Danube conquered outlying provinces. In 476, the last emperor was deposed and the Empire fell.

7 Papacy moves to Avignon
Following the departure of the papacy to France in 1309, the city became a backwater ruled by petty princes who built palaces out of marble from the great temples. In 1377 the papacy returned to Rome, and the city was reborn.

Papal Palace, Avignon

Top 10 Influential Popes

St Peter
The Apostle (AD 42–67) tapped by Jesus to lead the church. After his martyrdom in Rome the city became the epicentre of Christianity.

St Leo the Great
Rome's bishop (440–61) made himself *pontifex maximus* of the Christian church.

St Gregory the Great
Affirmed the papacy as the western secular leader and converted England to Christianity (590–604).

Innocent III
This medieval pope (1198–1216) hand-picked emperors and approved monkish orders.

Boniface VIII
Imperious, pragmatic and power-hungry, Boniface (1294–1303) instituted the first Jubilee to make money.

Alexander VI
Ruthless Borgia pope (1492–1503) used the pontificate to destroy rival families.

Julius II
Warrior pope and patron of the arts (1513–21), he hired Michelangelo for the Sistine Chapel and Raphael to decorate his apartment *(see p8)*.

Paul III
Scholarly and secular, but fighting Protestant reforms, Paul III (1534–49) founded the Jesuits and the Inquisition.

Sixtus V
Cleansed Papal States of corruption (1585–90) and masterminded a Baroque overhaul of Rome.

John Paul II
The first non-Italian Pope for over 400 years, John Paul II (1920-2005), was famed for his extensive travelling.

Sack of Rome
Rome was conquered for the first time in more than a millennium in 1527. Emperor Charles V's Germanic troops held the city for seven months until Pope Clement VII surrendered and promised to address concerns of the new Protestant movement.

Unification of Italy
Piemontese King Vittorio Emanuele II and his general, Garibaldi, spent years conquering the peninsula's kingdoms and principalities to create a new country called Italy. In 1870, Garibaldi breached the Aurelian walls and took the ancient capital, completing Italian Unification.

Mussolini Takes Power
Benito "Il Duce" Mussolini, leader of the nationalistic Fascist Party, marched on Rome in 1922 and was declared prime minister. Delusions of imperial grandeur led him to excavate many of the ruins we see today. He allied Italy with Hitler, but when the tides turned, Mussolini was deposed and Italy joined Allied troops. The current Republic was set up in 1946.

Left **Roman Forum and Colosseum** Centre **Palatine fresco** Right **Domus Augustana, Palatine Hill**

🔟 Ancient Sights

Roman Forum
In the centre of the Forum stands a humble ruined structure where fresh flowers are placed year-round. This is the foundation of the Temple to Julius Caesar, built by Augustus in the 1st century BC. The flowers indicate the exact spot of Caesar's cremation *(see pp16–17)*.

Pantheon
Originally worshippers approached this temple to all the gods by a steep staircase, but the street level has risen since the 2nd century. The present temple was built by Hadrian, after the 1st-century BC temple burned down *(see pp14–15)*.

Imperial Fora
The largest temple and one of the most commanding of this imposing zone was the 2nd-century AD Temple of Venus and Rome, its columns standing high on the hill between the Forum and the Colosseum. Its back-to-back design was Hadrian's, and when the great architect Apollodorus criticized it, Hadrian had him put to death *(see pp22–3)*.

Colosseum

Colosseum
The backbreaking labour to build the greatest of amphi-theatres was carried out by a horde of Jewish slaves, brought here following the suppression of their revolt in Judaea. The structure has been the archetype for the world's sports stadiums ever since *(see p22)*.

Palatine Hill
Most European languages derive their word for palace from the name of this hill. All-important in the history of early Rome, first as its birthplace, then as the home of its leaders' opulent homes, it now serves as a bucolic setting for a romantic stroll *(see pp18–19)*.

Baths of Diocletian
A large section of this huge 3rd-century AD complex now houses an excellent archaeo-logical museum, including a marble sculpture of Mithras that still retains its gold leaf and paint. A vast Michelangelo cloister is decorated with ancient statuary *(see p133)*.

Column of Marcus Aurelius
A 2nd-century AD commemo-ration of conquests along the Danube, this colossus stands 30 m (100 ft) high and is com-posed of 28 marble drums. The 20 spiral reliefs realistically chronicle scenes from two wars. A statue of the emperor and his

For more on Ancient Rome **See pp118–21**

wife once stood on top of the column, but it was replaced by one of St Paul in 1589 *(see p92)*.

8 Nero's Golden House

When the rooms of the mad emperor's house were discovered in the late 1400s, everyone thought they'd found mysterious grottoes. Consequently, the style of wall painting found here became known as "grotesque" and was much imitated by Renaissance artists, including Raphael *(see p23)*.

Nero's Golden House

9 Largo di Torre Argentina

Discovered in the 1920s, four Republican temples stand out distinctly, with the columns of a portico at the north end. The drainage gutters of an Imperial public latrine are behind one temple, and behind others stands the tufa-block platform of the Curia of the Theatre of Pompey. Caesar was killed here on 15 March 44 BC *(see p99)*.

10 Theatre of Marcellus

The theatre was inaugurated by Augustus in 23 BC and dedicated to his nephew and son-in-law Marcellus, who had just died, aged 19. Not much remains of the once huge structure, which held up to 20,000 people. In later ages, what was left of it was used as support for medieval and Renaissance fortresses and palaces *(see p101)*.

Top 10 Roman Emperors

1 Augustus
The first and most brilliant emperor (31 BC–AD 14) brought a reign of peace after 17 years of civil war.

2 Nero
The most notorious for his excesses, Nero (54–68) fancied himself a great singer and showman. He eventually committed suicide.

3 Vespasian
This emperor (69–79) ended civil war and the Jewish revolt, and started construction of the Colosseum.

4 Trajan
One of the most just rulers and successful generals, Trajan (98–117) pushed the Empire to its furthest reaches.

5 Hadrian
A great builder and traveller, Hadrian (117–38) revived Greek ideals, including the fashion of growing a beard.

6 Marcus Aurelius
The closest Rome came to having a philosopher-king of the Platonic ideal (161–80).

7 Septimius Severus
Brought order after civil war, promoted cultural life and left an important architectural legacy (193–211).

8 Diocletian
Diocletian (284–305) set up a governing system of multiple emperors. A virulent persecutor of the Christians.

9 Constantine
Constantine (306–37) established Christianity as the state religion and moved the capital to Constantinople.

10 Romulus Augustulus
The last of the emperors (475–6), deposed by the German warrior Odoacer.

Left **Sala dei Misteri, Vatican Museums** Right **Palazzo dei Conservatori, Musei Capitoline**

Museums and Galleries

Vatican Museums

Occupying papal palaces dating from the 13th century onwards, these galleries include the Graeco-Roman antiquities, the Etruscan Museum, four Raphael Rooms, the Collection of Modern Religious Art, the Sistine Chapel and the Picture Gallery *(see pp8–11)*.

Museo Nazionale Romano

Founded in 1889, this museum's holdings include archaeological finds and antiquities unearthed since 1870, plus pre-existing collections. The works are spread around five separate locations: the Baths of Diocletian, the Aula Ottagona – a part of the baths, nearby Palazzo Massimo, Palazzo Altemps, and the recently opened Crypta Balbi *(see pp28–31)*.

Galleria Borghese

A tribute to the unbridled power of favoured papal nephews in the 1600s, this pleasure-palace, its priceless collections of art, and its newly restored gardens comprise one of the most gorgeous sights in Rome *(see pp20–21)*.

Musei Capitolini

The glorious square, designed by no less than Michelangelo, is home to smaller papal art collections than the Vatican's, but equally invaluable *(see pp24–7)*.

Hellenistic faun, Galleria Borghese

Galleria Nazionale d'Arte Antica

This state art collection is now divided between two noble family residences: Palazzo Barberini *(see p133)* and Palazzo Corsini *(see p142)*. The first boasts the Gran Salone, with its dazzling illusionistic ceiling by Pietro da Cortona, along with works by Filippo Lippi, El Greco, Holbein and Caravaggio. The second houses a Fra Angelico triptych, and paintings by Rubens, Van Dyck and Caravaggio.

Villa Giulia

The building itself is a 16th-century country retreat designed for Pope Julius III by Vignola. Since 1889, it has housed the state collection of pre-Roman art, including Etruscan artifacts and relics of the Latins and other tribes. The prize Etruscan work is the 6th-century BC Husband and Wife Sarcophagus, a large terracotta showing a serenely smiling couple on a couch *(see p112)*.

Galleria Doria Pamphilj

This aristocratic family's palace is filled with masterpieces by such painters as Raphael, Titian and Veláz-quez, whose portrait of the Pamphilj pope is famous for its psychological depth. This exhibit is fortunate to have a superb audio-guide, narrated by the present-day Prince Jonathan Doria Pamphilj (in English) that gives rare insight into the history of the collection (see p91).

Palazzo and Galleria Spada

This superb 16th-century palace contains a specially built 17th-century gallery to hold the cardinals' collection of Renaissance, Baroque and later works, including paintings by Rubens and Jan Brueghel the Elder. One of the high points is Borromini's whimsical *trompe-l'oeil* gallery, a clever study in illusory perspective that appears to be four times longer that it really is (see p104).

Villa Giulia

Galleria Nazionale d'Arte Moderna

The *belle époque* home to this collection offers sculptures by Canova and an exhaustive view of 19th-century Italian and European painting. There is also an eclectic selection of modern works, including artists Rodin, Cézanne, Modigliani, Van Gogh, Monet, Klimt and Jackson Pollock. ⊗ *Viale delle Belle Arti, 131 • Map B2 • 06 323 4000 • Open 8:30am–7:30pm Tue–Sun • Adm*

Galleria Comunale d'Arte Moderna

Begun from a small donation to the city in 1883, this collection has grown to include examples of every major 19th- and 20th-century Italian artistic movement. Exhibitions include canvases by De Chirico, Morandi and Afro, as well as sculptures. ⊗ *Via Francesco Crispi 24 • Map P1 • 06 474 2848 • The gallery is undergoing restoration work, call ahead for opening times • Adm*

Left **Sarcophagus, San Clemente** Centre **Santa Maria Maggiore** Right **Santa Maria sopra Minerva**

🔟 Churches

1 St Peter's Basilica
Should the opportunity arise, don't miss seeing the basilica's cavernous interior when all the lights are on – only then can you fully appreciate this giant jewel-box of colour *(see pp12–13)*.

2 Santa Maria del Popolo
Legend recounts that on this spot, where a magnificent oak grew, Nero died and was buried. The site was thought cursed, but in 1099, in a vision, the Virgin told Pope Paschal II to fell the oak, dig up the evil emperor's bones and build a chapel *(see pp32–3)*.

3 San Clemente
This unpretentious yet compelling church provides a concise Roman history lesson in one concentrated location *(see pp34–5)*.

4 Santa Maria Maggiore
One of Rome's greatest basilicas, this richly decorated church dates from the 5th century, as do its earliest mosaics, full of Byzantine splendour. The 16th-century Cappella Sistina's rare marbles were "quarried" in typical papal fashion, by destroying an ancient wonder – in this case, the Palatine's Septizonium, a tower erected by Septimius Severus in AD 203 *(see p127)*.

5 Santa Maria sopra Minerva
Built over an ancient temple of wisdom, this is Rome's only Florentine Gothic church, built around 1280. In the 16th century it was the stronghold of the Inquisition in Rome. Among its great art is Michelangelo's *Risen Christ*, created nude but now sporting a skewed, gilt-bronze loincloth. The body of St Catherine of Siena, who convinced the papacy to return from France in 1377, reclines under the altar *(see p91)*.

6 San Giovanni in Laterano
The "Mother of All Churches", the cathedral of Rome's bishopric was founded by Constantine in the 4th century. It was the chief papal residence until 1309, and popes were crowned here up until the 19th century. Its most recent renovation was ordered in 1650, explaining the present-day Baroque bombast, with mammoth saints gesturing and gyrating. The remarkable cloisters are 13th-century Cosmatesque *(see p127)*.

San Giovanni in Laterano

San Luigi dei Francesi statue

7 Santa Maria in Trastevere

This is probably Rome's oldest church and certainly one of the most intimate and charming. Dating from the time of Pope Calixtus I (AD 217–222), it was an early centre of Marian devotion and is Rome's only medieval church that has not been transmogrified by either decay or enthusiastic Baroque renovators. Legend claims it was founded on a spot where olive oil miraculously sprang forth on the day of Christ's birth (see p139).

8 San Luigi dei Francesi

The national church of France in Italy really has only one star turn, but it is a priceless one at that – Caravaggio's famous trio of enormous paintings in the Chapel of St Matthew (see p49). The central oil on canvas, St Matthew and the Angel, is the second version. The first was rejected by the church because the saint was shown with dirty feet – and, some say, because his relationship with the young angel seemed inappropriately intimate (see p83).

9 San Paolo fuori le Mura

Despite its rather soulless 19th-century reconstruction following a fire, the grandeur of this 4th-century basilica can still impress. Some restored 5th-century and 12th- and 13th-century mosaics survive, along with the original 11th-century bronze door and a grand Paschal candlestick. Fortunately the cloisters of inlaid double columns (1214), considered the most beautiful in Rome, escaped the flames (see p151).

10 Sant'Andrea della Valle

Most visitors seek out this church as the setting of the first act of Puccini's opera *Tosca*, but the Counter-Reformation giant is also important in its own right. It has

Sant'Andrea della Valle

the city's second-largest dome, a flamboyant Baroque façade and some wonderful frescoes by Domenichino inside (see p99).

Left **Fontana delle Tartarughe** Right **Piazza San Pietro**

Top10 Squares and Fountains

1 Piazza Navona
The elongated oval of Rome's loveliest square hints that it is built atop Domitian's ancient stadium *(see p86)*. This pedestrian paradise is filled with cafés, street performers and artists, milling tourists, kids playing football, and splashing fountains. Bernini designed the central Fountain of Four Rivers, and added the Moor figure to the most southerly of the piazza's other two fountains, constantly altered from the 16th to 19th centuries *(see p83)*.

Trevi Fountain

2 Trevi Fountain
Tradition holds that if you throw coins into this 1732 Nicola Salvi fountain, you ensure a return to Rome. Ingeniously grafted on to the back of a palazzo (even the windowsills mutate into rough rocks), the Trevi marks the end of the Acqua Vergine aqueduct, built by Agrippa in 19 BC from a spring miraculously discovered by a virgin *(see p109)*.

3 Campo de' Fiori
This "field of flowers" bursts with colour during the morning market, and again after dark when its pubs and bars make it a centre of Roman nightlife. The dour hooded statue overlooking all is in honour of Giordano Bruno, a theologian who was burned at the stake here for his progressive heresies in 1600 during the Counter-Reformation *(see p99)*.

4 Piazza del Popolo
Architect Giuseppe Valadier expanded this site of festivals and public executions into an elegant piazza in 1811–23, adding four Egyptian-style lion fountains to the base of one of Rome's oldest obelisks. The 1200 BC Ramases II monolith was moved to the Circus Maximus by Augustus then placed here by Pope Sixtus V *(see p110)*.

5 Piazza San Pietro
Bernini's gargantuan colonnade, 196 m (640 ft) across, embraces the hordes of worshippers and tourists arriving at St Peter's. Its perfect ellipse is confirmed by the optical illusion of disappearing columns afforded by standing at one of the focus points – marble discs set between the central 1st-century BC obelisk, carved in Egypt for a Roman Prefect, and either fountain: Bernini's on the left, Domenico Fontana's on the right *(see p12)*. ◈ Map B3

Fontana delle Tartarughe

Giacomo della Porta designed this delightful fountain between 1581 and 1584. The turtles *(tartarughe)* struggling up over the lip, however, were added in 1658, perhaps by Bernini *(see p101)*.

Piazza Barberini

This busy piazza is centred on Bernini's Triton Fountain (1642–3), the merman spouting water from a conch shell. It was commissioned by Pope Urban VIII and features his family symbol (bees) on its base *(see p133)*.

Piazza Venezia

The de facto centre of Rome and convergence of traffic patterns, during evening rush hour conducted with balletic brio by a white-gloved policeman. The piazza is flanked by the Palazzo Venezia, from whose balcony Mussolini once exhorted hordes to the joys of Fascism *(see p104)*.

Fountain of the Naiads

The water spouting from Bernini's Triton is puny compared to the gushes rising from Glaucus in this huge fountain and traffic circle. The fountain is surrounded by naiads and horses in this 1888 confection by Mario Rutelli (grandfather of Francesco, the city's mayor from 1993 to 2001). ✆ *Piazza della Republica • Map C3*

Piazza del Popolo

Piazza Santa Maria in Trastevere

A perfect neighbourhood square: cafés, shops, a fine restaurant, and a 17th-century palazzo abutting a medieval church, its mosaics romantically floodlit at night. A fountain fitted with shells by Carlo Fontana (1682) atop a pedestal of stairs serves as benches for backpackers to strum guitars and tourists to eat ice cream *(see p139)*.

Left **Ceiling, Sistine Chapel** Right **Michelangelo's Pietà**

🔟 Artistic Masterpieces

1 Caravaggio's Deposition
Caravaggio strove to outdo Michelangelo's *Pietà* by making his Mary old and tired. Rather than a slender slip of a Christ, Caravaggio's muscular Jesus is so heavy (emphasized by a diagonal composition) that Nicodemus struggles with his legs and John's grasp opens Christ's wound *(see p9)*.

2 Raphael's Transfiguration
Raphael's towering master-piece and his final work was found, almost finished, in his studio when he died. It is the pinnacle of his talent as a syn-thesist, mixing Perugino's clarity, Michelangelo's colour palette and twisting figures, and Leonardo's composition *(see p8)*.

3 Michelangelo's Pietà
The Renaissance is known for naturalism, but Michelangelo warped this for artistic effect. Here, Mary is too young, her dead son, achingly thin and small, laid across her voluminous lap. Hear-ing the work being attributed to better known sculptors, the artist crept into the chapel of St Peter's one night and carved his name in the band across the Virgin's chest *(see p12)*.

4 Raphael's School of Athens
When Raphael first cast his con-temporary artists as Classical thinkers in this imaginary setting, one was missing. After he saw the Sistine ceiling Michelangelo was painting down the hall, Raphael added the troubled genius, sulking on the steps, as Heraclitus *(see p8)*.

5 Michelangelo's Sistine Chapel
Although he considered himself a sculptor first, Michelangelo managed to turn this almost flat ceiling into a soaring vault peopled with Old Testament prophets and *ignudi* (nude men). He did it virtually alone, firing all of his assistants save one to help him grind pigments *(see pp10–11)*.

Raphael's School of Athens

6 Bernini's Apollo and Daphne

Rarely has marble captured flowing, almost liquid movement so gracefully. Bernini freezes time, wind-blown hair and cloak, in the instant the fleeing nymph is wrapped in bark and leaves, transformed into a laurel by her sympathetic river god father *(see p20)*.

Caravaggio's Calling of St Matthew

7 Caravaggio's Calling of St Matthew

Caravaggio uses strong *chiaroscuro* techniques here. As a naturalistic shaft of light spills from Christ to his chosen chronicler, St Matthew, Caravaggio captures the precise moment of Matthew's conversion from tax collector to Evangelist *(see p83)*.

8 Leonardo da Vinci's St Jerome

Barely sketched out, yet compelling for its anatomical precision and compositional experimentation. Jerome forms a spiral that starts in the mountains, runs across the cave entrance and lion's curve, up the saint's outstretched right arm, then wraps along his left arm and hand into the centre *(see p9)*.

9 Michelangelo's Moses

This wall monument is a pale shadow of the elaborate tomb for Julius II that Michelangelo first envisaged and for which he carved this figure. Some claim there is a self-portrait hidden in the flowing beard. Moses is currently undergoing a long restoration but remains visible *(see p127)*.

10 Bernini's Ecstasy of St Teresa

The saint here is being pierced by a smirking angel's lance, and is Bernini at his theatrical best. He sets this religious ecstasy on a stage flanked by opera boxes from which members of the commissioning Cornaro family look on *(see p133)*.

Left **Palazzo Venezia** Right **Fresco, Villa Farnesina**

🔟 Villas and Palaces

1 Villa Farnesina
A little gem of gracious living, decorated by some of the greatest artists of the Renaissance, including Raphael. The loggias are now glassed in to protect the precious frescoes, but they were originally open, embodying the ideal of blending indoor and outdoor spaces – a concept borrowed from ancient Roman villa designers *(see p139)*.

2 Campidoglio Palazzi
When Emperor Charles V visited Rome in 1536, Pope Paul III was so embarrassed at the Capitol's state that he enlisted Michelangelo's help. Work started 10 years later, but Michelangelo died long before its completion. True to his design, however, are the double flight of steps for the Palazzo Senatorio, the addition of Palazzo Nuovo, the fine façades and placement of ancient sculptures *(see p99)*.

3 Palazzo Borghese
Called "the harpsichord" because of its unusual shape, this 17th-century palace was once the centre of fashionable entertainments for Rome's papal high society. Its Mannerist courtyard, in particular, was the stage for lavish affairs. You can peek in to see the oversize statuary, columns supporting the double loggias, and the "Bath of Venus" fountain *(see p94)*.

4 Palazzo Massimo alle Colonne
Architect Peruzzi overcame a number of technical problems to build this 16th-century masterpiece. Primarily, he had to follow the curve of the foundations of the ancient Theatre of Domitian. His colonnaded portico is an elegant solution along the street side; the other façade is decorated with monochrome frescoes, known as *grisaille (see p85)*.

5 Palazzo Farnese
Considered the Renaissance palace *par excellence*, reflecting the genius of both Antonio da Sangallo the Younger and Michelangelo. Home to one of Rome's most unscrupulous families, it was commissioned in 1517 by Alessandro Farnese, later Pope Paul III *(see p104)*.

Villa Farnesina courtyard

Villa Giulia

Intended for hedonistic pleasure, this was a perfect papal retreat where Pope Julius III could indulge his tastes for young boys and Classical statuary. Designed by Vignola, Ammannati and Vasari, this 16th-century marvel is all loggias, fountains and gardens *(see p112)*.

Palazzo Farnese

Palazzo Barberini

When Maffei Barberini became Pope Urban VIII in 1623, he decided to build a family palace on the (then) edge of town. Architect Carlo Maderno designed it as an outsize country villa with three floors of arcades. Bernini added the square staircase on the left; Borromini the spiral staircase on the right *(see p133)*.

Palazzo della Cancelleria

One of the loveliest palaces from the Early Renaissance (late 1400s) – the purity of its façade and courtyard is unparalleled. Several ancient monuments were pillaged to provide the marble and the 44 portico columns inside *(see p104)*.

Palazzo Spada

Built around 1550 for a wealthy cardinal, the architect unknown, this palace has one of the most ornate Renaissance façades in Rome, featuring reliefs evoking the city's glorious past. However, the inner courtyard is the masterpiece, decorated with stucco figures of the 12 Olympian gods and goddesses *(see p104)*.

Palazzo Venezia

Rome's first great Renaissance palace (1455–64) was built for the Venetian cardinal Pietro Barbo. It is attributed to one of two Florentine architects, Alberti or Maiano. You can admire the beautiful palm court with an 18th-century fountain from the museum café *(see p104)*.

Left **Mamertine Prison** Centre **Ceiling, San Clemente** Right **Nero's Golden House**

TOP 10 Underground Sights

1 San Clemente
The many layers of this fascinating church reveal the changing ideals of Rome in various eras *(see pp34–5)*.

2 Catacombs
The burial tunnels of Rome's early Christians are like a honeycomb beneath the consular roads out of Rome, especially along Via Appia Antica. Grave niches stacked like shelving along dark corridors are carved into the tufa, with some precious remnants of fresco and engraved marble slabs *(see pp151–2)*.

3 Vatican Grottoes
The famous Red Wall behind which Peter was supposedly buried was discovered under the Vatican in the 1940s *(see p13)*.

4 Nero's Golden House
Like most of "underground Rome", Nero's fabulous and vast palace was not originally buried. But when Renaissance worthies such as Raphael chopped holes in the roof and lowered themselves into the sumptuously decorated rooms on ropes, they called the spaces "grottoes", and named the intricate frescoed designs of foliage and fantastical creatures "grotesques" *(see p23)*.

5 Mamertine Prison
This was Rome's ancient central lockdown (built 7th–6th century BC). Among its celebrity inmates were Vercingetorix, a rebel Celtic chieftain, styled the last king of Gaul, who was brought to Rome in chains, and St Peter, who left an impression of his face where the guards reportedly slammed him against the stairwell wall. Downstairs is also the alleged column to which St Peter was chained. ◉ *Via S Pietro in Carcere/Via Tulliano • Map P5 • Open 9am–5pm (winter), 9am–7pm (summer) daily • Donation*

6 Crypta Balbi
A jumble of excavations from all eras, including a piece of 13 BC *crypta* (porticoed courtyard) attached to a destroyed theatre. The museum's didactic panels, which are an excellent introduction to Rome's layer effect, plus the medieval

Underground font, San Clemente

frescoes are more interesting than the rather plain excavations underneath. ◈ *Via delle Botteghe Oscure 31 • Map M4 • Open 9am–7:45pm Tue–Sun • Adm*

Casa di SS Giovanni e Paolo (Celian)

This house under an ancient church belonged to two Constantinian officials, martyred in AD 362. There is also a series of buildings, including a frescoed nymphaeum, dating from the 1st to 4th centuries. ◈ *Clivio di Scauro/ Piazza SS Giovanni e Paolo • Map E5 • 06 7045 4544 • Open 10am–1pm, 3–6pm Thu–Mon • Adm • DA*

Museo Barracco

The museum's basement dates from the 4th century AD: walls, flooring, column stumps, a bit of cornice and sculpted relief, a marble basin and a large double pestle for hand-grinding grains can be seen *(see p55)*.

Pompey's Theatre

Pompey's 61–55 BC theatre is still evident in the curve of medieval buildings on Largo del Pollaro. Its fabric is visible only in the basements, including the downstairs rooms of the da Pancrazio restaurant installed in the ancient travertine corridors. ◈ *Piazza del Biscione 92 • Map L4 • Open 12:30–2:30pm, 7:30–11pm Thu–Tue • Free*

Mithraeum under San Stefano Rotondo

Under this church lies a 2nd-century AD shrine to Mithraism, a popular religion among Rome's soldiers and lower classes while Christianity was gaining with patricians *(see p128)*. ◈ *Via di S Stefano Rotondo • Map F5 • Open by appt only on written application to the church • Free*

Top 10 Vistas

1 **Roman Forum from Campidoglio**
Walk around the right side of Palazzo Senatorio for a postcard panorama – floodlit at night. ◈ *Map P5*

2 **Il Vittoriano**
Climb the "Wedding Cake" for vistas across the Imperial Fora *(see p104)*.

3 **Gianicolo**
The Eternal City is laid out at your feet from a lover's lane perch across the Tiber *(see p141)*.

4 **The Spanish Steps**
Views spill down the steps to the tourist-filled piazza *(see p109)*.

5 **Musei Capitolini Café**
A bird's-eye sweep over the archaeological park at Rome's heart can be seen from here *(see p24)*.

6 **St Peter's Dome**
St Peter's colonnade and Castel Sant'Angelo can be seen from Michelangelo's dome *(see p12)*.

7 **Knights of Malta Keyhole**
St Peter's Dome is perfectly framed through a gate keyhole in this garden *(see p120)*.

8 **Castel Sant'Angelo Ramparts**
Lazy Tiber River vistas with the Ponte Sant'Angelo directly underneath *(see p140)*.

9 **Pincio**
Valadier carefully designed this view from his gardens, across Piazza del Popolo to St Peter's *(see p111)*.

10 **Villa Mellini**
A different panorama, near Rome's observatory above Piazzale Clodio, taking in the city and hills beyond from the northwest. ◈ *Map B1*

Left **Museo delle Anime del Purgatorio** Right **Museo Nazionale della Pasta Alimentari**

🔟 Hidden Rome

1 Capuchin Crypt

If you like a good haunted house, this is your first stop. The bones of thousands of deceased monks have been used to decorate every conceivable surface in the most ghoulish designs. Those corpses that weren't taken to bits have been hung on walls, decked out in cowled robes *(see p134)*.

2 Museo della Casina delle Civette

One of the restored buildings in Villa Torlonia, Mussolini's abode as prime minister, this Art Nouveau cottage displays ceramic and stained-glass decorations, including owl motifs, which gives it its name, "The Little House of the Owls." The setting is now a public park. ✎ *Via Nomentana 70 • Map G1 • Open 9am–1 hr before sunset daily (villa); Apr–Sep: 9am–7pm, Oct–Mar: 9am–6pm daily (museum) • Adm*

Façade, Museo della Casina delle Civette

3 Museo Nazionale delle Paste Alimentari

The National Museum of Pasta proudly proves that pasta was invented in Italy in the 12th century. Discover how pasta is made from durum wheat, which processes are used to create *pastasciutta* (dried pasta), and how eating it *al dente* (chewy) makes it easier to digest. ✎ *Piazza Scanderbeg 117 • Map P2 • Open 9:30am– 5:30pm daily • Adm • DA • www.pastainmuseum.com*

4 Museo delle Anime del Purgatorio

The Gothic Sacro Cuore del Suffragio church is host to a truly spooky display. A glass case preserves various types of physical "evidence" (mostly handprints somehow burned on to surfaces) of visitations from dead souls, waiting in Purgatory to move up into Heaven. ✎ *Lungotevere Prati 12 • Map L1 • Open 7–11am, 4:30–7pm Mon–Sat daily • Free*

5 Pyramid of Caius Cestius

Following the Egyptian fashion, many ancient Romans used to build their tombs as pyramids, but this is the only survivor. It was made to form part of the defensive wall around the city *(see p121)*.

6 Cat Sanctuary at Largo Argentina

Dr Silvia Viviani is the guiding genius of this loving undertaking, but what makes it work is the volunteers' enthusiasm. Tourists are welcome to visit the veterinary clinic, and are also encouraged to adopt one of the cats. The sanctuary has a "no-kill" policy. ⊗ *Largo di Torre Argentina (southwest corner of square)* • *Map M4* • *Open noon– 6pm daily* • *Donation*

7 Palazzo Zuccari
Noted for its door and window frames shaped into screaming mouths of grotesque ogres, this bit of 16th-century Mannerist fantasia was the atelier of the painters Taddeo and Federico Zuccari. ⊗ *Via Gregoriana 28* • *Map D2* • *Closed to public*

Doorway, Palazzo Zuccari

8 Museo Barracco
This select collection traces the development of sculptural art in the ancient world. Assyrian and Egyptian works are highlighted, along with Etruscan, Roman and paleo-Christian art. Its original Greek sculpture is second only to the Vatican's *(see p104).*

9 Museo della Civiltà Romana
A Fascist Art Deco Temple of Karnak is home to this fascinating museum. The most striking exhibit is a 1:250 scale model of what Rome looked like in the 4th century. There are also models of ancient furniture, musical instruments and other items. ⊗ *Piazza Giovanni Agnelli* • *Metro EUR Fermi* • *Open 9am–2pm Tue–Sun* • *Adm* • *DA*

10 Museo delle Mura
Porta San Sebastiano is the most impressive gate surviving in the Aurelian Wall *(see p152).* It now houses a museum containing prints and models illustrating the wall's history. Take a short walk along the restored parapets, which provide great views, especially along the Via Appia. ⊗ *Via di Porta San Sebastiano 18* • *Bus 118, 218* • *Open 9am–2pm Mon–Sat* • *Adm*

Left **Lord Byron** Right **Mark Twain**

🔟 Writers in Rome

1 Wolfgang Goethe
The first Grand Tourist, German author Goethe (1749–1832) rented rooms on the Corso, now a museum, between 1786 and 1788 *(see p112)*. His book *Italian Journey* laid the blueprint for later tourists who came to Italy to learn from its history and to complete their education.

Wolfgang Goethe

2 John Keats
The English Romantic poet (1795–1821) came to Rome in 1820 for the antiquities and Italian lifestyle – and to bolster his ailing health, which nevertheless failed. Keats died at age 25 of tuberculosis in an apartment by the Spanish Steps *(see p109)*.

3 Henry James
The New York author (1843–1916) spent half his life in Europe. Rome features in *Daisy Miller*, *A Roman Holiday*, *Portrait of a Lady* and his travelogue *Italian Hours*. In an 1869 letter he proclaimed "At last – for the first time – I live! It beats everything: it leaves the Rome of your fancy – your education – nowhere."

4 Nathaniel Hawthorne
During his Italian sojourn from 1857 to 1859, the American man of letters (1804–64) was so moved by an ancient sculpture in the Capitoline museums he crafted his final novel *The Marble Faun* around it.

5 Alberto Moravia
One of Italy's top modern authors (1907–90) wrote about Rome in *Raconti Romani*, *La Romana*, *La Ciociara*, *Gli Indifferenti* and *La Noia*, most of which have been translated.

6 Lord Byron
The ultimate Romantic poet (1788–1824) who lived, to varying degrees, the cavalier life so beloved by his genre. He spent years in Italy in the company of the Shelleys and other friends, and based a large part of *Childe Harold's Pilgrimage* and *Don Juan* on his experiences here.

7 Edward Gibbon
When English parliamentarian Gibbon (1737–94) stood in the Forum for the first time in 1764, he was struck by how "...each memorable spot where

Romulus stood, or Tully spoke, or Caesar fell, was at once present to my eye." He resolved to write the history of Rome, and by 1788 had finished his seminal work, *The Decline and Fall of the Roman Empire*.

Gore Vidal
The prolific American writer (b.1925) has been a resident of Rome and Ravello, south of Naples, for decades. His Roman experiences have informed such books as *The Judgment of Paris*, *Julian* and his memoir *Palimpsest*.

Mark Twain
The American writer (1835–1910) spent little time in the Eternal City during his Grand Tour, but his satirical impressions in *The Innocents Abroad* have become among the most quoted and memorable of any visitor.

Percy Bysshe Shelley
The English poet (1792–1822) lived in Italy with his wife Mary from 1818 until he drowned near Pisa. He visited Rome often, and penned the masterpiece *The Cenci* about the scandal of Roman patrician Beatrice Cenci.

Percy Bysshe Shelley

Top 10 Classical Writers in Rome

1 Plautus
Formulaic comedies of errors by Plautus (250–184 BC) influenced Shakespeare.

2 Caesar
General, dictator and writer (100–44 BC). *De Bello Gallico* describes his campaigns in Gaul (France), *The Civil War* his fight against Pompey.

3 Cicero
Great orator and staunch republican (106–43 BC). His speeches grant insight into Roman political life.

4 Virgil
Poet and propagandist (70–19 BC). His epic *The Aeneid* tied Rome's foundation to the Trojan War.

5 Ovid
Greatest Roman Classical poet (43 BC–AD 17). His *Metamorphoses* codified many Roman myths, but *Ars Amatoria* detailed how to entice women and got him exiled.

6 Tacitus
Tacitus (55–117) wrote *Annals and Histories* covering Rome's early Imperial history; *Life of Agricola* his father-in-law's governorship of Britain.

7 Juvenal
Romans invented satire; Juvenal (60–130) perfected the form in his poems.

8 Pliny the Younger
The letters *(Epistulae)* of Pliny (61–113) to prominent figures give us a glimpse of imperial society.

9 Suetonius
Historian (70–125) who wrote the lives of the Caesars.

10 Petronius
Petronius (70–130) parodied Roman life in *Satiricon*.

Left **Ben Hur** Right **La Dolce Vita**

🔟 Cinecittà Studio Films

1 La Dolce Vita
Fellini's 1960 classic on "the sweet life" of 1950s Rome, when the Eternal City was a hotspot for international glitterati. Marcello Mastroianni plays a reporter sucked into this decadent lifestyle, while a character named Paparazzo, snapping stars at Via Veneto cafés, gave a name to his occupation.

2 Fellini's Roma
Fellini's 1972 tribute to his adopted home town. Rome's heritage gets in the way of modernization, and the absurdity of the Vatican is shown in a frighteningly funny papal fashion show. Fellini built a highway at the Cinecittà studios so he could film rush hour without the bother of real traffic.

3 Ben Hur
The original big budget ($50 million) gladiator epic from 1959. William Wyler directed Charlton Heston as a Jewish prince betrayed into slavery. He bares his chest, wins his freedom and engages in a chariot race that has influenced every cinematic race since. The film won 11 Academy Awards.

4 The Bicycle Thieves
The ultimate neo-realist film, Vittorio de Sica's 1948 work is a recreated documentary of late 1940s Rome. An honest family man struggling to make ends meet in postwar Rome watches everything fall apart when his precious bicycle, so necessary for his livelihood, is stolen and he tries to track it down.

Roman Holiday

Cleopatra
Despite the lavish sets and costumes, a cast of thousands and Elizabeth Taylor and Richard Burton steaming up the place, Joseph Mankiewicz's 1963 epic was one of Hollywood's first spectacular box office flops.

Rome, Open City
Powerful 1946 drama about the Roman Resistance during World War II. Roberto Rossellini tried to create a documentary feel, filming in the streets mere months after the war ended, using real soldiers and recreating actual events. A young Fellini helped write the script.

Roman Holiday
Romantic comedy which made a star of newcomer Audrey Hepburn in 1953, when she won the Academy Award as a rebellious princess who runs around the city with Gregory Peck, a penniless writer.

Caro Diario
This most personal of films (1994) opens with the director, Nanni Moretti, riding his scooter around suburban Rome.

Life is Beautiful
Surprisingly successful 1998 mix of comedy and fable set against Nazi-occupied Italy. Writer/director Roberto Begnini's Jewish bookseller uses comedy to shield his son from the horror of their Nazi concentration camp by pretending it's all a big game. It won three Academy Awards.

Gangs of New York
Hollywood director Martin Scorsese spent $100 million to recreate 1840s New York and an ocean liner at the Cinecittà studios for his 2002 film.

Top 10 Italian Film Directors

Federico Fellini
The five-time Academy Award-winner (1920–1993) embodied styles from neo-realism to magico-realism.

Roberto Rossellini
Neo-realist master director (1906–77) of *Rome, Open City* and *Paisà*.

Vittorio De Sica
De Sica (1901–74) was the founder of neo-realism, with films such as *Shoeshine* and *Yesterday, Today and Tomorrow*.

Luchino Visconti
Visconti (1906–1976) is most famous for filming *The Leopard* and *Death in Venice*.

Pier Paolo Pasolini
Poet, Communist and filmmaker (1922–75). Filmed notorious versions of *Oedipus Rex* and *The Decameron*.

Sergio Leone
Leone (1929–89) turned Italy into America's Wild West and Clint Eastwood into a star with "spaghetti westerns" such as *A Fistful of Dollars*.

Michelangelo Antonioni
Antonioni (b.1912) helped create the Italian New Wave *(Red Desert)* and has enjoyed Hollywood success *(Blow Up)*.

Nanni Moretti
Often autobiographical writer/director (b.1953), likened to Woody Allen.

Bernardo Bertolucci
Poet and film-maker (b.1941). After great success outside Italy he returned home for *Stealing Beauty*.

Roberto Benigni
Writer-director-actor (b.1952), often using slapstick, achieved worldwide fame with *Life is Beautiful*.

Left **Villa Borghese** Centre **Casina Valadier, Pincio** Right **Church, Via Appia Antica**

🔟 Romantic Spots

Gianicolo
Saunter around arm-in-arm in this elegant park and take in a traditional puppet show, perhaps buy a puppet or two and check out the carousel. But most of all, enjoy the views, considered by many to be the best in the city. If you happen to be here at noon, get ready for a shock when the cannon booms – a daily routine *(see p141)*.

Pincio
These gardens are the other most famous view of Rome, much cherished by Romantic writers since the early 19th century, when the gardens were designed by Giuseppe Valadier. If the exclusive Casina Valadier café/restaurant should be open for business, no place is more romantic for a drink or a meal *(see p111)*.

Campidoglio at night

Rose and Orange Gardens, Parco Savello
The public Rose Gardens are a gracious, fragrant place to stroll in season, and then make your way on up the hill to the Orange Garden, where you can relax under umbrella pines and enjoy the view of the river, Trastevere and St Peter's. Take the ancient Clivo di Rocca Savella back down the hill. ◈ *Map A3*

Villa Borghese
A huge park with innumerable fountains, benches, shady lanes, niches and glades. But by far the most appealing activity is taking a rowboat out on the lake, around the island with its Classical temple *(see p111)*.

Arnaldo ai Satiri
Everything you might require for romance can be found in this candlelit hideaway restaurant on an ancient street. The poetic decor has a ballet theme and the atmosphere is suitably soft and subdued. *Rigatoni alla crema di cavoli* (fluted pasta with cream of cabbage sauce) is the unusual house speciality, and the turkey breast with mozzarella and mushrooms is equally delicious. ◈ *Via di Grotta Pinta 8 • Map L4 • 06 686 1915 • Closed Tue • €*

Lo Chalet del Lago

Believe it or not, the Fascist complex of EUR *(see p151)* has a truly charming restaurant with huge picture windows overlooking the lake, where during the day you can watch boaters go by and the ducks paddle about. The food is simple but is as elegant as its surroundings *(see p155)*.

Campidoglio by Night

With the subtle yet dramatic lighting, the three palaces on this hill take on an almost magical beauty at night *(see pp24–7)*. Make your way up the gentle incline, circumambulate the piazza once or twice, then head across and down to imbibe the vision of the Roman Forum and Colosseum, which are also evocatively floodlit.

Trevi Fountain

Too often thronged with tourists, yet the sheer beauty and power of this creation are nevertheless overwhelming, day or night. It's also a perfect opportunity to make any wishes you may have in mind, the more romantic the better. Have some coins ready for tossing in – backwards, of course – to ensure your return to Rome *(see p109)*.

Appian Way on a Sunday

One day a week, part of the old Via Appia Antica is closed to all traffic except tour buses, making it perfect for a bucolic bike ride, or a very long walk if you want to cover it all. Lined

Trevi Fountain

with pines and cypresses, this is where the ancient Romans came to bury their dead, and many tombs still remain along the roadside *(see p151)*.

Gelato at Tre Scalini

A triple-chocolate bomb with a cherry in the middle and topped with whipped cream is the famous *tartufo* produced by this café. If you get it "to go", it's a bargain, but it's probably more romantic to sit inside and share one – as long as you don't fight over the cherry *(see p88)*.

Left **Villa Doria Pamphilj** Right **Orto Botanico**

🔟 Green Spaces

Villa Borghese
Extensive, elegant and full of shady glades and beautiful fountains, this is a great park for a stroll, a picnic or a jog. You can also go boating on the artificial lake, rent a bicycle or in-line skates (see p111).

Pincio
The traditional time to enjoy the most famous panorama of Rome is at sunset. Other charms here include the water clock, the busts of various notables and an Egyptian-style obelisk Emperor Hadrian erected on the tomb of his beloved Antinous (see p111).

Villa Celimontana
Picnics have been a tradition here since 1552, when San Filippo Neri instituted the Visit of the Seven Churches and the Mattei family offered pilgrims a simple repast. In summer it's the venue for wonderful dinner-concerts. ◈ Piazza della Navicella 12 • Map E5 • Open dawn–dusk • DA

Villa Doria Pamphilj
Rome's largest green area, extending from the Gianicolo along the ancient Via Aurelia. It's a terrific place for a run and offers a course of exercise posts. Its hills are adorned with villas, fountains, lakes and

orangeries and are perfect for strolls; or enjoy a picnic under the umbrella pines (see p142).

Orto Botanico
The graceful botanical gardens and grounds of Palazzo Corsini now provide one of the most enjoyable places to while away an hour or two and breathe in air richly perfumed by more than 7,000 plant species that thrive here. The gardens, which now belong to the University of Rome, include indigenous and exotic varieties, grouped according to ecosystems (see p142).

Villa Sciarra
This small park is replete with fountains, gazebos, ponds, loggias and statuary. There are leafy lanes for walking and lawns

Villa Borghese

For squares and fountains in Rome See pp46–7

for relaxing. It's a good place for children, too *(see p64)*. ◈ *Via Calandrelli • Map C5 • Open dawn–dusk • DA*

Villa Ada
This huge public park, originally the hunting reserve of King Vittorio Emanuele III, has rolling lawns, serene waters and copses. It's worth the trip out if you need an antidote to the fumes and noise of the city. On summer nights the lake at the far end hosts food stalls and concerts. ◈ *Via Salaria • Map E1 • Open dawn–dusk • DA*

Water clock, Pincio

Piazza Cairoli
One of the very newest city parks makes an ideal break from this hectic district. Sitting on a bench by a well-tended lawn, with flowers in bloom and the gently splashing fountain, can go a long way towards restoring frayed nerves. ◈ *Via Arenula, Via dei Giubbonari • Map L5 • DA*

Colle Oppio
After hours of walking around the Forum and the Colosseum in the high summer heat, these green slopes can be a welcome sight. Most of the Colle Oppio park is actually the roof of Nero's Golden House *(see p41)*, and you can see skylight structures for its rooms. If you haven't had enough of sightseeing, you can also examine the massive remains of the Baths of Trajan scattered about the area. ◈ *Via Labicana, Parco Oppio • Map E4 • DA*

Parco della Resistenza dell'8 Settembre
This former dustbowl has now been turned into a pleasant slice of greenery, where local people picnic and children play. Since it's one of the few parks in the city without walls or gates, it's perfect for enjoying a moonlight stroll here after dinner. ◈ *Viale della Piramide di Cestia, Viale M Gelsomini • Map D5 • DA*

Left **Villa Borghese park** Right **Villa Borghese funfair**

🔟 Rome for Children

Villa Borghese
Scipione Borghese's private Renaissance park and the adjacent 19th-century Pincio gardens, with statues and fountains, are a joy to explore, especially on two wheels. There are bike rental stands scattered throughout the park. You can also rent paddle boats for the little lake or take the kids to the park's small funfair *(see p111)*.

Explora Museum
This museum near the city centre is specifically designed with children in mind. It allows youngsters to understand how things work through fascinating hands-on displays ✪ *Via Flamina 82 • Map C1 • Open 9:30am–6:45pm Mon–Fri (from 10am Sat, Sun & hols) • Book in advance (06 361 3776) • Adm*

Capuchin Crypt
Fantastically creepy chapels festively decorated with mosaics made from the bones of dead monks, a few of whose skeletons remain propped up in bone-built niches. It rarely fails to impress, and for adolescents and above can be a highlight of the trip, although it may be a bit too much for the very young or overly squeamish *(see p134)*.

Bioparco (Zoo)
Rome's zoo, once a depressing conglomeration of badly kept cement cubicles, has been overhauled to become a pretty "biological garden" set into a corner of Villa Borghese park. ✪ *Piazzale del Giardino Zoologico 1 • Map E1 • Open 9:30am–6pm Mon–Fri, 9:30am–7pm Sat & Sun (until 5pm Nov–Mar) • Adm*

Lunapark
This modest collection of rollercoasters, carnival rides and funhouses in the Fascist-built suburb of EUR *(see p151)* is a far cry from Disneyland Paris, but will fit the bill when only an amusement park will do. ✪ *Via delle Tre Fontane • Metro EUR Magliana • Open 4pm–1am daily (summer), 3–7pm Mon–Fri, 3pm–2am Sat, 10am–10pm Sun (winter) • Adm*

Puppet Shows on the Gianicolo
You don't need to understand Italian to appreciate a Punch and Judy show (the pugilistic characters are native to Italy). This is the last of the old puppet kiosks

Roman puppets

that once peppered Rome's public parks, offering a dying art form for free. ◈ *Teatro di Pulcinella, Gianicolo • Map B4 • Show times variable, Tue–Sun • Free • DA*

Villa Sciarra

This park, tucked into a bend in the Aurelian Wall where Trastevere fades into Monteverde Vecchio, features a playground and a small funfair with a tiny rollercoaster. ◈ *Via Calandrelli • Map C5 • Open dawn–dusk daily • Adm for fair • DA*

Roman children

Exploring the Catacombs

There is nothing more thrillingly spooky in Rome than wandering these mazes of tight, dimly lit corridors, roughly carved in the tufa and lined with thousands of tomb niches. At the San Domitilla complex, some guides even let you touch a few of the bones – at most others,

all human remains have been removed to ossuaries on lower levels *(see p151)*.

Piscina delle Rose

When traipsing around ruins has sapped your energy, spend some time cooling down with the locals. This open-air swimming pool in EUR is Rome's largest and most pleasant, with a special area for kids. ◈ *Viale America 20 • Metro EUR Palasport • Open Jun–mid-Sep 9am–7pm daily • Adm*

Climbing St Peter's Dome

A welcome break from all the art of the Vatican complex. You get great views not only from the lantern atop the dome, across Piazza San Pietro towards the River Tiber, but also from the drum halfway up, which offers a bird's-eye perspective down into the transept of St Peter's Basilica itself *(see p12)*.

Left **Piano recital, RomaEuropa Festival** Right **Easter, St Peter's Square**

🔟 Cultural Festivals

RomaEuropa Festival
A fast-growing performing arts festival with a pronounced emphasis on the provocative, held every autumn in various superlative venues, including the French Academy, Palazzo Farnese and the Spanish Academy. All kinds of music, dance and theatre, including several international artists. ◈ *end-Sep–early-Dec*

Testaccio Village
This well-run multi-event happens all summer long in a purpose-built area near an old slaughterhouse. Every evening there's live music until midnight, followed by several discos, each featuring a different type of music, and lots of food choices. There's a new decor theme every year, often quite elaborate. ◈ *Via Monte Testaccio 16 • Map D6 • 06 5730 1420 • Jun–Sep 8:30pm–3am nightly*

Festa dell'Unità
Put on by the DS, the former Communist Party, this is a lively evening event, featuring music, films, dancing, games and more. The venue changes every year, as do the dates, but it's usually held in a central park, sometime around July, for about a month.

Rome's Birthday
Every 21 April there's a gala civic observance in the Piazza del Campidoglio, celebrating Rome's traditional founding in 753 BC *(see p38)*. Music, fireworks and a speech by the mayor mark the event, but the best news is that the Musei Capitolini *(see pp24–7)* are free of charge and open until 10pm.

Summer Opera Festivals
Not only does the Rome Opera Company offer its usual summer programme in the Baths of Caracalla *(see p119)*, but there are also a number of other opera programmes all over the city, with singers from around the globe.

¡Fiesta!
Celebrating all forms of Latin music, this festival takes place every night throughout the summer. In recent years, world, jazz, rock and pop music have been added to the schedule. The event is held in the vast grounds of a converted racetrack. ◈ *Ippodromo delle Capannelle, Via Appia Nuova 1245 • Metro Colli Albani then bus • 06 718 2139 • mid-Jun–mid-Aug*

¡Fiesta!

Spring Festival
Orchestral and choral concerts in Trinita dei Monti and a mass of azaleas take over this popular gathering place. End of March. ◈ *Piazza di Spagna • Map D2*

International Horse Show
Villa Borghese's annual splash-out for the equestrian classes. International show-jumping in this gorgeous garden setting. Much of the park is closed off for the event and its gala parties.
◈ *Piazza di Siena, Villa Borghese • Map E1 • last week May*

International Horse Show

Villa Celimontana Jazz
A magnificent setting among dramatically lit umbrella pines, where you can enjoy gourmet cuisine and jazz every night all summer long. ◈ *Piazza della Navicella • Map E5 • 06 589 7807 • Jun–Sep • www.villacelimontanajazz.com*

May Day Concert
Held in front of the Basilica of San Giovanni in Laterano *(see p127)*, this is a vast, free event, boasting a line-up of top Italian popstars and the occasional international luminary. It's in celebration of socialist Italy's "Day of the Worker", when just about everything shuts down. ◈ *Piazza S Giovanni • Map F5 • 1 May*

Top 10 Religious Festivals

Pentecost
Rose petals shower down through the Pantheon's oculus *(see p14)*, followed by pageantry. ◈ *Map M3 • Whitsunday*

Christmas Market
Sugar candy, nativity figurines and all the Christmas trimmings. ◈ *Piazza Navona • Map L3 • 1 Dec–6 Jan*

White Night Festival
Museums, monuments and churches open through the night hosting a variety of cultural events. ◈ *Sep*

Easter Week
Events include the Good Friday Procession of the Cross at the Colosseum and the Easter Sunday blessing from the balcony of St Peter's.

Madonna della Neve
Commemorating a papal vision of an August snowfall in the 4th century, white petals float down from the ceiling of S Maria Maggiore. ◈ *5 Aug*

Christmas Eve Midnight Mass
Most churches celebrate the Saviour's birth, but tickets are required for St Peter's.

"Urbi et Orbi"
The noontime Christmas Day blessing by the pope from St Peter's balcony.

Carnival
Dressing up, parties and pranks. ◈ *Late Jan–Feb*

All Saints' Day
Romans visit the graves of loved ones. ◈ *1 Nov*

Feast of Sts Peter and Paul
Fireworks and partying to celebrate the founders of the Catholic Church. ◈ *Piazza S Paolo and Via Ostiense • Map D6 • 28–29 Jun*

Left **Dolce e Gabbana** Right **Via dei Condotti**

🔟 Shopping Streets

Via dei Condotti
The chicest of the chic shop here, where all the biggest names in *haute couture* have staked out their turf: Gucci, Bulgari, Prada, Hermès, Ferragamo, Armani, Trussardi, Valentino and more. It's a foregone conclusion that this street offers no bargains, but the staff will make you feel like visiting royalty *(see p111)*.

Via del Corso
Up and down Rome's central axis street, you'll find the entire range of shopping options. Music stores and trendy young styles predominate, but there are also good shoe shops and one of Rome's rare up-scale department stores, La Rinascente *(see p95)*.

Via Cola di Rienzo
This is Rome's best street for middle-range clothing. In addition, one of the few remaining Standa department stores is here, featuring inexpensive merchandise of all types. For hard-to-find international and traditional food items, Castroni is the city's best shop *(see p143)*.

Via Borgognona
The other major street for top-name fashion, second only and parallel to Via dei Condotti. Here's where Dolce e Gabbana, Fendi, Ferrè, Givenchy and Versace have all set up shop. Don't omit nearby Piazza di Spagna, which is home to Frette, Missoni and Krizia *(see p114)*.

Via dei Coronari
Named for the rosary makers and sellers that used to line the way when it was on the main pilgrimage route to St Peter's, this street now has a reputation for antiques. Only partly deserved, however, since prices are generally exaggerated and most pieces are imported *(see pp86–7)*.

Via del Babuino
An imposing blend of high fashion (Armani, Chanel, Tiffany & Co.) and antiques make this street one of Rome's most elegant. Worth a stroll just to peek into some of the finer antiques shops – they're full of Baroque furniture, paintings and antiquities *(see p113)*.

Via Margutta
A wonderful range of art, antiques and antiquities shops has made this little street famous. Nos. 45 and 86 often have stunning

Glassware, Via del Babuino

For shopping tips See p164

Antiques shop, Via Margutta

merchandise for sale, whereas No. 109 specializes in more affordable copies of antiquities (see p113).

Via Bocca di Leone
One of the side streets that joins Via dei Condotti and Via Borgognona itself has several high-style boutiques. A wonderful jewellery shop, Siragusa, creates unusual rings, bracelets and necklaces using ancient sardonyx seals, carved stones and coins (see p114).

Via Nazionale
A solidly mid-range shopping experience, lined with shoe and clothing boutiques, Oriental rug stores, an international bookshop and a reliable bag and luggage emporium. Frette, with its elegant range of bed linen, also has an outlet here. Map R2

Via dei Giubbonari
Named for the traditional giubbotti (jackets) whose makers and sellers used to populate this street, Via dei Giubbonari is still noted for its stylish clothing and down-to-earth prices. Sportswear, shoes, trendy styles and classics for men and women are all available here (see p105).

Top 10 Markets

1 Porta Portese
Rome's mammoth flea market, for genuine and fake antiques, memorabilia, art, clothing, plants and more. Sunday morning. Via Ippolito Nievo • Map C5

2 Campo de' Fiori
Rome's famous outdoor fruit, vegetable and fish market in one of the most authentic medieval squares (see p105).

3 Via Mamiani
Rome's largest market for the freshest meat and fish, as well as clothing and housewares. Monday to Saturday mornings (see p130).

4 Via Sannio
Vintage clothing and designer fakes. Weekday mornings and Saturday (see p130).

5 Antique Print Market
Antique and reproduction prints. Monday to Saturday mornings. Largo della Fontanella di Borghese • Map M1

6 Piazza Testaccio
A covered market with lavish displays of nature's bounty. Monday to Saturday mornings. Map D6

7 Via Trionfale Flower Market
Fresh cut flowers and all sorts of plants at bargain prices. Tuesday morning. Map B2

8 Parcheggio Borghese
Flea market specializing in children's goods. First weekend of month, Oct–Jun. Via Francesco Crispi 96 • Map E2

9 Piazza San Cosimato
Trastevere's lively fruit and vegetable market. Monday to Saturday mornings. Map C5

10 Quattro Coronati
Quaint produce market. Monday to Saturday mornings. Map E4

Left and centre **Antico Caffè Greco** Right **Giolitti**

Cafés and Gelaterie

Antico Caffè Greco

Rome's 1760 answer to all the famed literary cafés of Paris. Just off the Spanish Steps on the busiest shopping street in town, it is an elegant holdover from yesteryear, its tiny tables tucked into a series of genteel, cosy rooms plastered with photos, prints and other memorabilia from the 19th-century Grand Tour era. The A-list of past customers runs from Goethe to Byron, Casanova to Wagner *(see p116)*.

Café Sant'Eustachio

Rome's most coveted *cappuccini* come from behind a chrome-plated shield that hides the coffee machine from view so no one can discover the skilled owner's secret formula. All that is known is that the water comes from an ancient aqueduct and the brew is pre-sweetened. Always crowded *(see p96)*.

San Crispino

Navigate the glut of inferior ice cream parlours infesting the Trevi neighbourhood to reach this elegantly simple little *gelateria*. The signature ice cream contains honey but there are other velvety varieties made with fresh fruit or nuts and sinful delights laced with liqueurs. ◈ *Via della Panetteria 42 • Map P2*

Tre Scalini

This cafe's claim to fame is Rome's most decadent *tartufo* (truffle) ice cream ball, which is almost always packaged in other outlets. Dark chocolate shavings cover the outer layer of chocolate ice cream, with a heart of fudge and cherries *(see p88)*.

Giolitti

This 19th-century café is the best known of Rome's *gelaterie*. Touristy but excellent *(see p96)*.

Gran Caffè Doney

Still the top café on the famous Via Veneto, but long past its prime as the heartbeat (along with rival Café de Paris across the road) of Rome's 1950s heyday – when celebrities in sunglasses hobnobbed with starlets draped over the outdoor tables. The lifestyle was documented in

Giolitti

(and in part created by) Fellini's seminal film *La Dolce Vita (see p58)*, whose shutterbug character Paparazzo lent a name to his profession of bloodhound photographers *(see p136)*.

Caffè Rosati

The older, more left-wing of Piazza del Popolo's rival cafés (the other is Caffè Canova) was founded by two of the Rosati brothers (a third continued to manage the family's original Via Veneto café). It sports a 1922 Art Nouveau decor and its patrons park their newest Ferrari or Lotus convertibles out front *(see p116)*.

Harry's Bar

This Roman branch of the famed Venetian café opened at the top of Via Veneto in 1961, at the tail end of the neighbourhood's glory days. It has long been the haunt of politicians who appreciate the year-round pavement tables *(see p136)*.

Gelateria della Palma

Modern ice cream parlour with more than 100 flavours of *gelato* plus *semifreddi* (half-

La Tazza d'Oro

frozen mousse) and frozen yoghurt. It's open late and constantly thronged with Rome's young and beautiful. Mere steps from the Pantheon *(see p96)*.

La Tazza d'Oro

Strictly the highest quality Brazilian beans go into the coffee here. There's nothing fancy in this unassuming place and no touristy gimmicks (despite being just off the Pantheon's piazza). Just a long, undulating bar counter where regulars enjoy a heavenly *espresso* that, amazingly, manages to be both among the best and the cheapest in Rome *(see p96)*.

Left **Pizzeria da Ricci** Right **Pizzeria da Baffetto**

⑩ Pizzerias

1 Pizzeria da Baffetto

The best pizza in Rome but, as is traditional for a pizzeria, it is open only for dinner and, beyond pizza, only serves *bruschetta* and other simple appetizers *(see p162)*. The thin-crust, wood-oven pizzas come either *piccola* (small) or *grande* (large) *(see p89)*.

2 Pizzeria da Ivo

The most famous pizzeria in Trastevere, definitely discovered by the tourist crowds, but local fans never let them take it over completely. The pizza is great, but skip the other second-rate main meals *(see p148)*.

3 Pizzeria da Ricci

This Liberty-style pizzeria, in the Ricci family since 1905, is hidden away on a quiet dead-end street off Via Nazionale. The

pizzas are tiny (many people order two) but excellent; complement them with the sweet northern Lazio white wine Est! Est! Est!, after which the place is nicknamed *(see p77)*. ✆ Via Genova 32 • Map R2 • 06 488 1107 • Closed Mon • €

4 Pizzeria dar Poeta

There's a merry war between ultra thin-crust Roman pizza and thicker, chewier Neapolitan pizza. Dar Poeta goes its own road, letting the dough rise a full day (rather than the usual hour), resulting in a thin yet light and airy pie loaded down with the freshest of toppings. Tucked into a quiet Trastevere side street, with some coveted tables out front and more in the air-conditioned brick-walled dining room *(see p148)*.

Pizzeria da Ivo

For a guide to restaurant prices **See p89**

Pizzeria dar Poeta

Pizzeria da Vittorio
Vittorio Martini's unassuming little place with its wood beams and a few tables on the cobblestones out front serves fantastic Neapolitan-style pizza, courtesy of award-winning *pizzaiolo* Angelo Jezzi. The mixed *antipasti* plate is generous and a great bargain *(see p148)*.

Acchiappafantasmi
The award-winning pizza is shaped vaguely like a ghost with olives for eyes at this restaurant (the pizzeria's name means "ghostbusters"). A half-dozen Calabrese snacks are also available. The service can be slow. ⦿ *Via dei Cappellari 66 • Map K4 • 06 687 3462 • Closed Mon, Tue–Fri L • €*

PizzaRé
Roman mini-chain serving thicker, Neapolitan-style wood oven pies. Cheap lunch menus include cover charge, drink, and a pizza, a pasta, or a roast meat dish. ⦿ *Via di Ripetta 14 • Map D2 • 06 321 1468 • €*

Gaudì
Thick Neapolitan-style pizza in a modern room or on the roof terrace, with red lamps to click on for rapid service. Lots of pastas and desserts as well. No bookings and long queues, so arrive early. ⦿ *Via R Giovannelli 8–12 • Map F1 • 06 884 5451 • Closed Sat & Sun L • €*

Panattoni "L'Obitorio"
This Trastevere institution's nickname ("the morgue") refers to the chilly effect of the marble that sheathes the walls and acts as tabletops. The reception is as warm as the decor is cold, however, and the Roman pizza as excellent as the *supplì al telefono* (fried rice balls with a melted mozzarella heart that makes a long "telephone" cord when you pull them apart). Open late. ⦿ *Viale Trastevere 53 • Map C5 • 06 580 0919 • Closed Wed, L • No credit cards • €*

Pizzeria La Montecarlo
Late opening hours have kept this simple Roman-style pizzeria packed with locals and students for years *(see p89)*.

Left **Checchino dal 1887** Right **'Gusto**

⁵⁰ Restaurants

Checchino dal 1887

1 The premier restaurant of Testaccio since 1887 boasts Rome's largest wine cellar. Working-class dishes – this is the place that invented *coda alla vaccinara (see p77)* – and more elegant fare are prepared divinely, with the best selection of Italian and French cheeses in town *(see p125)*.

Agata e Romeo

2 Romeo Caraccio runs the dining room in this Liberty-style temple to creative Roman cuisine near Santa Maria Maggiore. His wife Agata Parisella reigns in the kitchen, preparing rich and highly original concoctions of meat, fish and fresh vegetables. Don't miss

Logo, Agata e Romeo

her heavenly desserts, including the *millefoglie* – puff pastry filled with cream *(see p131)*.

Alberto Ciarla

3 The quality of the cooking at Trastevere's famed fish restaurant has gone up and down over the years, but when it's good it can be outstanding. Prices are stratospheric, even for simple seafood, and the darkened atmos- phere of the modern rooms is somewhat overbearing, but it has loyal fans *(see p149)*.

Sabatini

4 One of Rome's most famed restaurants, favoured by the likes of Fellini in the days before it became too hyped for its own good. Killer location on the piazza, but terribly steep prices. The cuisine is refined Roman and seafood *(see p149)*.

Sapori del Lord Byron

5 The location, inside one of Rome's most exclusive small hotels, and the chef's renowned ability to turn both Italian classics and inventive new dishes into works of art, keeps this elegant restaurant on the A-list – and makes it a great place for celebrity-spotting. ⓢ *Via G. de Notaris 5, Hotel Lord Byron • Map E1 • 06 322 0404 • Closed Sun • €€€€€*

Terrace, Checchino dal 1887

Da Cesaretto

Also known as Fiaschetteria Beltramme, little has changed since this *osteria* opened in 1886. Prices are relatively low and dishes are solid Roman specialities *(see pp76–7)*. There is no phone and no reservations so come early. The tables are shared. ◈ *Via della Croce 39 • Map D2 • Closed Sun • No credit cards • €€*

Piperno

The best Roman Jewish cooking in the Ghetto since 1856 (although also the priciest). Hosts of TV shows have been seen sneaking in to try and unlock the chef's secrets. Service can be slightly off-hand, but the artichokes can't be beat *(see p107)*.

Da Augusto

Archetypal Trastevere *trattoria*. Block-style wooden tables and butchers' paper mats form the decor; the menu is recited by the busily indifferent waiters rather than printed. Good table wine and the food comprises excellent, simple traditional dishes. In fine weather there is seating on the tiny piazza-cum-car park out front *(see p148)*.

'Gusto

The latest see-and be-seen restaurant, kitschily installed in one of Mussolini's pompous travertine buildings lining the piazza. Glass walls and outdoor tables overlook Augustus's Mausoleum *(see p92)*. Several dining choices, each excellent: *cucina*

Piperno

creativa is served in the restaurant proper, and there's a pizzeria (open until 1am), and a wine bar (open 11am to 2am) serving Thai cuisine. Booking is recommended *(see p117)*.

Birreria Peroni

Local businessmen regularly take their lunchtime discussions to this 1906 beer hall sponsored by Italy's biggest brewery. The buffet snacks and scrumptious main dishes cross Roman and Germanic influences, and the Art Deco murals feature cherubs playing sports and promising "He who drinks beer lives to 100" *(see p117)*.

Left **Gnocchi alla Romana** Right **Spaghetti alla carbonara**

🔟 Roman Dishes

Saltimbocca
This savoury veal dish is so good they call it "jumps-in-the-mouth". A veal escalope is layered with sage leaves and prosciutto then sautéed in white wine.

Bucatini all'amatriciana

Bucatini all'amatriciana
Named after Amatrice, the northern Lazio town high in the Abruzzi mountains where it originated. The sauce consists of tomatoes mixed with Italian bacon – *guanciale* (pork cheek) or *pancetta* (pork belly) – laced with chilli pepper and liberally dusted with grated Pecorino romano cheese. The classic pasta accompaniment are *bucatini* (thick, hollow spaghetti). The original *amatriciana bianca* version (before tomatoes, a New World food, entered Italian cuisine) adds parsley and butter.

Carciofi alla romana
Tender Italian artichokes, often laced with garlic and mint, are braised in a mixture of olive oil and water.

Abbacchio scottadito
Roasted Roman spring lamb, so succulent the name claims you'll "burn your fingers" in your haste to eat it. When *abbacchio* (lamb) is unavailable, once the spring slaughter is over, they switch to less tender *agnello* (young mutton).

Spaghetti alla carbonara
The piping hot pasta is immediately mixed with a raw egg, grated Parmesan and black pepper so that the eggy mixture cooks on to the strands of spaghetti themselves. It is then tossed with pieces of *pancetta* (bacon). There's a local legend that the recipe was born out of US army rations after World War II (powdered bacon and eggs mix), but no one seems to have proven or discarded the theory.

Carciofi alla giudia

Carciofi alla giudia
Artichokes, first flattened then fried. This typical Roman Jewish dish is often accompanied by fried courgette (zucchini) flowers stuffed with mozzarella cheese and anchovies.

 For traditional Roman restaurants **See p125**

Pajata

7 It may sound revolting but it's actually delicious: suckling calf intestines boiled with its mother's milk still clotted inside. Usually the intestines are chopped, coated with a tomato sauce and served over pasta.

Coda alla vaccinara

8 Oxtail braised in celery and tomato broth. Like *pajata*, this is a product of trying to make something out of the *quinto quarto* (the unusable "fifth fourth" of the day's butchering), which was part of the take-home pay of 19th-century slaughterhouse workers.

Coda alla vaccinara

Checchino dal 1887, the restaurant that came up with this delicacy, is one of Rome's finest *(see p125)*.

Gnocchi alla Romana

9 These tiny potato-and-flour dumplings, dense and chewy, originated in northern Italy, but Rome has since adopted them as her own – the city even has a traditional "gnocchi day" every Thursday, when they are added to most restaurant menus. Gnocchi are best served with a fresh tomato sauce, although they're also good with a gorgonzola cheese sauce or simply with sage leaves and melted butter.

Cacio e Pepe

10 Sometimes the simplest dishes are among the best. Perfectly *al dente* ("with a bite") spaghetti is tossed hot with cracked black pepper and grated Pecorino romano (a local sharp, aged sheep's milk cheese rather similar to Parmesan).

Top 10 Wines and Liqueurs

1 Frascati
Lazio's only high profile wine, a dry, fruity, not always perfect white from the hills south of Rome.

2 Castelli Romani
Cousin to Frascati, from neighbouring hilltowns, also made with Trebbiano grapes.

3 Colli Albani
Another Trebbiano-based white from the slopes of Lazio's dormant volcano.

4 Orvieto Classico
Dry white from southern Umbria – so good that the Renaissance artist Signorelli once accepted it as payment.

5 Est! Est! Est!
A bishop's taste-tester, sampling this sweet white in a northern Lazio lakeside village, excitedly ran to the door and scribbled "*Est! Est! Est!*" (Latin for "This is it!").

6 Torre Ercolana
One of Lazio's unsung reds, made from Cabernet and Cesanese grapes.

7 Chianti
This old favourite from over the border in Tuscany is one of the most common reds you'll find in Rome's bars and restaurants.

8 Lacrima Christi
"Tears of Christ", a white wine from the slopes of the infamous Mount Vesuvius near Pompeii *(see p154)*.

9 Campari
A bitter red apéritif, best diluted in soda water, or lemonade for a sweet drink.

10 Grappa
The most powerful of Italy's *digestivi* (drunk after a meal), this is quite a harsh-tasting liqueur.

For eating and drinking tips **See p162**

Left **Big Mama** Centre **Alexanderplatz** Right **Roman carousers**

🔟 Pubs, Bars and Music Clubs

Alexanderplatz
This is definitely Rome's premier jazz venue. The management regularly books first-rate international talent as well as local musicians, and it serves excellent food, too. Advance reservations are highly recommended *(see p147)*.

Drunken Ship
One of the liveliest hubs of Campo de' Fiori's renowned nightlife, pumping out loud rock music. Very popular with young Romans and foreigners alike. Happy Hour is from 4 to 8pm; brunch is served at weekends *(see p106)*.

Jonathan's Angels
A must-see for its outlandish decor, which was the brainchild of the proprietor Jonathan, a former circus performer and also the artist. Taking a cue from his Baroque forbears, he's covered practically every square inch of the place with squirming colour. There's a piano bar and floor shows *(see p88)*.

Big Mama
Trastevere's historic jazz, blues, rhythm and blues and world music standby, with different acts performing every

Alexanderplatz

night. Membership is by the month or year, but unfortunately Friday and Saturday night concerts are open only to those with annual memberships *(see p147)*.

Fiddler's Elbow
One of the oldest Irish pubs in Rome and still going strong, frequented by both locals and out-of-towners. Italians seem to love everything Irish and the place really reels when some impromptu fiddlers get going.
Ⓢ *Via dell'Olmata 43 • Map F4*

Est'd dal 1976

IRISH PUB
THE FIDDLER'S ELBOW
ROME
Via dell'Olmata, n° 43 (S. Maria Maggiore)
tel. 06.4872110 fax 06.48916763

Fiddler's Elbow

Trinity College
Rather like entering a time-warp that lands you up in Ireland. A warm, inviting two-floor place that can get very noisy and packed, but always stays cheerful. A very eclectic menu of simple, tempting fare available until 1am, and brunch on Sunday *(see p96)*.

7 La Vineria

This historic wine bar is an established favourite with the locals. Smoky and definitely cosy during the winter, but spilling out onto the Campo de' Fiori in the summer. Prices for wine and beer are low, especially if you stand at the bar, and there are a few well -chosen snacks *(see p106)*.

Bar della Pace

8 Bar della Pace

For those who crave most of all to see and be seen, this is the place to drape your designer-clad self, especially on warm summer evenings when you can pose unashamed at an outdoor table. In the winter, it's a cosier, less self-conscious local favourite, although it's always pretty pricey, as are most places in the Piazza Navona area. ◉ Via della Pace 5 • Map L3

9 Rock Castle Café

This groovy hangout has a dungeon-themed, cavernous decor and is mostly frequented by foreign students. A fun atmosphere, with good rock music and a bit of dancing late at night, right in the heart of the Ghetto *(see p106)*.

10 Stardust

Voted Trastevere's most decadent venue by its loyal, discerning clientele. Whoever's on duty any given night sets the idiosyncratic musical tone, so there's always something unexpected happening here, including live jam sessions. The wildness doesn't really begin until after midnight, and then goes on until dawn. An excellent brunch is served at weekends *(see p147)*.

AROUND TOWN

Around Piazza Navona
82–89

Around the Pantheon
90–97

Campo de' Fiori to the
Capitoline
98–107

The Spanish Steps and
Villa Borghese
108–117

Ancient Rome
118–125

The Esquiline
and Lateran
126–131

The Quirinal and
Via Veneto
132–137

Trastevere and Prati
138–149

Beyond the City Walls
150–155

ROME'S TOP 10

Left **Piazza Navona** Right **Cornice, Palazzo Madama**

Around Piazza Navona

THIS IS BAROQUE ROME IN ALL ITS THEATRICAL GLORY, *a collection of curvaceous architecture and elaborate fountains by the era's two greatest architects, Bernini and Borromini, and churches filled with paintings by the likes of Caravaggio and Rubens. The street plan was largely overhauled by 16th- to 18th-century popes attempting to improve the traffic flow from St Peter's – in fact, a 19th-century plan to turn Piazza Navona into a boulevard from Prati across Ponte Umberto I was only killed when wiser heads widened*

Corso del Rinascimento instead. However, ancient Rome does peek through in the shape of Piazza Navona and the curve of Palazzo Massimo alle Colonne. This is also a neighbourhood of craftsmen, shopkeepers and antiques restorers and dealers who line Via dei Coronari (see p87). More recently the narrow alleys around Via della Pace have become a centre of Roman nightlife, with tiny pubs, trendy cafés and nightspots where the clientele spills out into the streets in summer (see p88).

The Ganges, Four Rivers Fountain

Sights

1. Piazza Navona
2. Four Rivers Fountain
3. San Luigi dei Francesi
4. Sant'Ivo
5. Sant'Agostino
6. Santa Maria della Pace
7. Palazzo Altemps
8. Pasquino
9. Palazzo Massimo alle Colonne
10. Palazzo Madama

Piazza Navona

1 One of Rome's loveliest pedestrian squares *(see p46)* is studded with fountains and lined with palaces, such as the Pamphilj, the church of Sant'Agnese, and classy cafés such as Tre Scalini *(see p88).* ⦿ *Map L3*

Four Rivers Fountain

2 The statues ringing Bernini's theatrical 1651 centrepiece symbolize four rivers representing the continents: the Ganges (Asia, relaxing), Danube (Europe, turning to steady the obelisk), Rio de la Plata (the Americas, bald and reeling), and the Nile (Africa, whose head is hidden since the river's source was then unknown). The obelisk, balancing over a sculptural void, is a Roman-era fake, its Egyptian granite carved with the hieroglyphic names of Vespasian, Titus and Domitian. ⦿ *Piazza Navona • Map L3*

San Luigi dei Francesi

3 France's national church in Rome has some damaged Domenichino frescoes (1616–17) in the second chapel on the right, but everyone bee-lines for the last chapel on the left, housing three large Caravaggio works. His plebeian, naturalistic approach often ran foul of Counter-Reformation tastes. In a "first draft" version of the *Angel and St Matthew*, the angel guided the hand of a rough labourer-type saint; the commissioners made the artist replace it with this more courtly one *(see p45)*. Underlying sketches in

Piazza Navona

Martyrdom of St Matthew and *Calling of St Matthew (see p47)* show how Caravaggio was moving away from symbolic compositions in favour of more realistic scenes. ⦿ *Piazza S Luigi dei Francesi 5 • Map L2 • Open 8:30am–12:30pm, 3:30–7pm (closed Thu pm) • Free*

Sant'Ivo

4 Giacomo della Porta's Renaissance façade for the 1303 Palazzo della Sapienza, the original seat of Rome's university, hides the city's most gorgeous courtyard. The double arcade is closed at the far end by Sant' Ivo's highly original façade, an intricate Borromini interplay of concave and convex curves. The crowning glory is the upward spiralling ellipse of the dome. The interior is disappointing, despite its Pietro da Cortona altarpiece. When the courtyard is closed, you can see the dome from Piazza Sant' Eustachio. ⦿ *Corso Rinascimento 40 • Map L3 • Courtyard: Open 8am– 6pm Sun–Fri; Church: Open 10am–4:30pm Mon–Fri, 10am–1pm Sat, 9am–noon some Sun • Free*

Spire and lantern, Sant'Ivo

Stone relief, Palazzo Madama

first chapel on the right is frescoed with *Sibyls* (1514) influenced by the then recently unveiled Sistine ceiling *(see pp10–11)*. Peruzzi decorated the chapel across the aisle and Bramante's first job in Rome was designing a cloister based on ancient examples. It now hosts frequent concerts. ® *Via della Pace • Map L2 • Open 10am–12:45pm Mon–Fri • Free*

5 Sant'Agostino

Raphael frescoed the prophet Isaiah (1512) on the third pillar on the right, and Jacopo Sansovino provided the pregnant and venerated *Madonna del Parto*; but Sant'Agostino's pride and joy is Caravaggio's *Madonna del Loreto* (1603–1606). The master's strict realism balked at the tradition of depicting Mary riding atop her miraculous flying house (which landed in Loreto). The house is merely suggested by a travertine doorway and flaking stucco wall where Mary, supporting her overly large Christ child, is venerated by a pair of scandalously scruffy pilgrims. ® *Piazza di Sant'Agostino • Map L2 • Open 8am–noon, 4–7:30pm daily • Free*

6 Santa Maria della Pace

Baccio Pontelli rebuilt this church for Pope Sixtus IV in 1480–84, but the lovely and surprising façade (1656–7), its curved portico squeezed into a tiny piazza, is a Baroque masterpiece by Pietro da Cortona. Raphael's

7 Palazzo Altemps

This 15th-century palace was overhauled in 1585 by Martino Longhi, who is probably also responsible for the stucco and travertine courtyard (previously attributed to Antonio da Sangallo the Younger or Peruzzi). It now makes an excellent home to one wing of the Museo Nazionale Romano, its frescoed rooms filled with ancient sculptures *(see pp28–31)*.

8 Pasquino

That this faceless, armless statue was part of "Menelaus with the body of Patroclus" (a Roman copy of a Hellenistic group) is almost irrelevant. Since this worn fragment took up its post here in 1501, it has been Rome's most vocal "Talking Statue" *(see box)*. ® *Piazza Pasquino • Map L3*

Pasquino, Piazza Pasquino

Rear view, Palazzo Massimo alle Colonne

9 Palazzo Massimo alle Colonne

This masterpiece of Baldassare Peruzzi marks the transition of Roman architecture from the High Renaissance of Bramante and Sangallo into the theatrical experiments of Mannerism that would lead up to the Baroque. The façade is curved for a reason; Peruzzi honoured Neo-Classical precepts so much he wanted to preserve the arc of the Odeon of Domitian, a small theatre incorporated into the south end of the emperor's stadium *(see p50)*. ⊗ *Corso Vittorio Emanuele II 141 • Map L3 • Open 7am–1pm 16 Mar only • Free*

10 Palazzo Madama

Based around the 16th-century Medici Pope Leo X's Renaissance palace, the Baroque façade of unpointed brick and bold marble window frames was added in the 17th century. Since 1870 it's been the seat of Italy's Senate, so public admission is obviously limited.
⊗ *Piazza Madama 11 • Map L3 • Open for guided tours 10am–6pm 1st Sat of month • Free*

A Morning around Piazza Navona

🕐 Start in the courtyard of the Sapienza, marvelling at the remarkable façade of **Sant'Ivo** *(see p83)*. Head around the church's right side and out the back exit on to Via della Dogana Vecchia. If you need a morning pick-me-up, turn left and then right into Piazza Sant'Eustachio (if the namesake church is open, pop in for an early 18th-century interior). In the elongated piazza to the left are fine views of Sant'Ivo's dome and two great cafés to choose from, Camillo and Sant' Eustachio.

Return to Via della Dogana Vecchia and turn right to visit the Caravaggio works inside **San Luigi dei Francesi** *(see p83)*. Continue up the street to Via delle Coppelle and turn left for more Caravaggio at **Sant'Agostino**. Continue into Piazza della Cinque Lune and walk a few yards to the left down Corso del Rinascimento to **Ai Monasteri** *(see p87)* and browse the quality liqueurs and old-fashioned beauty products, all made by monks.

Around the corner is **Palazzo Altemps**, now full of Classical statuary. Spend a good hour inside. Then relax from the morning's sightseeing with a stroll amid the street performers and splashing fountains of **Piazza Navona** *(see p83)*. Enjoy a *tartufo* ice cream or a full lunch at the wonderful **Tre Scalini** *(see p88)*, before ending the morning window-shopping along the antiques of **Via dei Coronari** *(see pp86–7)*.

Left **Palazzo Pamphilj** Right **St Agnes statue, Sant'Agnese in Agone**

Best of the Rest

Sant'Agnese in Agone

This church was built in honour of a 13-year-old girl who was stripped in a brothel but whose hair miraculously grew to cover her nakedness. Borromini's façade is a wonderful play of concave and convex shapes. ◈ *Piazza Navona • Map L3 • Closed for restoration • Free*

Domitian's Stadium

The outline of this AD 86 stadium is echoed in Piazza Navona, built on top of its remains. ◈ *Piazza di Tor Sanguigna • Map L3 • Open special occasions only • Adm*

Via dei Coronari

Lined with antiques shops, this street is at its torch-flickering best during the May and October antiques fairs *(see p68)*. ◈ *Map K2*

Palazzo Pamphilj

This 17th-century palace has a wonderful Pietro da Cortona fresco upstairs. ◈ *Piazza Navona 14 • Map L3 • Open by appointment only • Free*

Chiesa Nuova

Pietro da Cortona painted the dome and apse and Rubens three sanctuary canvases for this 1575 church. ◈ *Piazza della Chiesa Nuova/Corso Vittorio Emanuele II • Map K3 • Open 8am–1pm, 4:30–7pm daily • Free*

Palazzo Braschi

The last papal family palace, built 1791–1811. Cosimo Morelli used a Renaissance design to match the piazza. Inside is a small museum dedicated to Roman history. ◈ *Via San Pantaleo 10 • Map L3 • Open 9am–7pm Tue–Sun • Adm*

Sant'Antonio dei Portoghesi

A Baroque gem of a church. Out front is the Torre della Scimmia, a rare remnant of medieval Rome. ◈ *Via dei Portoghesi • Map L2 • 8:30am–1pm, 3–6pm • Free*

Santa Maria dell'Anima

Highlights in this gilded church are a Giulio Romano altarpiece and Peruzzi's Hadrian VI tomb (1523). ◈ *Vicolo della Pace 20 • Map L2 • Open 8am–1pm, 2–7:30pm daily • Free*

Museo Napoleonico

A collection of paintings, furnishings and *objets d'art* that once belonged to the extensive Bonaparte clan. ◈ *Piazza di Ponte Umberto I • Map L2 • Open 9am–7pm Tue–Sun • Adm*

San Salvatore in Lauro

A chapel in this 1594 church houses da Cortona's *Adoration of the Shepherds* (1630). ◈ *Piazza S Salvatore in Lauro 15 • Map K2 • Open 9am–noon, 4–7pm daily • Free*

Left **Antiques shop, Via dei Coronari** Right **Ai Monasteri**

Antiques Shops

1 Antica Cappelleria Troncarelli
Don't be fooled by the tiny size of this shop – it is still one of the best haberdashers in Rome, established in 1857. *Via della Cuccagna 15 • Map L2*

2 Ai Monasteri
Monasteries from all across Italy supply their homemade honey, liqueurs, beauty products, elixirs and other products to this shop. *Corso Rinascimento 72 • Map L2*

3 Antiqua Domus
Bring some of Rome's elegance into your own home. This sizeable showroom has mostly 18th- and 19th-century furnishings on sale; some nice Empire pieces are particularly worth a look. *Via dei Coronari 39 • Map K2*

4 Gea Arte Antica
Own your own piece of ancient Rome. Choose from a range of objects, from simple oil lamps to exquisite painted vases. *Via dei Coronari 233A • Map K2*

5 Massimo Maria Melis
This unique jewellery studio wraps 21-carat gold around coins, glass and stones preserved from the Etruscan, Roman and medieval eras. *Via dell'Orso 57 • Map L2*

6 Galleria Il Colibri
Small but worthy gallery presenting group and solo shows of contemporary painters, as well as historic posters and other types of art media. *Via dell'Orso 92 • Map L2*

7 Dott. Sergio de Sanctis
Exclusively Italian antiques, mostly elegant 18th- to early 20th-century furnishings and gilt-framed mirrors. *Via dei Coronari 218–19 • Map K2*

8 L'Art Nouveau
Antiques shop devoted to Art Nouveau and Liberty style furnishings, lamps, *objets d'art* and *chinoiserie* silk tapestries and gowns. *Via dei Coronari 221 • Map K2*

9 Calzoleria Petrocchi
Bruno Ridolfi keeps alive the high fashion, excellent quality, made-to-measure cobbler traditions of his uncle Tito Petrocchi, who regularly shod glamorous stars of stage and screen in the "*dolce vita*" heyday of the 1950s and 1960s. *Via dell'Orso 25 • Map L2*

10 Nardecchia
Prints, old photographs and watercolours are on sale here, from Piranesi originals to 20th-century works. *Piazza Navona 25 • Map L3*

Left **Tre Scalini** Right **Abbey Theatre Irish Pub**

Chic Cafés and Bars

Tre Scalini
This historic café, right on Piazza Navona, is renowned for its delectable chocolate home-made *tartufo* ice cream ball *(see p70)*. ◈ *Piazza Navona 28 • Map L3*

Jonathan's Angels
Perhaps Rome's most unique and kitsch nightspot, which should be seen to be believed. Run by a former circus acrobat, it is eccentrically decorated, with a piano bar, tables out on the narrow alley strung with fairy lights, and the occasional impromptu floor show. ◈ *Via della Fossa 16 • Map K3*

Abbey Theatre Irish Pub
Comfortable, cosy Guinness pub, pleasantly removed from the hubbub of the nightlife core that has recently sprouted down the road. Basic snacks are also served and there's an Internet terminal. ◈ *Via del Governo Vecchio 51–53 • Map K3*

Cul de Sac
One of Rome's oldest wine bars, with lots of labels on offer. A bit of a squeeze inside and out, but a better option than the near-by bars of the Piazza Navona. ◈ *Piazza Paquino 73 • Map L3*

Bull Dog Pub
American style bar positively hopping nightly with plenty of lively young students

both foreign and Italian ◈ *Corso Vittorio Emanuele II 107 • Map L4*

Bloom
The former Clochard nightclub was reborn in 2001 as a jazzy modern bar, with a sushi restaurant upstairs – a rare find in Rome. ◈ *Via del Teatro Pace 30 • Map L3*

Bramante
Café/bar with a quirky elegance amid this sea of pubs. Light dishes are served to a chic young crowd. ◈ *Via della Pace 25 • Map K3*

Bar del Fico
An alternative, chic hangout in the shade of the legendary fig tree in a tiny square, where you can sit inside or out and enjoy a morning *cappuccino* or a very late liqueur. ◈ *Piazza del Fico • Map K3*

La Botticella
Small, always crowded *birreria* (beerhouse) with some tables outside, in the heart of the area's nightlife action. Devil's Kiss and Castlemaine XXXX beer are on tap. ◈ *Via di Tor Millina 32 • Map L2*

Old Bear
Eclectic but good food accompanies a wide range of beers here, with live music played in the basement. ◈ *Via dei Gigli d'Oro 2–4 • Map L2*

Above **Pizzeria da Baffetto**

Places to Eat

1 Pizzeria da Baffetto
By many folks' reckoning, the best pizzeria in Rome (see p72). ◈ Via del Governo Vecchio 114 • Map K3 • 06 686 1617 • €

2 Terra di Siena
One of the best Tuscan restaurants in Rome. The family imports ingredients and classic seasonal recipes from the farmers around their hometown near Siena. ◈ Piazza Pasquino 77–8 • Map L3 • 06 6830 7704 • Closed Sun • €€

3 Lilli
An ex-footballer runs this ultra-traditional restaurant hidden away in a cul-de-sac next to the riverside boulevard. If you are looking for a true taste of Rome's cuisine, the recipes don't get more Roman than this. ◈ Via Tor di Nona 23 • Map L2 • 06 686 1916 • Closed Sun • €

4 Il Convivio
For a special night out. One of the historic centre's best restaurants, with strictly seasonal cuisine based on Italian traditions and an excellent wine list. ◈ Vicolo dei Soldati 28 • Map L2 • 06 686 9432 • Closed Sun • €€€€€

5 Insalata Ricca 2
Rome's mini-chain of vegetarian-orientated eateries. Huge, inventive salads are the mainstay, although they also offer good pasta dishes. Seating outdoors. ◈ Piazza Pasquino 72 • Map L3 • 06 6830 7881 • €

6 Pizzeria La Montecarlo
The offspring of Baffetto's owners run this joint. Has less ambience than its famous parent, but benefits from shorter queues (see p73). ◈ Vicolo Savelli 12 • Map K3 • 06 686 1877 • Closed Mon • €

7 Tre Archi
A local trattoria with two small rooms and a famed Roman set menu. ◈ Via dei Coronari 233 • Map K2 • 06 686 5890 • Closed Sun • €

8 Fraterna Domus
Communal dining in a hospice run by nuns. The set menu offers soup or pasta, a meat course, salad and fruit for dessert. ◈ Via di Monte Brianzo 62 • Map L1 • 06 6880 5475 • Closed Thu • €

9 Zio Ciro
This pizzeria is popular both for its al fresco dining and the chance to order extra-large pizzas with two or three different toppings. ◈ Via della Pace 1 • Map K3 • 06 686 4802 • €

10 Antica Taverna
The owners here get the goat's milk ricotta and rabbit from their hometown in the Sabine Hills. ◈ Via Monte Giordano 12 • Map K3 • 06 6880 1053 • Closed Tue • €

Left **Piazza Sant'Ignazio** Right **Frieze, Ara Pacis**

Around the Pantheon

DURING THE ROMAN EMPIRE the Tiber Bend area was a public training ground for soldiers called the Campo Marzio. With Rome's fall, the city turned its back on this riverside neighbourhood and, aside from a few foreign settlements, it wasn't until the 15th century that anything other than a few churches was built here. The Baroque boom gave the area's palaces their distinctive look. Mussolini cleaned up the neighbourhood in the 1920s and 1930s to bring out its ancient character. He cleared away the debris surrounding Augustus's Mausoleum, reassembled the Ara Pacis and surrounded the lot with reviled Fascist buildings, complete with self-aggrandizing bas-reliefs.

Marcus Agrippa, Ara Pacis

🏛 Sights

1. The Pantheon
2. Santa Maria sopra Minerva
3. Galleria Doria Pamphilj
4. Ara Pacis
5. Sant'Ignazio di Loyola
6. Column of Marcus Aurelius
7. Augustus's Mausoleum
8. Piazza di Sant'Ignazio
9. Bernini's Elephant Obelisk
10. Piazza della Rotonda

1 The Pantheon

"Simple, erect, severe, austere, sublime" – even Lord Byron struggled to find words to express this marvel of ancient Roman architecture, the only ancient Roman temple to survive the millennia virtually intact *(see pp14–15).*

Relieving arches, Pantheon

2 Santa Maria sopra Minerva

The only truly Gothic church in Rome, possibly built, as the name suggests, atop a temple to Minerva. Michelangelo's bold *Risen Christ* (1514–21) is a muscular rendition of the Saviour so shockingly nude that church officials added the bronze wisp of drapery. Filippino Lippi frescoed the last chapel on the right; the lower scene on the right wall includes portraits of young Giovanni and Giulio de' Medici (better known as Popes Leo X and Clement VII), who are buried in tombs by Antonio Sangallo the Younger, in the apse, along with Fra' Angelico and (most of) St Catherine of Siena *(see p44).*
🕲 *Piazza della Minerva • Map M3 • Open 8am–7pm daily • Free • DA*

3 Galleria Doria Pamphilj

The best of the private collection galleries in Rome. In addition to paintings by Rubens, Correggio, Tintoretto, Carracci and Brueghel, star works include Caravaggio's *Mary Magdalene, Rest on the Flight into Egypt,* and *Young St John the Baptist* (a copy he made of his Capitoline version); Titian's *Salome with the Head of John the Baptist*; and Bernini's bust of Pope Innocent X *(see p43).* 🕲 *Piazza del Collegio Romano 2 • Map N3 • Open 10am–5pm Fri–Wed • Adm €8.00 • DA • www.doriapamphilj.it*

4 Ara Pacis

Augustus Caesar built this "Altar of Peace" between 13 BC and 9 BC to celebrate the famed *pax romana* (Roman peace) he instituted – largely by subjugating most of Western Europe, the Levant and North Africa. Fragments of the altar were excavated over several centuries, and in the 1920s Mussolini placed the reconstituted Ara Pacis by Augustus's Mausoleum. The altar is now housed in a Richard Meier-designed museum, the first modern structure to rise in the centre of Rome in 70 years. 🕲 *Piazza Augusto Imperatore & Lungotevere Augusta • Map D2 • 06 8205 9127 • Open 9am–7pm Tue–Sun • Adm €6.50 • www.arapacis.it*

Nave, Santa Maria sopra Minerva

Relief, Column of Marcus Aurelius

career of Marcus Aurelius. The spiral of reliefs celebrates his campaigns against the Germans (169–73) on the bottom and the Sarmatians (174–76) on the top. In 1588, Pope Sixtus V replaced the statues of the emperor and his wife with that of St Paul.
🔊 *Piazza Colonna • Map N2*

Sant'Ignazio di Loyola
5 When the Jesuits' new Baroque church was finished in 1685, it still lacked a dome. Master of *trompe-l'oeil* Andrea Pozzo used his flawless technique to create the illusion of an airy dome on the flat circle of ceiling over the church's crossing; stand on the yellow marble disc for the full effect, then walk directly under the "dome" to see how skewed the painting actually is. Pozzo also painted the nave vault with the lovely *Glory of Sant'Ignazio.* 🔊 *Piazza di S Ignazio • Map N3 • Open 7:30am–12:30pm, 3–7:15pm daily • Free*

Column of Marcus Aurelius
6 Trajan's Column was such a success *(see p22)* that this 29.5-m (97-ft) one was erected in AD 180–93 to honour the military

---

Recycled Temples
Romans are ingenious recyclers. The Pantheon became a church, Hadrian's Temple a stock exchange; San Clemente was built atop a temple to Mithras, Santa Maria sopra Minerva one to Minerva. In the 11th century, the walls of San Lorenzo in Miranda in the Forum and San Nicola in Carcere on Via Teatro di Marcello were both grafted onto temple columns.

Augustus's Mausoleum
7 Augustus built this grand imperial tomb in 27 BC, his ashes later joined by those of emperors Tiberius and Nerva, and worthies such as Agrippa and Marcellus. Barbarian invaders later made off with the urns and locals mined its travertine facing for their palaces. The ancient rotunda has served time as a hanging garden, fortress, circus for bear-baiting, and concert hall. In the 1920s its crown was restored to the ancient style, covered with grass and cypress, and Mussolini laid out the Fascist piazza around it. Major architectural work is planned for this area.
🔊 *Piazza Augusto Imperatore • Map D2 • Open by appt only • Adm*

Piazza di Sant'Ignazio
8 Francesco Raguzzini laid out this masterpiece of Baroque urban design for the Jesuits in

Augustus's Mausoleum

Piazza della Rotonda

1727–8, creating piazza carefully planned right down to the ornate iron balconies and matching dusty pink plaster walls. ◈ *Map M2*

Bernini's Elephant Obelisk
An example of Bernini's fun-loving side. This baby elephant, carved to the master's designs by Ercole Ferrata in 1667, carries a miniature 6th-century BC Egyptian obelisk on its back. It is a tongue-in-cheek reference to Carthaginian leader Hannibal's war elephants, which carried tall siege towers across the Alps to attack the Roman Empire in 218 BC. ◈ *Piazza della Minerva • Map M3*

Piazza della Rotonda
The square in front of the Pantheon was filled with a boisterous daily market until 1847; some of the Pantheon's portico columns still bear square holes from the stall posts once set into them. The square is now filled with tourists, outdoor tables of cafés, and horse-drawn carriages, all ranged around Giacomo della Porta's 1575 fountain, which supports a tiny Egyptian obelisk dedicated to Ramses II. ◈ *Map M3*

A Morning Stroll around the Pantheon

Start with a *cappuccino* at **Café Sant' Eustachio** *(see p96).* Follow Salita de' Crescenzi into **Piazza della Rotonda** and the stunning beauty of the **Pantheon** *(see pp14–15).* Head down to Piazza di Minerva, with **Bernini's Elephant Obelisk** and the façade of **Santa Maria sopra Minerva** *(see p91),* hiding masterpieces by Filippino Lippi and Michelangelo inside.

Via S Caterina da Siena becomes Via Pie' di Marmo (look right to see the famous ancient marble foot). The street spills into the long piazza in front of **Galleria Doria Pamphilj** *(see p91).* After paying homage to works by Caravaggio, Tintoretto and Bernini continue out the east end of the piazza on Via Lata, then on to the Corso to **Santa Maria in Via Lata** *(see p94).* Turn left up the Corso to the Baroque **Piazza Sant' Ignazio**, backed by Rome's best *trompe-l'oeil* frescoes in **Sant'Ignazio di Loyola**. Work your way behind the square's mini palaces onto Piazza di Pietra. A narrow alley leads to the **Column of Marcus Aurelius**. Head to **Giolitti** for a delicious ice cream *(see p96).*

Walk west on Via del Leone into Piazza Borghese, home to an antiques print market and the **Palazzo Borghese** *(see p94).* Two blocks north it opens out on to Piazza Augusto Imperatore, home to many churches, **Augustus's Mausoleum** and the **Ara Pacis** *(see p91).* End your morning with lunch at trendy **'Gusto** *(see p117).*

Left **Fontanella del Facchino** Right **Hadrian's Temple**

🔟 Best of the Rest

1 Hadrian's Temple
Eleven huge, worn columns still stand from a Temple to Hadrian built in AD 145 by his son. ❧ *Piazza di Pietra 9A • Map M2 • Free*

2 Santa Maria Maddalena
The church is an elliptical Baroque gem. The 1735 façade by Giuseppe Sardi is Rome's best Rococo monument. ❧ *Piazza della Maddalena • Map M2 • Open 8am–noon, 5–7:30pm daily • Free*

3 Pie' di Marmo
This oversized, well-worn sandalled marble foot belonged to an unidentified ancient statue. ❧ *Via S Stefano del Cacco, Via Pie di Marmo • Map N3*

4 San Lorenzo in Lucina
Founded in the 5th century, and overhauled in 1090–1118. Guido Reni did the Crucifixion altarpiece, Bernini the second chapel on the right. ❧ *Piazza S Lorenzo in Lucina • Map M2 • Open 9am–noon, 5pm–7:30pm daily • Free*

5 Palazzo di Montecitorio
Bernini's 1670 palace has housed Parliament's Chamber of Deputies since 1871. The south façade is original; the north is Art Nouveau. ❧ *Piazza di Montecitorio & Piazza del Parlamento • Map M1 • 06 676 01 • Open 10am– 6pm 1st Sun of month • Free*

6 Piazza di Montecitorio
The square's obelisk was once part of the Augustus's giant sundial, which used to be flanked by the Ara Pacis *(see p91)*. ❧ *Map M1*

7 Palazzo Borghese
The oddly shaped "harpsichord of Rome", begun by Vignola in 1560, was finished with a Tiber terrace by Flaminio Ponzio. ❧ *Via Borghese & Via di Ripetta • Map M1 • Free*

8 Santa Maria in Via Lata
Pietro da Cortona designed the façade and vestibule (1660); Bernini the high altar (1639–43). Its 6th-century frescoes are now in the Crypta Balbi *(see p52)*. ❧ *Via del Corso 306 • Map N3*

9 Fontanella del Facchino
This small wall fountain (probably from the 1570s) is fashioned as a water-seller whose barrel forever spouts fresh water. ❧ *Via Lata, off Via del Corso • Map N3*

🔟 Piazza Sant'Eustachio
A lovely square, home to two cafés competing for Rome's "best *cappuccino*" title, as well as an 1196 bell tower, and an excellent view of Sant'Ivo *(see p93)*. ❧ *Map M3*

Left **Davide Cenci** Right **Il Papiro**

🔟 Shops

Davide Cenci
Men's and women's clothes designer since 1926. Their own slightly conservative but eminently fashionable line is sold alongside international labels such as Ralph Lauren, Church's, Brooks Brothers and Fay. ⓢ *Via di Campo Marzio 1–7 • Map M2*

Vittorio Bagagli
Purveyor of fine houseware since 1855, including design-led Alessi kitchen gadgets and Pavoni *espresso* machines. ⓢ *Via di Campo Marzio 42 • Map M2*

M Simotti Rocchi
Specialist in Greek, Etruscan and Roman antiquities, selling everything from coins to vases to statuary at a fraction of the prices auction-goers pay (simple coins or terracotta heads start at around €75). ⓢ *Largo Fontanella Borghese 76 • Map M1*

Mercato dell'Antiquariato
Lovely antiquarian market consisting of about 17 stalls specializing in antique prints and books. ⓢ *Piazza Borghese • Map M1*

Città del Sole
Part of an Italian chain of high-class toy stores with the very best in educational playthings. ⓢ *Via della Scrofa 65 • Map L1*

Pane & Company: Forno
This tiny bakery sells an array of local pastries and sweets. The delicious pistachio biscuits are a house speciality. ⓢ *Via della Stelletta 2 • Map M2*

Il Papiro
Rome branch of the renowned Florentine chain, selling marbled paper products, souvenir pens and calligraphy tools. ⓢ *Via del Pantheon 50 • Map M3*

Campo Marzio Roma
Here they sell their own line of fountain pens, covered in silver plating, as well as other writing and calligraphy utensils. Beautiful leather-bound notebooks make great presents. ⓢ *Via di Campo Marzio 41 • Map M2*

Maria Teresa Nitti Valentini
This lovely shop sells stunning antique jewellery from the 1800s up to the 1940s, as well as original brooches based on the design of older pieces. ⓢ *Via della Stelletta 4 • Map M2*

Amarena Chic
Stylish women's shoe shop selling good quality boots and shoes at affordable prices. The unique designs are highly distinctive and are available in a wide selection of colours. ⓢ *Via di Campo Marzio 9 • Map M2*

Left **Café Sant'Eustachio** Right **Gelateria della Palma**

🔟 Cafés, Gelaterie and Bars

Giolitti
This 19th-century landmark café is widely regarded as serving Rome's best ice cream *(see p70).* ◈ *Via degli Uffici del Vicario 40 • Map M2*

Café Sant'Eustachio
Another best – this time the best *cappuccino*. Not surprisingly, the recipe is a closely guarded secret *(see p70).* ◈ *Piazza Sant'Eustachio 82 • Map M3*

Trinity College
Ever-popular pub off the Corso, with tasty food served upstairs and standard bar downstairs. Outdoor seating *(see p78).* ◈ *Via del Collegio Romano 6 • Map N3*

Black Duke
A passably genuine Irish pub in a cosy basement, with pub food and, in summer, outdoor seating. ◈ *Via della Maddalena 29B • Map M2*

Gelateria della Palma
A wide selection of ice cream flavours, just off the Pantheon's square, and open late *(see p71).* ◈ *Via della Maddalena 20–23 • Map M2*

Tazza d'Oro
Rome's "House of Coffee" since 1946. A die-hard locals' joint, serving what devotees swear

is Rome's best coffee *(see p71).* ◈ *Via degli Orfani 84 • Map M2*

Enoteca al Parlamento
Atmospheric and stylish wine bar frequented by politicos from the nearby Italian parliament buildings. ◈ *Via dei Prefetti 15 • Map M1*

Capranica
This wine bar-cum-restaurant is just the place for a quick *aperitivo* or a more leisurely alfresco lunch. The impressively bottle-lined interior shows that this is a serious wine bar with a well-stocked cellar offering a great choice of labels.
◈ *Piazza Capranica 99 • Map M2*

Cremeria Monteforte
A prime tourist position (next to the Pantheon) doesn't always sound the death knell. This joint guarded by a wooden Pinocchio doorman serves the best *fragola* (strawberry) ice cream in town and interesting variations such as orange chocolate. ◈ *Via della Rotonda 22 • Map M3*

Pascucci
This is the place with the frothiest milk shakes and smoothies in town. They come in all flavours and in any combination. ◈ *Via di Torre Argentina 20 • Map M4*

Price Categories

For a three-course
meal for one with half
a bottle of wine (or
equivalent meal), taxes
and extra charges.

€	under €30
€€	€30–40
€€€	€40–50
€€€€	€50–60
€€€€€	over €60

Above **Il Delfino**

Places to Eat

1 L'Eau Vive
Amid 16th-century frescoes, lay sisters from around the world dressed in native costume serve refined French cuisine and dishes from their own countries. Everyone sings "Ave Maria of Lourdes" before their *crêpes flambées*. Perhaps a little kitsch but all the profits do go to charity. ◎ *Via Monterone 85* • *Map M3* • *06 6880 1095* • *Closed Sun* • *€€*

2 Il Bacaro
Booking is essential at this tiny *osteria*. Although the design is contemporary inside, it feels like old Rome when sitting at an outdoor table against the ivy-covered walls. The cuisine is traditional dishes from across Italy. ◎ *Via degli Spagnoli 27* • *Map M2* • *06 687 2554* • *Closed Sun* • *€€*

3 Osteria dell'Ingegno
This popular modern wine bar also serves huge meat and cheese platters. ◎ *Piazza di Pietra 45* • *Map N2* • *06 678 0662* • *Closed Sun* • *€€€*

4 Ristorante Enoteca Corsi
This wine shop has grown into a thriving restaurant (lunch only) serving delicious traditional cuisine at affordable prices. Check the blackboard for the daily specials. ◎ *Via del Gesù 87* • *Map N3* • *06 679 0821* • *Closed Sun* • *€*

5 Maccheroni
The fans and airy rooms wrapped around an open kitchen have a Parisian bistro look. The menu is staunchly Roman, though. ◎ *Piazza delle Coppelle 44* • *Map M2* • *06 6830 7895* • *€€*

6 Ristorante Boccondivino
Classy, modern restaurant with a contemporary art collection and outdoor seating. ◎ *Piazza in Campo Marzio 6* • *Map M2* • *06 6830 8626* • *Closed Sat L, Sun* • *€*

7 Enoteca Corsi
Cheap, filling Roman fare. Limited daily blackboard menu and communal tables. ◎ *Via del Gesù 87–8* • *Map M3* • *06 679 0821* • *Closed evenings and Sun* • *€*

8 Settimo all'Arancio
Hectic, but excellent classic Roman cuisine. ◎ *Via del Arancio 50–52* • *Map M1* • *06 687 6119* • *Closed Sun (Jul–Aug)* • *€€*

9 Da Gino
Visit these *trompe-l'oeil* vaults for food like *nonna* (grandma) used to make. ◎ *Vicolo Rosini 4* • *Map M1* • *06 687 3434* • *Closed Sun* • *€*

10 Il Delfino
Self-service Roman dishes at good prices and friendly staff. ◎ *Corso Vittorio Emmanuele 67* • *Map M4* • *06 686 4053* • *€*

Left **Campo de' Fiori market** Right **Campidoglio square**

Campo de' Fiori to the Capitoline

THIS WEDGE-SHAPED AREA *holds the dubious distinction of being the place where Caesar was assassinated – but it is also home to the Capitoline Hill, Rome's finest glory right up to the present day. In ancient times, the zone was full of important public monuments, but in the 14th century, when the papacy moved to France, Rome sank close to extinction and it was along this bend in the river that the remaining 15,000 citizens huddled, in abject squalor. With the popes' return, serious gentrification took place – papal palaces sprang up, long avenues were laid to connect them with the basilicas, and commerce thrived. Today, you can find clear signs of the long history of Rome's most authentic neighbourhood.*

Sights

1. Campo de' Fiori
2. Capitoline Hill
3. Largo di Torre Argentina
4. Sant'Andrea della Valle
5. Santa Maria in Cosmedin
6. Foro Boario
7. Gesù
8. Santa Maria in Aracoeli
9. Fontana delle Tartarughe
10. Theatre of Marcellus

Palazzo Senatorio

1 Campo de' Fiori
The "Field of Flowers" *(see p46)* occupies what was, in ancient times, the open space in front of the Theatre of Pompey. Since the Middle Ages, it has been one of Rome's liveliest areas, a backdrop for princes and pilgrims alike. On the darker side, it was also the locus of the Inquisition's executions, as attested to by the statue of the hooded philosopher Giordano Bruno, burned here in the Jubilee celebrations of 1600. ✪ *Map L4*

2 Capitoline Hill
The basic principle for comprehending Rome is that everything is built on top of something else. For example, the Capitoline *(see p24)* was originally two peaks: one, called the Arx, graced by the Temple of Juno, and the other, the Cavo, with the Temple of Jupiter, now mostly occupied by the Palazzo dei Conservatori *(see pp26–7)*. The huge Tabularium (Record Office) was built between them in 78 BC, thus forming one hill, called the Capitol; and over that the Palazzo Senatorio was built in the 12th century. ✪ *Map N5*

3 Largo di Torre Argentina
The important ruins of four Republican temples (one dating back to the 4th century BC) were uncovered here in 1925 *(see p41)*. On the northwest side is the pleasing façade of the 18th-century Teatro Argentina, with its

Santa Maria in Cosmedin

LargTo di Torre Argentina

inscription to the Muses. Many operas received their debuts here in the 19th century, including Rossini's *Barber of Seville*. It was a crashing flop on its first night, but only because his enemy, Pauline Bonaparte, had paid a gaggle of hecklers. ✪ *Map M4*

4 Sant'Andrea della Valle
How could one of the most impressive 17th-century Baroque churches have been left with an asymmetrical façade? The answer is artistic temperament. Looking at the grandiose pile, it is quickly apparent that only one angel, on the left, supports the upper tier. Upon its completion, Pope Alexander VII dared to criticize the work, and sculptor Cosimo Fancelli refused to produce an angel for the right side. "If he wants another he can make it himself!" was his rejoinder to His Holiness *(see p45)*. ✪ *Piazza di Sant' Andrea della Valle • Map L4 • Open 7:30am–12:30pm, 4:30–7:30pm daily • Free*

5 Santa Maria in Cosmedin
Originally a bread distribution centre, the site became a church in the 6th century and, 200 years later, the focus of Rome's Greek exile community. The Greek epithet "in Cosmedin" means "decorated". Very little of the earliest ornamentation

The Jews in Rome

Since the 2nd century BC, Jews have been a significant presence in Rome. They thrived throughout the Middle Ages, until, in 1556, Pope Paul IV, founder of the Inquisition, confined them to the squalid Ghetto, where they remained until 1870. Sixty years later they again suffered deadly persecution under the Fascists, but today Roman Jews are an integral part of civic life and number about 16,000.

St Ignazio chapel, Gesù

remains; most of it is from the 12th and 13th centuries, although there is a graceful altar screen characteristic of Eastern Orthodox churches. The most popular element, however, is the "*Bocca della Verità*" ("Mouth of Truth"), an ancient cistern cover. Legend has it that the mouth snaps shut on the hands of liars. ✪ Piazza della Bocca della Verità 18 • Map N6 • Open daily 9am–5pm (6pm summer) • Free

Foro Boario

The name refers to the ancient cattle market that was once here. Now the area is a mini-archaeological park, with two 2nd-century BC temples and a later Arch of Janus. If not for the ferocious traffic, it would be a wonderful place to linger. Dating from the reign of Constantine or later, the arch is unprepossessing, but the temples are amazingly well preserved. The rectangular shrine is to Portunus, god of rivers and ports, while the circular one is a Temple of Hercules. ✪ Map N6

Gesù

A windy piazza hosts the prototype Counter-Reformation church. Enormous and ornate, it's meant to convince the wayward of the pre-eminence of the Jesuit faith. The façade is elegant, but the interior is the major dazzler – first impressions are of vibrant gold, bathed in sunlight. Then there's the vision of angels and saints being sucked into heaven through a miraculous hole in the roof. The tomb of Ignatius, the order's founder, is adorned with the world's largest chunk of lapis lazuli. ✪ Piazza del Gesù • Map N4 • Open daily 6am–12:30pm, 4-7:15pm • Free

Santa Maria in Aracoeli

The 6th-century church stands on the site of the ancient Temple of Juno Moneta (Juno the Sentinel), but it was also the Roman mint – and the origin of the word "money". Superstition claims you can win the lottery by climbing on your knees up the 14th-century staircase leading to the unfinished façade – but what you will definitely gain is a fine view. Inside, the nave's 22

Santa Maria in Aracoeli

columns come from various ancient structures; the third one on the left is inscribed "a cubiculo Augustorum" ("from the emperor's bedroom"). ◎ *Scala dell'Arca Capitolina, 12 • Map N4 • Open daily 9am–12:30pm, 3–6pm • Free*

⑨ Fontana delle Tartarughe
The "Fountain of the Tortoises" is the work of three artists. First created in the late 1500s for the Mattei family, it was designed by Giacomo della Porta. The four bronze boys, however, were sculpted by Taddeo Landini. The crowning touch came almost a century later, when an unknown artist (some say Bernini) added the tortoises and gave the fountain its name *(see p47).* ◎ *Piazza Mattei • Map M5*

Fontane delle Tartarughe

⑩ Theatre of Marcellus
One of three ancient theatres in this district *(see p41),* dating back to the 1st century BC, and probably the most frequented of all Imperial theatres until the Colosseum captured the public's favour. The lower archways once housed picturesque medieval shops, until cleared away by archaeologists in the 1920s. To the right of the theatre stand three columns and a frieze fragment that belonged to a Temple of Apollo, also dating to the 1st century BC. ◎ *Via del Teatro di Marcello • Map N5 • Open 9am–6pm daily*

Roman Culture, Layer upon Layer

🕐 Because of church opening times, you should take this walk (two to four hours) starting at about 10am or at 4pm. Starting with the **Theatre of Marcellus**, notice the soaring buttresses that support the palace, added in the 16th century. Heading round the next corner, in **Santa Maria in Campitelli** *(see p102)* use binoculars to espy the oak leaves depicted in the altar's tiny icon. Continuing west, as you approach the **Fontana delle Tartarughe**, listen for the sound of splashing water echoing off the medieval walls. To the north, the **Crypta Balbi Museum** *(see p53)* has fascinating displays about the neighbourhood's history. One block north is the awe-inspiring **Gesù**.

🍴 For one of the best *cappuccino-cornetto* combinations in town, stop off at Bernasconi *(Piazza Cairoli, 16).*

At **Sant'Andrea della Valle** *(see p99)* look up at the unusual barrel-vaulted ceiling. Then head south to Via di Grotta Pinta for the remains of the **Theatre of Pompey** *(see p53).* A block northwest, in the piazza of the **Palazzo Farnese** *(see p104),* admire the twin fountains, composed of stone tubs from the Baths of Caracalla. Walk across **Campo de' Fiori** *(see p99)* to **Palazzo della Cancelleria** *(see p51)* to contemplate its Renaissance perfection.

🍷 End with a drink at **La Curia di Bacco** *(see p106)* set in 1st-century BC vaults of the Theatre of Pompey.

Left **Synagogue** Right **Tabernacle, Santa Maria in Campitelli**

10 Best of the Rest

1 Palazzo Farnese
One of Rome's largest palaces is graced by superlative Michelangelo creations, such as the wonderful cornice *(see p50)*. ◈ *Piazza Farnese • Map K4 • 06 686 011 • Open by appt - call ahead to book • Adm*

2 Palazzo Spada
Home in the 17th century to two brothers, Bernardino and Virginio Spada, who amassed a fine collection of paintings. The building now houses the Council of State and a gallery *(see p51)*. ◈ *Piazza Capo di Ferro 13 • Map L5 • Open 8:30am–7:30pm Tue–Sun • Adm*

3 Il Vittoriano
The pastiche of motifs on this monument to Victor Emmanuel II is so out of sync with the city that Romans give it nicknames such as "The Wedding Cake". ◈ *Piazza Venezia • Map N4 • Open 9:30am–4:30pm (winter), until 5:30pm (summer) daily*

4 Palazzo Venezia
Pope Paul II, who built this palace, watched the carnival horse races from the balcony. From the same, Mussolini shouted his Fascist harangues *(see p51)* . ◈ *Piazza Venezia • Map N4 • 06 6999 4318 • Open 8:30am–7:30pm Tue–Sun • Adm*

5 Portico d'Ottavia
Built in honour of Octavia, Augustus's sister, this was an entrance to the Circus Flaminius. Despite the archaeological digs, you can pass through the ruins on scaffolding. ◈ *Map M5*

6 Museo Barracco
This delightful palazzo houses a small but important collection of ancient sculpture *(see p53)*. ◈ *Corso Vittorio Emanuele II 166 • Map L4 • 06 6880 6848*

7 Via Giulia
Fashionable street laid out by Bramante in the early 16th century. The ivy-hung viaduct was designed by Michelangelo, but never completed. ◈ *Map K4*

8 Synagogue
This 1904 synagogue has a museum that traces the history of Rome's Jewish community *(see p100)*. ◈ *Lungotevere dei Cenci • Map M5 • Open Jun–Sep: 10am–7pm Sun–Thu (until 4pm Fri); Oct–May: 9am–5pm Sun–Thu (until 2pm Fri) • Adm*

9 Palazzo della Cancelleria
Sublime Renaissance structure, once the Papal Chancellery. ◈ *Piazza della Cancelleria • Map L4 • Open by appt only • Adm*

10 Santa Maria in Campitelli
Home to one of the most lavish tabernacles in Rome. ◈ *Piazza Campitelli • Map N5 • Open 7:30am–noon, 4–7pm daily • Free*

Left **Libreria Babele** Right **Libreria Rinascita**

🔟 Shops

Marble and Tile Bottega
This is certainly one of the most fascinating of a nest of authentic workshops. Particularly appealing are the 18th-and 19th-century Neapolitan floor tiles.
◈ *Vicolo Cellini 16 • Map J3*

Il Goccetto
Considered by connoisseurs to be Rome's premier wine shop, more than 500 labels are available to try by the glass. The proprietor's expertise is at your disposal when selecting which bottles to take home. ◈ *Via dei Banchi Vecchi 14 • Map J3*

Antichità
One of the most appealing antiques shops on this street. An assortment of furniture and small knick-knacks, at good prices.
◈ *Via dei Banchi Vecchi 47 • Map J3*

Libreria Babele
Rome's first gay and lesbian shop has a selection of books in English, plus information concerning goings-on about town.
◈ *Via dei Banchi Vecchi 116 • Map J3*

Sciam
This incredible shop has a Middle Eastern bazaar atmosphere. Hand-blown glass is a speciality. ◈ *Via del Pellegrino 55 • Map K3*

Fahrenheit 451
Cinema, art and photography books galore. ◈ *Campo de' Fiori 44 • Map L4*

Brooks
Modern classics for men in this little boutique, on the street known to have the best, most fashionable bargains in town.
◈ *Via dei Giubbonari 69 • Map L4*

Inn Sport
Whatever he or she may need in active wear, from jeans and tops to gear designed for specific sports, it's all here at prices that make shops in other parts of Rome seem outrageous.
◈ *Via dei Giubbonari 99 • Map L4*

Orologeria Mazzella
Looking for a nice watch that won't blow your budget? This friendly proprietor sells name brands at about 30–50 per cent below regular retail prices. Strong on Swatch watches.
◈ *Via dei Pettinari 41 • Map L4*

Libreria Rinascita
Once the Communist Party's headquarters, this building now houses a well-stocked bookshop. Every Sunday one section of the store is entirely devoted to children, who are free to play and read.
◈ *Via delle Botteghe Oscure 1 • Map N4*

Left **La Vineria** Right **Rock Castle Café**

TOP 10 Nightspots

The Drunken Ship
Currently the top spot, with a sea of energetic carousers night after night in this jumping piazza. Mainstream rock inside. Outside you queue at the service window to get your drinks. ⬡ *Campo de' Fiori 20–21 • Map L4*

I Giganti della Notte
A newcomer to the Campo scene, but already a favourite with a young, good-looking crowd. Great outsize hi-tech decor and modern rock music inside; lots of tables and standing room outside. ⬡ *Campo de' Fiori 26 • Map L4*

Taverna del Campo
Occupying as it does the crucial corner position, this lively drinking and gourmet eating establishment is always a winner and perpetually jammed with merrymakers. Tables inside and out. ⬡ *Campo de' Fiori 16 • Map L4*

La Vineria
This tiny wine bar has long-time regulars lounging at the outside tables. ⬡ *Campo de' Fiori 15 • Map L4*

Caffè Farnese
A more chic place is hard to imagine. On a corner facing elegant Piazza Farnese, some of Rome's smartest young beautiful people sip their glasses of wine at outside tables. Yet, it's also really friendly. ⬡ *Piazza Farnese 106 • Map K4*

Sciam
A taste of Arabia awaits you here. A turquoise-glazed fountain splashes gently at the entrance, and inside all is inlaid wood and tiles. Teas and sweetmeats complement the dreamy music. ⬡ *Via del Pellegrino 56 • Map K4*

La Curia di Bacco
This long, narrow space is a vaulted corridor of the ancient Pompey's Theatre *(see p53)*. ⬡ *Via del Biscione, 79 • Map L4*

Mad Jack's
A classic Irish pub offering all the brews you can imagine, especially Guinness, along with decent light snacks. ⬡ *Via Arenula 20 • Map L4*

Rock Castle Café
A medieval dungeon, with tables tucked into odd nooks. Rock music in the background, plus a dance floor. ⬡ *Via Beatrice Cenci 8 • Map M5*

Shanti
An Arabian night out: hookah pipes, exotic teas, live music and belly-dancing. ⬡ *Via dei Funari 21 • Map M5*

Price Categories

For a three-course meal for one with half a bottle of wine (or equivalent meal), taxes and extra charges.	€ under €30
	€€ €30–40
	€€€ €40–50
	€€€€ €50–60
	€€€€€ over €60

Above **Traditional Roman-Jewish breads**

🔟 Roman-Jewish Restaurants

Piperno
1 Roman-Jewish cuisine at its finest, in a beautiful piazza hidden away from the hubbub. Traditional dishes include *carciofi alla giudia* (Jewish-style fried artichokes). Booking is a must. ✪ *Via Monte de'Cenci 9 • Map M5 • 06 686 1113 • Closed Sun D, Mon • €€€€*

Da Giggetto
2 Famous for its first-rate cookery and grand setting, right next to the soaring columns of the Portico d'Ottavia (see p104). Try chicory shoots *(puntarelle)* with anchovy dressing, a typical Roman dish. ✪ *Via del Portico d'Ottavia 21a–22 • Map M5 • 06 686 1105 • Closed Mon • €€€*

Vecchia Roma
3 One of Rome's finest institutions, noted for its historic interior, excellent service and superb wine list. ✪ *Piazza Campitelli 18 • Map N5 • 06 686 4604 • Closed Wed & 2 weeks Aug • €€€€*

La Taverna del Ghetto
4 Kosher cooking in remodelled medieval rooms, or outside on the piazza. Grilled fish is their forte. ✪ *Via Portico d'Ottavia 8 • Map N5 • 06 6880 9771 • Closed Fri D • €€€*

Sora Margherita
5 Wonderful Jewish-Roman delicacies. No sign; look for the red streamers in the doorway. Weekday lunches only. ✪ *Piazza delle Cinque Scole 30 • Map M4 • 06 686 4002 • No credit cards • €*

Zi Fenizia
6 A pizzeria and a Jewish café all rolled into one outlet. ✪ *Via dell'Umiltà 31 • Map N3 • 349 252 5347 • Closed Fri D, Sat • No credit cards • €*

Filetti di Baccalà
7 A Roman tradition, little changed for centuries. Juicy fried cod fillets, served with similar Roman standards. ✪ *Largo dei Librari 88 • Map M4 • 06 686 4018 • Closed Sun • No credit cards • €*

Da Sergio alle Grotte
8 A simple, traditional Roman dining experience: *spaghetti alla carbonara, gnocchi,* tripe and more. ✪ *Vicolo delle Grotte, 27 • Map M4 • 06 686 4293 • Closed Sun • €*

Osteria ar Galletto
9 An old favourite, tables spilling out into the piazza every summer. Good, honest cooking. ✪ *Piazza Farnese 102 • Map K4 • 06 686 1714 • Closed Sun • €€*

Yotvata
10 Kosher cuisine in a historic palazzo. Good for pizza, fresh fish and hearty pasta dishes. Excellent desserts. ✪ *Piazza Cenci 70 • Map L5 • 06 6813 4481 • Closed Sat L, Fri D • €€*

Left **Piazza del Popolo** Right **Pinturicchio fresco, Santa Maria del Popolo**

The Spanish Steps and Villa Borghese

ERE IS ROME AT ITS MOST ORDERLY AND ELEGANT, *carefully laid out under 16th-century papal urban planning schemes. Baroque popes such as Leo X and Sixtus V redeveloped the all but abandoned area around the Corso, the extension of the ancient Via Flaminia from northern Italy, for their rapidly growing city. Romans now call it the Tridente after the trident of streets – Corso, Ripetta and Babuino – diverging from Piazza del Popolo. It's an area stamped by a love of theatricality: the beautifully symmetrical Piazza del Popolo; long vistas that stretch down arrow-straight roads; the carefully landscaped Pincio gardens and the lush expanse of Villa Borghese; the stage-set backdrop of the Spanish Steps; the oversized and overwrought Trevi Fountain. It's also Rome's most stylishly self-conscious district, famous for its boutiques hawking frighteningly expensive high fashion. Artists have long made their home along Via Margutta, as numerous galleries and antiques shops attest, and Rome's most elegant passeggiata (the traditional early evening see-and-be-seen stroll) unfolds down the length of Via del Corso.*

Bust, Keats-Shelley Memorial

🔟 Sights

1. Galleria Borghese
2. Santa Maria del Popolo
3. The Spanish Steps and Piazza di Spagna
4. Trevi Fountain
5. Keats-Shelley Memorial
6. La Barcaccia
7. Piazza del Popolo
8. Trinità dei Monti
9. Villa Borghese
10. Via dei Condotti

Galleria Borghese

One of Europe's greatest small museums, worth seeing for its setting alone, is home to Rome's best collection of early Bernini sculptures *(see pp20–21)*.

Santa Maria del Popolo

A priceless lesson in Renaissance and Baroque art, architecture and sculpture can be found in this spectacular church *(see pp32–3)*.

The Spanish Steps and Piazza di Spagna

The Spanish Steps and Piazza di Spagna

This elegant, off-centre sweep of a staircase is Rome's most beloved Rococo monument. It is at its most memorable in May, when it is covered in azaleas, but all year round it is littered with people drinking in *la dolce vita* (sweet life) and musicians strumming guitars until late into the night. Francesco De Sanctis designed the steps in 1723–6 for King Louis XV, and their true name in Italian is Scalinata della Trinità dei Monti, after the church at the top. The hourglass-shaped Piazza di Spagna, with its Bernini Barcaccia fountain and milling tourists, was named after the Spanish Embassy to the Vatican located nearby. ✇ *Map D2*

Trevi Fountain

Anita Ekberg bathed in it in *La Dolce Vita*; *Three Coins in a Fountain* taught us to throw coins backwards over our shoulder to ensure a return visit to Rome (healthier than the original tradition of drinking the water for luck) – thanks to the world of cinema this beautiful fountain is one of the most familiar sights of Rome. The right relief shows a virgin discovering the spring from which Augustus (left relief) built the Acqua Vergine aqueduct, which still feeds the fountain. Nicola Salvi paid homage to these ancient origins by grafting his exuberant Baroque confection onto the Classical architectural framework of a triumphal arch *(see p46)*.
✇ *Piazza di Trevi • Map P2*

Keats-Shelley Memorial

The pink-stuccoed apartment overlooking the Spanish Steps, where 25-year-old John Keats breathed his last, consumptive breath in 1821, has been turned into a modest little museum dedicated to the Romantic-era British poets who lived part of their lives in Rome *(see p56)*. Main displays include documents, letters, copies of publications, and Keats' death mask. Companion Joseph Severn cradled Keats' head as he died; his resultant drawing of *Keats on his Deathbed* is also on exhibit.
✇ *Piazza di Spagna 26 • Map D2 • 06 678 4235 • Open 9am–1pm, 3–6pm Mon–Fri, 11am–2pm, 3–6pm Sat • Adm*

6 La Barcaccia

Bernini's father Pietro possibly helped train his son in making this tongue-in-cheek 1629 fountain of a sinking boat. The design ingeniously solved the low water pressure problem by having a boat sprouting leaks rather than jets and sprays.
⊕ *Piazza di Spagna • Map D2*

7 Piazza del Popolo

Rome's elegant public living room started as a trapezoidal piazza in 1538. In 1589, Sixtus V had Domenico Fontana build a fountain crowned with a 3,200-year-old obelisk – the 25-m (82-ft) megalith from Heliopolis, honouring Ramses II, was brought to Rome by Augustus. Napoleon's man in Rome hired Giuseppe Valadier to overhaul the piazza to its current Neo-Classical look in 1811–24, a giant oval that grades up the steep slope of the Pincio via a winding road. Valadier also added the fountain's Egyptian-style lions *(see p46)*. • *Map D2*

8 Trinità dei Monti

This church, crowning the French-commissioned Spanish Steps, was part of a convent founded by Louis XII in 1503. The twin-towered façade (1584) is by Giacomo della Porta; the double staircase (1587) by Domenico Fontana. The Baroque interior has three chapels. Daniele da Volterra frescoed the third chapel on the right and painted the *Assumption* altarpiece (which includes a portrait of his teacher Michelangelo as the far right figure), as well as the *Deposition* in the second chapel on the left. The nearby 16th-century Villa Medici (open for special exhibits) has housed the French Academy since 1803.
⊕ *Piazza Trinità dei Monti • Map D2*
• *Open 10am–1pm, 4–6:30pm daily • Free*

9 Villa Borghese

Rome's largest green space is made up of 688 ha (1,700 acres) of public park, landscaped gardens, statuary, fountains, groves, path-ways, pavilions and a water clock. There are also three world-class museums: Renaissance and Baroque art at Galleria Borghese *(see pp20–21)*, ancient Etruscan artifacts at Villa Giulia *(see p51)*, and modern art at the Galleria Nazionale d'Arte Moderna *(see p43)*. In addition, the Museo Carlo Bilotti, which

Trinità dei Monti

Via dei Condotti

opened in 2006, houses a permanent collection of contemporary works by the Italian artist Giorgio de Chirico (1888–1978). It's all thanks to Cardinal Scipione Borghese, who in 1608 turned these vast family lands just outside the Aurelian walls into a private pleasure park, opened to the public in 1901. In 1809–14, Giuseppe Valadier had turned the adjacent space within the city walls into the terraced Pincio gardens, a favourite *passeggiata* destination studded with statues of great Italians *(see p62)*. There's an elaborate tea house and an obelisk commissioned by Hadrian to honour his lover.
◆ Entrances on Piazza Flaminio, Piazza del Popolo, Via Trinità dei Monti and Corso Italia • Map D2

Via dei Condotti
The "Fifth Avenue" of Rome, lined with chic shops and fashion boutiques of top-name designers. After flirting with high street retail chains in the 1990s, the street has been re-conquered by the *haute couture* that made it famous *(see p68)*. ◆ Map D2

An Afternoon Roman Passeggiata

Begin in Piazza SS Apostoli to see its namesake church *(see p112)* and the 2nd-century AD relief of an Imperial eagle against the portico's right wall. Then continue straight across Via dell'Umiltà and through the elaborate iron, glass, and frescoed 1880s pedestrian passage. Turn right on Via di Muratte to the **Trevi Fountain** *(see p109)*. Your three coins tossed over your shoulder should ensure a return trip. Leave the square on Via di Lavoratore and turn left on Via di Panetteria for some of Rome's best *gelato* at **San Crispino** *(see p70)*.

Turn right up Via del Tritone and left on Via Francesco Crispi for the **Galleria Comunale d'Arte Moderna** to enjoy a rare glimpse in Rome of contemporary art *(see p43)*. Walk down Via Capo le Case and right on Via Due Macelli into **Piazza di Spagna** and the **Spanish Steps** *(see p109)*. Spend as long as you like window-shopping along the grid of streets west of the piazza, but try to finish up by 5pm so you can work your way north, weaving between Via del Babuino and Via Margutta to see the art and antiques shops *(see p113)*, to **Piazza del Popolo**.

Pause for a *cappuccino* at **Caffè Canova** *(see p116)*, then cross to **Santa Maria del Popolo** *(see pp32–3)*, with its works by Caravaggio, Raphael and Bernini. Try to get to **Santa Maria in Montesanto** *(see p112)* around 7pm to hear the Gregorian chant, before heading off for a special dinner at **Dal Bolognese** *(see p117)*.

Around Town – The Spanish Steps & Villa Borghese

Left **German author Goethe lived in Via del Corso** Right **SS Ambrogio e Carlo al Corso**

Best of the Rest

1 Villa Giulia
Contains Italy's top Etruscan collection, celebrating the peninsula's first great civilization (8th to 3rd centuries BC). ✎ *Piazzale di Villa Giulia 9 • Map D1 • Open 8:30am–7:30pm Tue–Sun • Adm • DA*

2 Galleria Nazionale d'Arte Moderna
The national modern art museum covers 19th-and 20th-century works. Strongest in Italian art, although foreigners feature too.
✎ *Viale delle Belle Arti 131 • Map D1 • Open 8:30am–7:30pm Tue–Sun • Adm • DA*

3 Galleria Comunale d'Arte Moderna
The museum covers Italian art from the late 1800s to mid-1900s.
✎ *Via S Francesco Crispi 24 • Map P1 • Open 9am–6:30pm Tue–Sat, 9:30am–1:30pm Sun • Adm • DA*

4 SS Ambrogio e Carlo al Corso
Roman Baroque church (1669) by Pietro da Cortona, who designed the tribune, cupola and stuccoes. ✎ *Via del Corso 437 • Map N1 • Open 7am–12:30pm, 5–7:30pm daily • Free*

5 Santa Maria dei Miracoli and in Montesanto
Carlo Fontana was responsible for these late 17th-century "twin" churches, although Bernini guided him in the decoration of the more elaborate Montesanto. ✎ *Piazza del Popolo • Map D2 • Open 6:30am–1pm, 5–7pm Mon–Sat; 8am–1pm, 4:30–8pm Sun • Free*

6 Canova's Studio
The artist's studio walls are embedded with fragments of statuary. ✎ *Via del Babuino 150a • Map D2 • Open 8:30am–8:30pm Mon–Sat • Free*

7 Palazzo Colonna
The gallery features work by Tintoretto, Lotto and Veronese. ✎ *Via della Pilotta 17 • Map N2 • Open 9am–1pm Sat • Closed Aug • Adm*

8 Porta del Popolo
Michelangelo used the Arch of Titus as the model for this gateway. ✎ *Piazza del Popolo • Map D2*

9 Casa di Goethe
German author Goethe lived here from 1786 to 1788 (see p56), and his letters are on display.
✎ *Via del Corso 18 • Map D2 • Open 10am–6pm Tue–Sun (guided tours available on request) • Adm*

10 Santissimi Apostoli
This 6th-century church, restructured in 1702–08, has a *trompe-l'oeil* vault above the altar.
✎ *Piazza SS Apostoli • Map N2 • Open 7am–noon, 4–7pm • Free*

Left **Galleria Veneziani** Right **Dott. Cesare Lampronti**

🔟 Art and Antiques Shops

1 Dott. Cesare Lampronti
Although it resembles an art museum, you can buy the work on show here: still lifes, religious paintings, mythological compositions, scenes of Roman life and Neo-Classical statues, variously dating from the 16th to 19th centuries. ◈ *Via del Babuino 174–5 • Map D2*

2 Benucci
Heavy duty art and antiques of the type more usually found in museums – 15th-century Roman and Florentine Virgin and Childs, works by artists such as Luca Giordano or Fra' Bartolomeo – plus beautiful furnishings inlaid in mother-of-pearl and hardwoods.
◈ *Via del Babuino 151–3 • Map D2*

3 Galleria Veneziani
A large gallery selling a wide range of high-quality antiques, from furnishings and old oil paintings to statuary, vases and various *objets d'art*. Definitely worth a browse.
◈ *Via Margutta 45
• Map D2*

4 Maurizio Grossi
Maurizio Grossi is a specialist in marble. This is just the place to buy a reproduction Roman bust or an astoundingly life-like sculpted fruit.
◈ *Via Margutta 109
• Map D2*

5 Alberto di Castro
Etching, lithographs and other prints mostly from the 1660s to the 1920s are on sale in this lovely shop. ◈ *Via del Babuino 71 • Map D2*

6 Galleria Augusto Consort
Regularly changing exhibitions of contemporary paintings, watercolours and prints are held here. ◈ *Via Margutta 52 • Map D2*

7 Galleria Antiquaria
A small selection of artworks, mostly sculpture, paintings and *objets d'art*.
◈ *Via Margutta 67 • Map D2*

8 Nomades
This eclectic, funky gallery housed in a former convent sells wood, stone and ceramic *objets d'art* from around the globe.
◈ *Via di Ripetta 224 • Map D2*

9 E&R Danon
Mostly 18th- to early 20th-century Oriental carpets and prayer rugs, from Persia and India, Tibet and China. ◈ *Via Margutta 36–37 • Map D2*

10 La Bottega del Marmoraro
Homespun Italian homilies carved into scraps of marble are hung pell-mell around a characteristic old workshop. ◈ *Via Margutta 53B • Map D2*

Left **Gucci** Right **Giorgio Armani**

🔟 High Fashion Boutiques

Giorgio Armani
Stylishly cool service for one of Italy's top names. Emporio Armani branch (Via del Babuino 140) sells the designer's couture line at lower prices. The lowest-end line, Armani Jeans, is at Via del Babuino 70A. ◈ *Via dei Condotti 77 • Map D2*

Prada
The most highly priced of the top Italian designers. A Milan fashion house making minimalist, slightly retro clothing. ◈ *Via dei Condotti 92–5 • Map D2*

Gucci
The Florentine saddle-maker turned his leather-working skills into one of Italy's early fashion successes. The era of ostentatious interlocking "G's" on everything is over, but the accessories are still top notch. ◈ *Via dei Condotti 8 • Map D2*

Valentino
Boutique for the *prêt-à-porter* collection of this native Roman designer in the top echelon of fashion since Jackie Kennedy and Audrey Hepburn donned his clothes in the 1960s. ◈ *Via del Babuino 61 • Map D2*

Ferragamo
The shoemaker to the stars during Hollywood's Golden Age of the 1950s hasn't lost its touch, but it now mass-produces styles rather than creating unique works. ◈ *Via dei Condotti 73–4 • Map D2*

Gianni Versace
The house of the late fashion designer never compromises the clothing's flamboyant cuts and garish use of colour. ◈ *Via Bocca di Leone 27 • Map D2*

Fausto Santini
Gorgeous, classically styled shoes at stratospheric prices. ◈ *Via Frattina 120 • Map D2*

Fendi
Five sisters founded this Roman fashion empire from their parents' workshop and reign over Italy's rage for furs. ◈ *Largo Goldoni 420 • Map D2*

Philosophy di Alberta Ferretti
Well-cut women's clothing that is feminine yet powerful and modern. ◈ *Via Condotti 34 • Map D2*

Laura Biagiotti
Designer who has made stylish fashions for women since 1972. In menswear, she uses the soft wool that has earned her the moniker "Queen of Cashmere". ◈ *Via Borgognona 43–4 • Map D2*

Left **Messaggerie Musicali** Right **Firmastock**

🔟 Discount and Specialist Shops

1 Il Discount dell'Alta Moda
This stock house sells mostly men's and women's clothing, plus accessories. The staff are genuinely helpful. There are discounts of up to 50 per cent on Versace, Donna Karan, Armani, Dolce & Gabbana and more. ✆ *Via di Gesù e Maria 14–16A • Map D2*

2 Firmastock
Small, eclectic collection of designer men's and women's suits, dresses, coats and shoes at up to 50–70 per cent off the usual retail prices. ✆ *Via delle Carrozze 18 • Map D2*

3 Buccone
Historic wine shop with a vast selection and excellent prices. Speciality Italian foods are on sale as well. ✆ *Via di Ripetta 19–20 • Map D2*

4 Enigma
Owned by Bulgari, this intriguing shop sells a highly exclusive line of watches and jewellery. ✆ *Via Margutta 61 • Map D2*

5 Vertecchi
The queen of Rome's stationery stores, with hundreds of types of pens (the fancier ones are sold next door at No. 72), thousands of notebooks, and the very best in art supplies. ✆ *Via della Croce 70 • Map D2*

6 C.U.C.I.N.A.
The motto of this shop, carrying the best in minimalist kitchenware, is "How a kitchen inspires new appetites". ✆ *Via Mario de' Fiori 65 • Map D2*

7 Messaggerie Musicali
Huge, ultra-modern music store with dozens of listening stations so you can better select your choice of cassettes and CDs. Tastes range from Italian pop to classic opera. ✆ *Via del Corso 472 • Map D2*

8 Tebro
Founded in 1867, this department store specialises in luxury bed linens, towels and lingerie. A made-to-measure service is also available. ✆ *Via dei Prefetti 46–54 • Map M1*

9 Remainders
Does exactly what the name says: sells overstock books at up to 50 per cent off their original price, including lots of luxurious art catalogues and coffee table tomes. ✆ *Piazza S Silvestro 27–8 • Map D2*

10 Cravatterie Nazionali
Beautiful ties from Valentino, Gigli, Givenchy, Zenga, Gucci and Les Copains at reasonable (for designer) prices and all in one spot. ✆ *Via Vittoria 62 • Map D2*

Left & Right **Babington's Tea Rooms**

TOP10 Pubs, Cafés and Bars

1 L'Antica Cantina
Delicious antipasti and wine by the glass, are served in this old-fashioned lively establishment. ◎ *Via della Croce 76b • Map D2*

2 Gilda
Rome's most central disco has remained popular for years, with a pizzeria in the evening and dance music cranking up at midnight. High cover charge on weekends, but always an A-list crowd. ◎ *Via Mario de' Fiori 97 • Map D2*

3 Antico Caffè Greco
Rome's premier literary café since 1760, best known for its popularity with the 19th-century English Romantic poets *(see p70)*. ◎ *Via Condotti 86 • Map D2*

4 Thé Verde
Owned by a family of tea traders since 1890, this tranquil, Oriental-style tea-house stocks over two hundred types of tea. Home-made cakes and light meals are also available. ◎ *Via Bocca Leone 46 • Map D2*

5 The Victoria House Pub
Every British ex-pat seems to have adopted this Victorian-style pub as his or her own, lending it an air of authenticity. ◎ *Via Gesù e Maria 18 • Map D2*

6 Nag's Head
Self-styled "Scottish pub" with an occasional DJ and, Monday to Wednesday, live music. ◎ *Via IV Novembre 138B • Map P3*

7 Café Rosati
Art Nouveau rival to the right-wing Canova across the piazza, this café has long been the haunt of left-wing intellectuals *(see p70)*. ◎ *Piazza del Popolo 4–5 • Map D2*

8 Caffè Canova
The right-wing bastion in the long-standing Piazza del Popolo café war, with cheaper *espresso*, better ice cream and a restaurant upstairs (the Rosati is more stylish, though). ◎ *Piazza del Popolo 16–17 • Map D2*

9 Shaki
Post-Modern wine bar serving salads and sandwiches with a few tables outside. They also have a very good speciality foods store at Piazza di Spagna 65. ◎ *Via Mario de' Fiori 29A • Map D2*

10 Babington's Tea Rooms
Good for a very pricey spot of tea and other daintily British edibles. Opened in 1893 by a Derbyshire lady, it was the ex-pat hub of the later Grand Tour era. ◎ *Piazza di Spagna 23 • Map D2*

For Rome's Top 10 Pubs, Bars and Music Clubs See **pp78–9**

Price Categories

For a three-course meal for one with half a bottle of wine (or equivalent meal), taxes and extra charges.

€	under €30
€€	€30–40
€€€	€40–50
€€€€	€50–60
€€€€€	over €60

Above 'Gusto

Places to Eat

1 Fiaschetteria Beltramme (da Cesaretto)

Regulars and tourists are fitted into communal tables at this ultra-traditional *trattoria* just down the block from the Spanish Steps. ® *Via della Croce 39* • *Map D2* • *Closed Sun* • *No credit cards* • *€€*

2 Edy

Some of the best food and lowest prices in this high-rent neighbourhood. Mix of seafood and Roman dishes. The candlelit tables out front are a nice touch. ® *Vicolo del Babuino 4* • *Map D2* • *06 3600 1738* • *Closed Sun, Mon L* • *€€*

3 'Gusto

Trendiest thing going: combo restaurant, pizzeria and Thai wine bar *(see p75)*. ® *Piazza Augusto Imperatore 9* • *Map D2* • *06 322 6273* • *€€€*

4 Birreria Peroni

Beer hall with excellent, cheap food sponsored by Italy's premier brewery – try their "Blue Ribbon" Nastro Azzurro label *(see p75)*. ® *Via San Marcello 19/Piazza SS Apostoli* • *Map N3* • *06 679 5310* • *Closed Sun* • *€*

5 Dal Bolognese

This restaurant's popularity roller-coaster is currently on the upswing, with international celebrities again gracing its tables on Piazza del Popolo for classic Roman cuisine in view of the Ferraris parked out front. ® *Piazza del Popolo 1* • *Map D2* • *06 361 1426* • *Closed Mon* • *€€€€*

6 Abruzzi

The cuisine here hails from the owners' home in the nearby Abruzzi mountains, as the name suggests. ® *Via del Vaccaro 1* • *Map D2* • *06 679 3897* • *Closed Sat* • *€*

7 Hosteria St Ana

Warren of basement rooms plastered with photos of famous patrons. Classic Roman cookery. ® *Via della Penna 68–9* • *Map D2* • *06 361 0291* • *Closed Sat L, Sun* • *€€*

8 Al 34

Excellently priced menus featuring inventive Italian cooking. ® *Via Mario de' Fiori 34* • *Map D2* • *06 679 5091* • *Closed Mon* • *€*

9 Il Brillo Parlante

Popular basement eatery packed with locals enjoying huge plates of salad and delicious pizzas. ® *Via della Fontanella 12* • *Map D2* • *06 324 3334* • *Closed Mon L* • *€*

10 L'Archetto

The cast from nearby Teatro Quirino head here for more than 100 pasta sauces. ® *Via dell'Archetto 26* • *Map D2* • *06 678 9064* • *€*

Note: *Unless otherwise stated, all restaurants accept credit cards and serve vegetarian meals*

Left and right **San Teodoro**

Ancient Rome

THIS AREA HAS ALWAYS BEEN A CONTRASTING MIX *of the highest and the lowest, from the most extravagant luxury to the toughest work-a-day world. In ancient times, the emperor's lavish palaces were built on the Palatine, but they weren't far from the docks, where roustabouts heaved the tons of goods that were imported to the wealthy city from around the world. There are three hills in the zone: the Palatine and the Aventine are two of the original seven, but Monte Testaccio is entirely man-made. Legend has it that the Aventine was where Remus formed a populist settlement, to rival his twin brother Romulus's dictatorial encampment (see p38). Over the centuries it has been an area inhabited by poor workers and religious institutions. Today, it has returned to being an enclave of greenery and smart dwellings, studded with hidden art treasures and some of the world's finest ancient monuments and priceless archaeological finds.*

Capital, Baths of Caracalla

🔟 Sights

1. Roman Forum and Palatine Hill
2. Colosseum and Imperial Fora
3. Musei Capitolini
4. Santa Sabina
5. Baths of Caracalla
6. Piazza of the Knights of Malta
7. San Saba
8. Pyramid of Caius Cestius
9. San Teodoro
10. Protestant Cemetery

Roman Forum and Palatine Hill

Once the heart of the Roman empire, this mass of ruins is an eerie landscape that seems gripped by the ghosts of an ancient civilization *(see pp16–19)*.

Colosseum and Imperial Fora

These monuments memorialize Imperial supremacy. The Forum of Trajan was declared a Wonder of the World by contemporaries; the only remnant is Trajan's Column, considered to represent Roman sculptural art at its peak. The Colosseum embodies the Romans' passion for brutal entertainment *(see pp22–3)*.

Musei Capitolini

Notwithstanding their great beauty, the original motivation for these museums was purely political. When the popes started the first museum here in 1471, it laid claim to Rome's hopes for civic autonomy – the Palazzo dei Conservatori was the seat of hated papal counsellors, who ran the city by "advising" the Senators. Today the museums are home to a spectacular collection of art *(see pp24–7)*.

Santa Sabina

This church was built over the Temple of Juno Regina in about 425 to honour a martyred

Santa Sabina

Roman matron. In 1936–8 it was restored almost to its original condition, while retaining 9th-century additions such as the Cosmatesque work and the bell tower. Twenty-four perfectly matched Corinthian columns are surmounted by arcades with marble friezes and light filters through the selenite window panes. The doors are 5th-century carved cypress, with 18 panels of biblical scenes, including the earliest known Crucifixion – strangely without any crosses.
◈ *Piazza Pietro d'Illiria 1 • Map D5 • Open 6:30am–12:45pm, 3:30–7pm daily • Free • DA*

Baths of Caracalla

Inaugurated in 217 and used until 546, when invading Goths destroyed the aqueducts. Up to 2,000 people at a time could use these luxurious *thermae*. In general, Roman baths included

Gymnasia, Baths of Caracalla

➤ *Carry a bottle of water with you, which you can refill at little fountains around the area* social centres, art galleries, libraries, brothels and *palestrae* (exercise areas). Bathing involved taking a sweat bath, a steam bath, a cool-down, then a cold plunge. The Farnese family's ancient sculpture collection was found here, including *Hercules*, a signed Greek original. Today, ruins of individual rooms can be seen. ✍ *Via delle Terme di Caracalla 52 • Map E6 • Open 9am–2pm Mon, 9am–1 hr before sunset Tue–Sun • Adm • DA*

Pyramid of Caius Cestius

6 Piazza of the Knights of Malta

Everyone comes here for the famous bronze keyhole view of St Peter's Basilica, ideally framed by an arbour of perfect trees *(see p53)*. However, it's also worth a look for the piazza's wonderful 18th-century decoration by Giambattista Piranesi, otherwise renowned for his powerful engravings of fantasy-antiquity scenes. To honour the ancient order of crusading knights (founded in 1080), the architect chose to adorn the walls with dwarf obelisks and trophy armour, in the ancient style. Originally based on the island of Rhodes, then Malta, the knights are now centred in Rome. ✍ *Map D5*

7 San Saba

Originally a 7th-century oratory for Palestinian monks fleeing their homeland, the present church is a 10th-century renovation, with many additions. The portico of the beautiful 15th-century loggia houses a wealth of archaeological fragments. Greek style in floorplan, with three apses, the interior decoration is mostly Cosmatesque *(see p35)*. The greatest oddity is a 13th-century fresco showing St Nicholas about to toss a bag of gold to three naked girls lying on a bed, thus saving them from prostitution. ✍ *Via di San Saba • Map E6 • Open 7am–noon, 4–6:30pm daily • Free*

Class Divisions and Power Struggles

The ceaseless struggle between the governing and the working classes is typified by the history of this area. Romulus on the Palatine versus Remus on the Aventine gave rise to patricians and plebeians respectively. The contrast still exists, between wealthy Aventine and down-to-earth Testaccio.

Portico carving, San Saba

Take a torch (flashlight) and binoculars when visiting churches to see the architectural details close up

8 Pyramid of Caius Cestius

This 12 BC edifice remains a truly imposing monument to the wealthy Tribune of the People for whom it was built. It stands 36 m (118 ft) high and took 330 days to erect, according to an inscription carved into its stones. Unlike Egyptian originals, however, it was built of brick then covered with marble, which was the typically pragmatic, Roman way of doing things. ◈ *Piazzale Ostiense • Map D6*

9 San Teodoro

At the foot of the Palatine, this small, circular, 6th-century church is one of Rome's hidden treasures. St Theodore was martyred on this spot, and his church was built into the ruins of a great *horrea* (grain warehouse) that stood here. The apse mosaic showing Christ seated upon an orb is original, but the Florentine cupola (1454) and other treatments are mostly 15th-century restorations ordered by Pope Nicholas V. The courtyard was designed by Carlo Fontana in 1705. ◈ *Via di San Teodoro • Map P6*

Keats' tombstone

10 Protestant Cemetery

Also called the Acattolica (Non-Catholic) Cemetery, people of many faiths have been sepulchred here since 1738. The most famous denizens are the English poets Keats and Shelley (see pp56–7). Until 1870, crosses and references to salvation were forbidden. ◈ *Via Caio Cestio 6 • Map D6 • Open 9am–4:30pm Tue–Sun • Donation*

A Morning Parkland Stroll

🕐 The parkland on the other side of the Circus Maximus from the Palatine Hill conceals exquisite early churches and other gems. Start on the south side of the Circus Maximus, now a sunken patch of dust and weeds, but once a majestic racecourse until the popes plundered its stones to build their palaces. Head up the hill to the **Rose Garden** *(see p60)*. In spring and summer few places in Rome radiate such beauty. Continue along the old wall and enter Parco Savello's **Orange Garden** *(see p60)* to take in the view from the parapet. Next door is **Santa Sabina** *(see p119)*. Use a torch and binoculars to scrutinize carved wooden doors and the Crucifixion scene. Stop next at Piranesi's **Piazza of the Knights of Malta** and peer through the celebrated keyhole.

Wind down Via di San Alessio until Viale Aventino and **San Saba**. Take time to appreciate the notorious St Nicholas fresco on the left wall. In the **Parco della Resistenza dell'8 Settembre** *(see p63)* you can get a *gelato* in the park's café and gaze at length on the 3rd-century **Aurelian Wall** *(see p152)*.

Cross over to the lovely **Protestant Cemetery**, pay your respects at the graves of Shelley, Keats and friends, pause to reflect on the splendid **Pyramid of Caius Cestius**, and leave your donation in the box as you exit.

🍴 **Volpetti** *(see p125)* is a fabulous choice for lunch with a made-to-order gourmet sandwich.

Following pages Palatine Hill

Left **Alpheus** Right **L'Alibi**

Rome's Trendiest Nightlife

Alpheus
Alpheus contains three individual discos, each of which plays different music, plus a garden. It holds special shows too, plus theme nights and the occasional live concert. The entrance ticket includes one free drink. ◈ *Via del Commercio 36 • Map D6 • DA*

Nazca
This is the place where Rome's bright young things sip a well-mixed cocktail or two before sampling the other delights of the Testaccio-Ostiense area. It has a good sound system and an equally trendy restaurant. ◈ *Via del Gazometro 40 • Map D6*

Radio Londra
One of Rome's perennial favourites for an energetic night out. This is a noisy, buzzing rock-and-roll venue with an air-force theme and occasional up-and-coming live bands. Food is also available. ◈ *Via di Monte Testaccio 65B • Map D6 • DA*

L'Alibi
This is Rome's largest and most famous gay disco, with several dance floors, lounges and a huge terrace garden to cool off in in summer. ◈ *Via di Monte Testaccio 44 • Map D6*

Villaggio Globale
Occupying part of an old slaughterhouse, the "Global Village" offers great world music, plus ethnic snacks. Winter only. ◈ *Lungotevere Testaccio • Map C6*

Caffè Latino
Films, cabaret and disco with a great, eclectic mix of music. ◈ *Via di Monte Testaccio 96 • Map D6 • DA*

Café de Oriente
Occasional Brazilian bands rock the samba, while the rest of the time Latin-tinged disco gets you going. ◈ *Via di Monte Testaccio 36 • Map D6 • DA*

Four XXXX Pub
One of Rome's more popular English-style pubs, but featuring South American-inspired food. Jazz and Latin music on occasion. ◈ *Via Galvani 29 • Map D6 • DA*

Mount Gay
Very relaxed, two-room disco-bar, named after the Caribbean rum, featuring occasional live jam sessions and DJ gigs. ◈ *Via Galvani 54 • Map D6*

Clamur
This pub projects a genuine English atmosphere with a zippy Italian twist. Guinness is on offer, along with snacks. ◈ *Piazza dell'Emporio 2 • Map D5 • DA*

Price Categories

For a three-course meal for one with half a bottle of wine (or equivalent meal), taxes and extra charges.

€	under €30
€€	€30–40
€€€	€40–50
€€€€	€50–60
€€€€€	over €60

Above **Checchino dal 1887**

🔟 Traditional Roman Restaurants

1 Checchino dal 1887

Among the great Roman restaurants *(see p74)*, the menu offers offal-based delicacies such as *rigatoni alla pajata* (pasta with calf intestine). ◎ *Via di Monte Testaccio 30 • Map D6 • 06 574 6318 • Closed Sun–Mon • €€€*

2 Agustarello

Roman-style, heavy-duty dishes are the standard here. Sample tripe, *coda alla vaccinara* (oxtail), *lingua* (tongue) and other peasant fare *(see pp76–7)*. ◎ *Via G Branca 98 • Map D6 • 06 574 6585 • Closed Sun • No credit cards • €€*

3 Da Remo

One of Rome's quintessential pizzerias. Authentic, cheap and always packed. ◎ *Piazza S Maria Liberatrice 44 • Map D6 • 06 574 6270 • Closed Sun • No credit cards • €*

4 Volpetti

Rome's premier delicatessen and the ideal place to have a lunchtime sandwich or a whole picnic made to order. ◎ *Via Marmorata 47 • Map D6 • 06 574 4306 • Closed Sun • €*

5 Felice

This simple *trattoria* is one of the best places in the city to try the traditional *carciofi alla romana (see p76)*. ◎ *Via Mastro Giorgio 29 • Map D6 • 06 574 6800 • Closed Sun • €€*

6 Il Ristoro dei Cocci

The speciality here is delicious pizza, and the *focaccia* bread is among Rome's best. ◎ *Via di Monte Testaccio 34/B • Map D6 • 06 572 88940 • Closed Mon in winter • No credit cards • €*

7 Di Pietro

Good traditional Roman fare is served at this neighbourhood favourite, close to the Caius Cestius Pyramid. Take-away *(tavola calda)* is available from the buffet. ◎ *Piazza di Porta San Paolo 6A • Map D6 • 06 578 0252 • Closed Tue • €€*

8 Acqua e Farina?

At "Water and Flour?" practically everything on the menu, from savouries to sweets, is pastry-based and made to an original recipe. ◎ *Piazza O Giustiniani 2 • Map C6 • 06 574 1382 • Closed L • €*

9 Il Seme e la Foglia

Great for large salads and inventive sandwiches, such as goats' cheese, radicchio and olive spread. ◎ *Via Galvani 18 • Map D6 • 06 574 3008 • No credit cards • Closed Sun • €*

10 Né Arte ne Parte

Run by two Italian TV actors, the menu features such Roman classics as carbonara and roast lamb. ◎ *Via Luca della Robbia 15–17 • Map D6 • 06 575 0279 • Closed Tue L, Wed L, 3 wks July • €€*

 Note: Unless otherwise stated, all restaurants accept credit cards and serve vegetarian meals

125

Left **Mosaic, Santa Prassede** Right **Nave, Santi Giovanni e Paolo**

The Esquiline and Lateran

IN ANCIENT TIMES THE LARGEST OF ROME'S SEVEN HILLS *was almost entirely residential, consisting mostly of upper-class villas. The western slope of the quarter, just behind the Imperial Fora (see pp22–3) was considered rather unhealthy as it was densely populated – the massive wall at the back of the Fora was intended to keep the squalid slum out. However, in the 4th century, this zone became central to the development of Christianity. In setting up the religion as the official faith, Constantine did not dare step on too many pagan toes, so he established Christian centres outside of town, on the sites of holy tombs. The main one was what is now San Giovanni in Laterano (Saint John in Lateran). Other churches quickly followed, culminating in the striking Santa Maria Maggiore, built in the 5th century. The district remains steeped in history and religious mystique.*

Statue, San Giovanni in Laterano

🔟 Sights

1 San Clemente
2 Palazzo Massimo alle Terme
3 Santa Maria Maggiore
4 San Giovanni in Laterano & Scala Santa
5 San Pietro in Vincoli
6 Nero's Golden House
7 Santa Prassede
8 Santo Stefano Rotondo
9 Santi Giovanni e Paolo
10 Oriental Art Museum

San Clemente

Architectural layers of this church unravel Rome's history, from the 2nd century BC to the 15th century AD *(see pp34–5)*.

Palazzo Massimo alle Terme

Housing an extraordinary collection of ancient frescoes, mosaics and sculpture, this branch of the Museo Nazionale Romano is perhaps the most inspiring. The building itself was erected by the Massimo family at the end of the 19th century and later served as a Jesuit college *(see pp28–9)*.

Santa Maria Maggiore

This church is a unique blend of architectural styles. The nave and its mosaics are original 5th-century; the Cosmatesque work, the apse mosaics and the Romanesque bell tower are medieval; the coffered ceiling (of New-World gold) is Renaissance; and the twin domes and front and back façades are Baroque. Pope Sixtus V erected the Egyptian obelisk in 1587 as part of his overall town-planning, to provide landmarks for pilgrims. The column in front was taken from the Basilica of Maxentius and Constantine in 1615 *(see p44)*. ◈ Piazza di S Maria Maggiore • Map F3 • Open 7am–7pm daily • Free

Catacomb, San Clemente

San Giovanni in Laterano and Scala Santa

Besides its grandiose Baroque bulk, visible from all over Rome, this former papal complex boasts the world's very first baptistry, its octagonal shape the model for all those to come. A building on the piazza houses the Scala Santa, claimed to be the staircase from Pontius Pilate's house that Jesus ascended to face his trial – devout believers climb the 28 steps on their knees. Tradition says that the stairs were brought from Jerusalem by St Helena, mother of Emperor Constantine *(see p45)*. ◈ Piazza di S Giovanni in Laterano • Map F5 • Open 7am–7pm daily (cloisters: 7am–6pm; baptistry 7:30am–12:30pm, 4–7pm) • Adm to cloisters

San Pietro in Vincoli

Michelangelo's *Moses* is the unmissable experience here. Weirdly horned and glaring, the

Façade, Santa Maria Maggiore

righteously indignant patriarch is about to smash the tablets down in outrage at his people's idolatry. This powerful sculpture was just one of 40 the artist planned, but never finished, for the tomb of Pope Julius II *(see p49)*. It has recently been restored. The original shrine was built in the 4th century to house the chains supposedly used to bind St Peter in prison. It has been rebuilt since, first in the 8th century and again in the 15th century. ◈ *Piazza di S Pietro in Vincoli 4A • Map R4 • Open 7am– 12:30pm, 3:30–7pm daily (until 6pm Oct–May) • Free • DA*

Statuary, San Pietro in Vincoli

Nero's Golden House
Subsequent emperors were so embarrassed by Nero's gargantuan profligacy that they went to great lengths to undo as much of it as they could. One way was to give some of the land Nero took for himself back to the use of the Roman people. The Flavians drained his lake and built the Colosseum *(see p22)*, to provide the citizenry with a suitable place for their gladiatorial spectacles. Then Trajan built Rome's first great bath complex by cutting through Nero's original house and building right over it *(see p41)*. ◈ *Viale della Domus Aurea • Map E4 • Currently closed for restoration • Adm • DA*

Establishment of the Church
This area played a central role in early Christianity. Although Constantine himself was not a convinced convert, his mother, St Helena, was indefatigable in her promotion of the new religion. She convinced her son to found the official seat of the Bishop of Rome on the site of the ancient Laterani family villa, which his wife Fausta had inherited.

Santa Prassede
Built in the 9th century over a 2nd-century oratory, the original design is still discernible despite restorations. In the central nave, a stone slab covers the well where St Prassede is said to have buried 2,000 martyrs. Byzantine artists decorated the apse with mosaics depicting saints, lambs, palm trees and poppies. The walls and vaults of the Chapel of St Zeno also have mosaics from the same period, and there is a fragment of the column Christ was bound to when he was flogged. ◈ *Via S Prassede 9A • Map F4 • Open 7am– noon daily • Free • DA*

Santo Stefano Rotondo
The unusual shape of this early church (468–83) may mean it was built over Nero's round *Macellum Magnum* (meat market). Or perhaps its form was inspired by Jerusalem's Church of the Holy Sepulchre. Whatever the case, recent digs have found a Mithraeum underneath *(see p53)*. The structure is a peaceful, delightful sanctuary, situated far from urban uproar, although

16th-century frescoes by Niccolò Pomarancio depict martyrdoms in sadistic fashion. ◎ *Via di S Stefano Rotondo 7* • *Map F5* • *Open 2–4:15pm Mon, 9am–1pm, 2–4:15pm Tue–Fri* • *Free*

Santi Giovanni e Paolo

The eponymous saints were 4th-century martyrs and their home is still seen under the 5th-century structure. They were beheaded here in 361 on orders from Emperor Julian. Except for the Late Baroque interior, much of the church is pure medieval. The base of the bell tower is that of the 1st-century Temple of Claudius that once stood here. ◎ *Piazza SS Giovanni e Paolo 13* • *Map E5* • *Open 8:30am–noon, 3:30–6:30pm daily* • *Free*

Oriental Art Museum

A fine, though small collection of Middle and Far Eastern art, ranging from prehistoric Persian ceramics to 18th-century Tibetan paintings. The most fascinating works are the Ghandharan. These 3rd-century BC to 10th-century AD Indian Buddhist works display both Asian and Greek influences, due to the conquest of the area that is now Pakistan by Alexander the Great. ◎ *Via Merulana 248* • *Map F4* • *Open 8:30am–7:30pm Tue, Thu & Sun; 8:30am–2pm Mon, Wed, Fri, Sat (closed 1st & 3rd Mon of month)* • *Adm* • *DA*

Santo Stefano Rotondo

Exploring Rome's Early Churches

Morning

⏱ Start with **San Clemente** (see pp34–5), with its fascinating layers. At the lowest level use a torch (flashlight) to appreciate the beautiful fresco of the head of a bearded man.

🍴 Walk one block over to the **Via dei Santi Quattro Coronati** to glimpse the produce market (see p69); turn left and walk up the hill to Santi Quattro Coronati, a rich and little visited 4th-century church with remarkable frescoes in the chapel (1246). Continue on until you reach **San Giovanni in Laterano** (see p127). The cloisters with gorgeously twisted columns and mosaic inlays will make your visit truly memorable.

🍴 For an equally memorable lunch, head to **Cannavota** (see p131).

Afternoon

After lunch, it's time for another of the great basilicas, **Santa Maria Maggiore** (see p127). Check out the ancient column in front and inside use binoculars to examine the 5th-century mosaics lining the upper reaches of the nave. Finally, cut over to **Santa Prassede,** where you can take in some of Rome's most radiant Byzantine mosaics and a powerful painting of the Flagellation in the sacristy.

🍴 For sustenance after your spiritual journey, continue down the hill, past Santa Maria Maggiore's grand staircase and enjoy a drink at **L'Angolo di Napoli** (see p131), or stay for a dinner of Neapolitan-style pizza.

Left **Via Mamiani Market** Right **Via Sannio Market**

Clothing and Discount Shops

Via Sannio Market
The market is a good bet for new leather jackets at great savings. Otherwise there is a lot of quite junky fakes, good-condition second-hand clothing, and other miscellaneous items *(see p69).* ◎ *Map G5*

Via Mamiani Market
Exotic foodstuffs, spices, flowers, clothing, luggage – you can find all that and more around this huge market square. Under the porticoes there are even more stalls to check out *(see p69).* ◎ *Map F4*

Oviesse
Fairly well-made clothing at bargain prices, plus a large selection of cosmetics and toiletries. This is the largest of several branches of Oviesse in Rome. ◎ *Piazza Vittorio Emanuele 108–10 • Map F4*

Coin
A fashionable department store, with reasonable prices. It's mostly clothing, shoes and accessories, but they also carry kitchenware and more general furnishings. ◎ *Piazza Appio 7 • Map G5*

MAS
MAS stands for *"Magazzini allo Statuto"* ("Statutory Warehouses"). Shopping here is like one vast rummage sale. There's tons of merchandise piled up in bins, but the prices are ludicrously low and the staff are friendly and helpful. ◎ *Piazza Vittorio Emanuele 138 • Map F4*

Barrita Boutique
The lovely, hand-made leather shoes are good value for money. Stock includes boots, shoes and leather bags. A boot-stretching service is also available. ◎ *Via Appia Nuova 41 • Map G5*

UPIM
A mid- to low-range department store that carries clothing, toiletries and practical items for the home. ◎ *Via Gioberti 74 • Map F3*

Leam
An extremely trendy clothing emporium with a factory outlet on the top floor selling Prada and D&G. ◎ *Via Appia Nuova 26 • Map G5*

Exotic Foods
One of the few places in the city where you can find Chinese, Thai and Indian spices and cooking pastes. ◎ *Via Napoleone III 95 • Map F3*

International Trade Corp
One of many Chinese shops in Rome's Chinatown. This one specializes in women's wear. ◎ *Piazza Vittorio Emanuele 61/A • Map F3*

Price Categories

For a three-course meal for one with half a bottle of wine (or equivalent meal), taxes and extra charges.

€	under €30
€€	€30–40
€€€	€40–50
€€€€	€50–60
€€€€€	over €60

Above **Agata e Romeo**

🔟 Places to Eat

1 Agata e Romeo
The eponymous couple divide the labour expertly, she as chef and he as *maître d'*. Try the *menu degustazione* for a sampling of each day's masterworks. Reservations a must *(see p74)*. ⊗ Via Carlo Alberto 45 • Map F3 • 06 446 6115 • Closed Sat–Sun, 2 weeks Jan & Aug • DA • €€€€€

2 Baia Chia
Cuisine from Sardinia, which adds up to lots of fish and lots of flavour. ⊗ Via Machiavelli 5 • Map F3 • 06 7045 3452 • Closed Sun • DA • €€

3 Cannavota
A traditional neighbourhood restaurant. Try *risotto alla pescatore* (seafood risotto). ⊗ Piazza S Giovanni in Laterano 20 • Map F5 • 06 7720 5007 • Closed Wed, Aug • DA • €€

4 Trattoria Monti
This friendly, intimate restaurant serves creative dishes from the Marche region. The *tagliatelle con ragù* is excellent, and the house Verdicchio wine is above average. Booking in advance is advised. ⊗ Via di San Vito 13A • Map F4 • 06 446 6573 • Closed Mon, Sun D, Aug • €€

5 F.I.S.H.
Seafood and fusion cuisine served by a bilingual staff. ⊗ Via dei Serpent 16 • Map Q3 • 06 478 24 962 • Closed Aug, Mon L • €€€

6 Little India
Rome's best value Indian restaurant, is set in two attractive medieval rooms. Tandoori cooking is a speciality ⊗ Via Principe Amedeo 303–05 • Map F3 • 06 446 4980 • €

7 Monti D.O.C.
This cosy wine bar has a full menu of hearty Tuscan soups, cous cous, tuna steaks and, for dessert, delicious carrot cake. ⊗ Via G Lanza 93 • Map F3 • 06 487 2696 • €

8 Enoteca Cavour 313
A clubby old wine bar. Bottles from around the world to choose from, as well as a decent menu of salads, pastas, sandwiches and more. ⊗ Via Cavour 313 • Map R4 • 06 678 5496 • Closed Jul–Sep: Sun • €

9 L'Angolo di Napoli
Head here for lunch in this light and airy establishment with cafeteria-style service. Great hot or cold buffet selections. ⊗ Via Agostino Depretis 77A • Map E3 • 06 474 6866 • Closed Sun L • €€

10 Il Guru
Elegant Indian restaurant, a cut above the rest. The food is superbly prepared in north-Indian style. ⊗ Via Cimarra 4/6 • Map R4 • 06 474 4110 • Closed L • €

Left **Palazzo del Quirinale** Right **Via Veneto**

The Quirinal and Via Veneto

THE ORIGINAL HILL OF ROME, *the Quirinal was mainly residential in Imperial times, noted for its grand baths and temples. In the Middle Ages, it reverted to open countryside and it wasn't until the 16th century that it again became important, when the crest of the hill was claimed for the pope's new palace. Following that, important papal families built their large estates all around the area, including the Barberini, the Corsini and the Ludovisi. The Quirinal Palace has passed through many metamorphoses but the biggest change to the area came after 1870. The Ludovisi sold off their huge villa to developers, and Via Veneto and the smart area around it became an instant success with the wealthy classes of the newly unified country. This quarter speaks of elegance and power throughout all its ages.*

🔟 Sights

1. Baths of Diocletian & Aula Ottagona
2. Santa Maria degli Angeli
3. Santa Maria della Vittoria
4. Palazzo Barbarini
5. Piazza Barbarini
6. Via Veneto
7. Capuchin Crypt
8. Palazzo del Quirinale
9. Sant'Andrea al Quirinale
10. San Carlo alle Quattro Fontane

Baths of Diocletian

1 Baths of Diocletian and Aula Ottagona

The main collection of this museum is dedicated to rather academic holdings, principally inscriptions and *stele* (funeral stones). The Aula Ottagona features two 2nd-century BC bronze sculptures of great beauty, which were discovered lovingly hidden in a trench 6 m (20 ft) below the concrete floor of the Temple of the Sun, on the steep hillside of the Quirinal *(see p40)*. ✎ Baths of Diocletian: piazza dei Cinquecento 78, Map F3, Open 9am–7:45pm Tue–Sun, Adm • Aula Ottagona: via Romita, piazza della Repubblica, Map F3, Open 9am–2pm Tue–Sun, Free

2 Santa Maria degli Angeli

In 1561 the pope commissioned Michelangelo to transform the central hall of Diocletian's Baths, the *frigidarium* (cold plunge room), into a church. The result is this overwhelming space, which gives a clearer idea than anywhere else in Rome of how vast these public bathing palaces were. Even then, the finished church takes up only half of the original. Michelangelo had to raise the floor 2 m (6 ft) in order to use the ancient 15-m (50-ft) rose-red granite columns the way he wanted to. ✎ Piazza della Repubblica • Map F3 • Open 7:30am–6:30pm daily • Free • DA

3 Santa Maria della Vittoria

This 17th-century Baroque extravaganza has perhaps Rome's most ornate decor, most of it executed by Bernini and his students. The most indulgent corner is the Cornaro Chapel, to the left of the altar, home to Bernini's shocking *Ecstacy of St Teresa* *(see p49)*. ✎ Via XX Settembre 17 • Map E2 • Open 8:30am–11am (10am Sun), 3:30–6pm daily • Free • DA

Santa Maria della Vittoria

4 Palazzo Barberini

The Barberini sold their palace to the Italian State in 1949 to house part of the National Gallery, which was founded in 1893 with the purchase of the Corsini Palace. The number of pictures in the collection now exceeds 1,700 and has been added to through the acquisition of collections from Rome's noble families over the ensuing years. Among the most famous works are Filippo Lippi's *Madonna and Child*, the controversial *La Fornarina* (supposedly Raphael's mistress, probably painted by Giulio Romano, his favourite pupil), and Caravaggio's *Judith and Holofernes* *(see p51)*. ✎ Via delle Quattro Fontane 18 • Map Q1 • 06 328 101 • Open 9am–7pm Tue–Thu • Adm • DA

Palazzo Barberini

Power and Elegance

Since the 16th century, the Quirinal Hill has been the elemental expression of temporal power and dominion in Rome: first the popes, then the kings, and now the Presidents of the Republic. Since the late 1800s, Via Veneto has complemented that raw clout with the charisma and glamour of great wealth and all that money can buy.

Piazza Barberini

This could be called the "piazza of the bees", the Barberini family symbol (judiciously upgraded from horseflies when their fortunes improved). Both of the piazza's fountains by Bernini have large, mutant-like versions of the busy insects carved onto them, to let everyone know who sponsored their creation. The central figure of a triton blowing his conch is one of Rome's most appealing and memorable, made of travertine that takes on a warm honey colour. The other fountain is a simple scallop shell (see p47). ✎ Map Q1

Via Veneto

This lazy curve of a street sports a number of belle époque grand hotels and canopied pavement cafés. It enjoyed its famous dolce vita (sweet life) heyday in the 1950–60s, when movie stars supped, sipped and simpered here for the paparazzi. Today, the allure is sadly limited for anybody other than tourists, but every visitor to Rome should come at least once to take a stroll here. ✎ Map E2

Fountain, Piazza Barberini

Capuchin Crypt

A taste for the macabre may be all you need to enjoy this place. A cast-iron stomach doesn't hurt, either. Perhaps the most fascinating thing about this intense memento mori is its position, at the bottom of what was the most sophisticated of streets when la dolce vita was in full swing (see p64). ✎ Via Veneto 27 • Map E2 • Open 9am–noon, 3–6pm Fri–Wed • Donation

Palazzo del Quirinale

The highest of the original seven hills, the Quirinal was also the enclave of the ancient Sabines (see p38) in Rome's earliest days. Today, it is graced by 5.5-m (18-ft) Roman copies of 5th-century BC Greek originals of the Dioscuri and their prancing horses. The hill's stark, imposing palace, Rome's largest, was built in 1574 as a summer papal residence, to escape the endemic malaria around the Vatican. In 1870 it became the residence of the kings of Italy and, since 1947, Italy's presidents have held official functions here.
✎ Piazza del Quirinale • Map P2 • Open Sep–Jun: 8:30am–12:30pm Sun (gardens open to the public on 2 Jun, Italian Republic Day) • Adm • DA

Sant'Andrea al Quirinale

This may represent Bernini's architectural peak, built between 1658 and 1670, the only construction over which he was able to exercise total artistic control. The wide, shallow space needed an oval plan, counterpoised in the concave curving entrance. The eye is masterfully drawn around the elliptical interior, where canonical elements are blended

Sant'Andrea al Quirinale

with sculptural decoration to produce an elegant harmony. For so small a church, the impact is surprisingly grand, made richer by the columns of red marble from Sicily. ✪ *Via del Quirinale 29 • Map Q2 • Open 8am–noon, 4–6pm Wed–Mon • Donation • DA*

San Carlo alle Quattro Fontane

Borromini's masterpiece appears about as radically freeform as architecture could be in the 17th century. His response to this small space was to fill it with fluid undulations, which have complex geometrical relationships. Borromini succeeded in blurring the line between architecture and sculpture, resulting in a homogeneous interior topped by an oval dome. ✪ *Via del Quirinale 23 • Map R2 • Open 10am–1pm daily, 3–6pm Mon–Sat • Free • DA*

One of the Quattro Fontane statues

Exploring the Quirinal

Morning

Start on Quirinal Hill, also known as Monte Cavallo after the horse sculptures, here. Sadly, the vast blandness of the **Palazzo del Quirinale** does little to spur the imagination. Walk halfway down Via del Quirinale and across from a gate, you'll find Bernini's architectural tour de force, **Sant' Andrea al Quirinale**. Inside, note the many maritime motifs, symbolic of Andrew the fisherman.

Continue on to Borromini's **San Carlo alle Quattro Fontane**. Don't miss the masterful crypt and the exquisite cloister. Two blocks along, take a right to the **Aula Ottagona** *(see p133)*. The ancient bronzes of the Prince and the Boxer are amazing expressions of controlled power.

Now take Via Bissolati to **Via Veneto**. Check out the cafés, shops and hotels before enjoying lunch at the elegant **Gran Caffè Doney** *(see p136)*.

Afternoon

After lunch, admire the *belle époque* **Excelsior Hotel** *(see p171)* for its appealing architecture, especially its cupola and sexually ambiguous caryatids. And don't miss the public rooms of the sublime **Regina Baglioni** *(see p170)*, which positively reek of luxury.

Finally, after soaking up all the opulence, walk down to visit the eerie **Capuchin Crypt** to put things back in perspective. Round off your tour with a stop at **Piazza Barberini** and Bernini's marvellously life-affirming Triton Fountain.

Left **Pavement café, Via Veneto** Right **Café de Paris**

TOP10 La Dolce Vita Venues

1 Gran Caffè Doney
One of the best spots in the world to sit under the magnolias, sip *cappuccino* and watch passers-by – although they're mostly tourists now not the celebrities of old *(see pp70–71)*. ✪ *Via Veneto 145 • Map E2 • DA*

2 Café de Paris
This café has always been the landmark of *dolce vita* life-style along this glossy strip. It's still a magical place to sip an *espresso* or partake of a light snack. ✪ *Via Veneto 90 • Map E2 • DA*

3 Harry's Bar
Noted for its clubby American style – a dry Martini, tuxedo and cigar sort of place, featuring a piano bar, a restaurant with gourmet cuisine, and a café with tables outside. Be prepared to spend lavishly *(see p71)*. ✪ *Via Veneto 150 • Map E2*

4 La Terrazza dell'Eden
At the top of the erstwhile premier celebrity hotel, this bar-restaurant has perhaps the best views in Rome. It's perfect for a romantic *tête-à-tête* or any special do *(see p170)*. ✪ *Via Ludovisi 49 • Map E2*

5 Gran Caffè Roma
Located in an elegant curve of the street, with outdoor tables at the bottom of a broad staircase. A great spot to linger over your *cappuccino* and news-paper. ✪ *Via Veneto 32 • Map E2 • DA*

6 R & Co
Nothing short of fabulous is this collection of designer shoes, leather goods and other fashions. ✪ *Via Veneto 104 • Map E2 • DA*

7 Brioni
This legendary Italian tailor was established in 1945. The beautifully cut suits have been used in recent James Bond films. ✪ *Via Veneto 129 • Map E2 • DA*

8 Jackie O'
As the name implies, this was a leading watering-hole and club in the 1960s. It still attracts international stars. Call ahead if you are not world-famous. ✪ *Via Boncompagni 11 • Map E2 • DA*

9 Hard Rock Café
It was inevitable that this international chain would choose Via Veneto for its Roman home. Serves standard American fare. ✪ *Via Veneto 62/A/B • Map E2 • DA*

10 Arion
Independent bookstore specializing in exquisite art books. It stays open until 10pm on Sundays. ✪ *Via Veneto 42 • Map E2 • DA*

Price Categories

For a three-course		
meal for one with half	**€**	under €30
a bottle of wine (or	**€€**	€30–40
equivalent meal), taxes	**€€€**	€40–50
and extra charges.	**€€€€**	€50–60
	€€€€€	over €60

Above **Supplí, Andrea**

Places to Eat

1 Café Veneto
Right in the heart of the famous street, habitués find elegance and carefully prepared fare. Specialities include game and truffles. ⊗ *Via Veneto 120 • Map E2 • 06 482 7107 • Closed Mon • DA • €€€€€*

2 La Scala
A most inviting setting, with wood panelling and stained-glass skylights, situated at the top of a grand staircase. Unusual dishes such as *bombolotti spada e melanzane* – pasta tubes with swordfish and aubergine (eggplant). Dinner only; reserve. ⊗ *Via di S Isidoro 5 • Map E2 • 06 481 9264 • Closed Tue • €€*

3 La Giara
A traditional *trattoria* with an unpretentious charm. The menu includes mussels with port and curry. ⊗ *Via Toscana 46, at Via Sardegna • Map E2 • 06 4274 5421 • Closed Sun • DA • €€*

4 Colline Emiliane
The speciality here is Emilia-Romagna cuisine, which highlights a variety of *prosciutto* (ham) dishes and *tortellini in brodo* (meat-filled pasta in broth). ⊗ *Via degli Avignonesi 22 • Map E2 • 06 481 7538 • Closed Sun dinner, Mon • DA • €€*

5 Andrea
Very congenial and featuring a wide-ranging menu. The *supplì* (rice croquette) is a classic starter. ⊗ *Via Sardegna 28 • Map E2 • 06 482 1819/474 0557 • Closed Sat lunch, Sun • DA • €€€€€*

6 Trimani
A classy wine bar with a full menu of soups, pastas, cheeses and cured meats. ⊗ *Via Cernaia 37/B • Map F2 • 06 446 9630 • Closed Sun • DA • €*

7 Doublé
One of the best bargains in town, Fish specialities on Fridays. Lunch only. ⊗ *Salita di S Nicola da Tolentino 19–21 • Map E2 • 06 474 0029 • Closed Sun • €*

8 Dagnino
Rome's favourite spot for sampling Sicilian pastries, like *cassata* (iced cake). ⊗ *Via Vittorio Emanuele Orlando 75 & Via Torino 95 • Map E3 • 06 481 8660 • DA • €*

9 Mariano
A pleasant setting with fine roasted game or *abbacchio* (lamb). ⊗ *Via Piemonte 79 • Map E2 • 06 474 5256 • Closed Sat L, Sun • DA • €€*

10 Africa
Scoop up tantalizingly spicy vegetables and meats with spongy bread at this fantastic restaurant. ⊗ *Via Gaeta 26 • Map F2 • 06 494 1077 • Closed Mon • DA • €*

Left **Fresco, Castel Sant'Angelo** Right **Mosaic, Santa Maria in Trastevere**

Trastevere and Prati

TRASTEVERE, WHICH LITERALLY MEANS "ACROSS THE TIBER", *is Rome's left bank and Bohemian neighbourhood. The former working-class ghetto has retained its medieval character better than any other part of Rome, despite having become one of the most restaurant- and nightlife-packed zones of the city. The Borgo is Vatican turf, a largely uninspired grid of streets strung with kitsch religious souvenir shops and bad, tourist-orientated restaurants. Its medieval character was ruined when Mussolini laid out the grand Via della Conciliazione leading to St Peter's. North of the Borgo however stretches Prati, developed in the 19th century and one of Rome's most genuine, non-touristy, middle-class neighbourhoods. Its widest boulevards, Via Cola di Rienzo, Viale Giulio Cesare and Viale delle Milizie, are where Romans shop for everything from sporting goods to CDs to imported foods and the best fresh-baked calzone in town.*

Statue, Ponte Sant'Angelo

🔟 Sights

1. Vatican City
2. St Peter's Basilica
3. Villa Farnesina
4. Santa Maria in Trastevere
5. Santa Cecilia in Trastevere
6. Vatican Gardens
7. Castel Sant'Angelo
8. San Francesco a Ripa
9. Gianicolo
10. Ponte Sant'Angelo

Vatican City
One of the great museum complexes of the world includes Michelangelo's Sistine Chapel and the extensive Raphael Rooms *(see pp8–11)*.

St Peter's Basilica
The capital of Christendom is packed with works by Bernini, statues by Michelangelo and panoramic views from the dome *(see pp12–13)*.

Villa Farnesina
Peruzzi's sumptuous villa (1508–11) was built for papal banker Agostino Chigi, whose parties were legendary – he would toss silver platters into the Tiber after each course. In a downstairs room, Peruzzi painted Chigi's horoscope on the ceiling, Sebastiano del Piombo painted scenes from Ovid's *Metamorphoses*, and Raphael painted the sensual *Galatea*. Peruzzi's upstairs hall features a *trompe-l'oeil* balustrade overlooking hills. The 1527 graffiti by Charles V's troops is now historic vandalism, protected under glass. The bedroom contains Sodoma's *Wedding Night of Alexander the Great* (1517) *(see p50)*. ◈ *Via della Lungara 230 • Map J5 • Open 9am–1pm Mon–Sat & afternoons by appt • Adm €4.15*

Dome, St Peter's Basilica

Santa Maria in Trastevere
Rome's oldest church dedicated to the Virgin was founded in 337 on the site where a miraculous font of oil spouted the day Christ was born. The miracle is depicted in the stupendous *Life of the Virgin* mosaics (1291) by Pietro Cavallini, covering the lower half of the apse. The current 12th-century church has 13th-century mosaics, 22 mismatched ancient columns and a Cosmatesque pavement. There's also a rare 7th-century panel painting of the *Madonna della Clemenza* in the chapel left of the altar *(see p45)*. ◈ *Piazza S Maria in Trastevere • Map K6 • Open 7:30am–8pm daily • Free*

St Cecilia statue, Santa Cecilia in Trastevere

View of the Tiber from Castel Sant'Angelo

Santa Cecilia in Trastevere

Built atop the saint's house, some of which is visible in the crypt excavations. A Guido Reni painting of Cecilia's decapitation sits off a right-hand corridor of the nave. Under the apse's glittering 9th-century mosaics rests a *baldacchino* (1293) by Arnolfo di Cambio and Carlo Maderno's 1600 statue of the saint (he saw her incorrupt body when her tomb was opened in 1599). Ring the bell on the left aisle to see the top half of Pietro Cavallini's *Last Judgment* (1289–93), his only remaining fresco in Rome.
🔊 *Piazza di S Cecilia • Map D5 • Open 9:30am–12:30pm, 4–6:30pm daily (summer 4:15–6pm) • Adm €2.50 for crypt*

Vatican Gardens

Typical 16th-century Italianate gardens of lawns, woods, grottoes and fountains. Structures include the first Vatican radio tower, designed by Marconi in 1931, Pier Luigi Nervi's shell-shaped audience hall (1971) and the Mannerist Casina of Pius IV (1558–61), home to the Pontifical Academy of Sciences. 🔊 *Viale Vaticano • Map A2 • Open for tours 10am Tue, Thu, Fri (06 6988 4676) • Adm €9.00 • DA*

Castel Sant'Angelo

Hadrian designed his massive circular tomb in 123–39. Aurelian fortified it in 271 as part of his city walls *(see p152)*. It was the papal castle for 1,000 years – a viaduct from the Vatican let the popes scurry here in times of crisis. Gregory the Great named it in 590 after a vision of St Michael announced the end of a plague from its tower, commemorated by the bronze statue of a sword-bearing archangel. There are frescoed Renaissance papal apartments and a small arms and armour collection (Etruscan through to the 1900s), plus stunning panoramas from the ramparts.
🔊 *Lungotevere Castello 50 • Map J1 • Open 9am–7:30pm Tue–Sun • Adm €8.00*

San Francesco a Ripa

Though altered during the Renaissance and Baroque eras, the church was built just 12 years after St Francis stayed at this hospice in 1219. Ask the sacristan's permission to visit the

---

St Cecilia

Cecilia was a Roman patrician and secret Christian. In 230 she was locked in steam baths for three days by political enemies. She came out singing (hence becoming patron saint of music), so they tried to behead her, but the requisite three strokes initially failed and Cecilia lingered for three days, converting hundreds to her faith.

---

cell in which St Francis stayed, bearing a copy of his portrait by Margaritone d'Arezzo. The last chapel on the left houses Bernini's *Beata Ludovica Albertoni* (1671–4), in a state of religious ecstasy bordering scandalously on the sexual. ◈ *Piazza di S Francesco d'Assisi • Map C5 • Open 7am–noon, 4–7pm daily • Free*

Gianicolo

This long ridge separating Trastevere from the Vatican offers some of the best views of Rome *(see p60)*. Its two equestrian monuments celebrate Garibaldi and his wife Anita, who is buried underneath. ◈ *Map B4*

Ponte Sant'Angelo

Hadrian built this bridge in 133–4 to access his mausoleum, but only the three central arches of that span remain. Clement VII had the statues of St Peter (by Lorenzetto) and St Paul (by Paolo Taccone) installed in 1534. Clement IX hired Bernini in 1688 to design the statues of 10 angels holding symbols of the Passion. ◈ *Map J2*

Bernini sculpture, San Francesco a Ripa

A Tour of Trastevere

Morning

Begin at **San Crisogno** *(see p142)*; ask the custodian to let you into the excavations downstairs. By 10am be at **San Francesco a Ripa** for the five minutes it takes to see Bernini's stunning sculpture. Head down Via Anicia Antica, right on Via Madonna dell'Orto, and left on Via di S Michele to reach **Santa Cecilia**. Explore the crypt and pay the nuns a small donation to get up to see the Cavallini frescoes. Head out of the courtyard left onto Via di Genovesi, which leads to Viale Trastevere.

Crossing Piazza S Maria in Trastevere, bear right into Piazza S Egidio and fork left onto Via della Scala. Continue past Santa Maria della Scala and up Via della Lungara to **Villa Farnesina** *(see p139)*. You'll be here before noon, time enough to spend 30 minutes admiring the frescoes. Take a breather amid the greenery of the **Orto Botanico** *(see p142)*, then return to the heart of Trastevere to enjoy a pizza at **Dar Poeta** *(see p148)*.

Afternoon

After lunch, peruse the collections of the **Museo di Roma** *(see p142)*, visit the marvellous medieval church of **Santa Maria in Trastevere** *(see p139)* and walk up Via Garibaldi to peek through the grille at Bramante's Tempietto in the courtyard of **San Pietro in Montorio** *(see p142)*. Or simply spend the afternoon wandering the medieval streets shrouded by washing lines, awaiting the dinner hour when Trastevere comes to life.

Left **Palazzo Corsini** Right **Ponte Rotto**

Best of the Rest

1 San Pietro in Montorio
Bramante designed the mini-temple in the courtyard to mark the spot where St Peter was supposedly crucified. ✪ *Via Garibaldi 33 • Map C4 • Open 9am–noon, 4–6pm (winter 2–4pm) Tue–Sun • Free*

2 Palazzo Corsini
Small painting collection, featuring works by Fra' Angelico, Van Dyck, Titian, Rubens and Caravaggio. ✪ *Via della Lungara 10 • Map J5 • Open 8:30am–1:50pm Tue–Sun • Adm*

3 Tiber Island
It is said that the serpent of medical god Aesculapius jumped ship and swam ashore here in 293 BC. Rome's maternity hospital is still here. ✪ *Map M6*

4 Orto Botanico
Palazzo Corsini's beautiful gardens are now the University of Rome's botanical museum. ✪ *Via Corsini 23a • Map J5 • Open Sep–Jul: 9:30am–6:30pm Tue–Sat • Adm • DA*

5 Ponte Rotto
Rome's first stone bridge, (181–142 BC) was ruined in 1598. It retained three arches until 1886, when two were destroyed to make room for Ponte Palatino (*Rotto* means broken in Italian). ✪ *Map N6*

6 Santa Maria della Scala
A charming Renaissance church, whose claim to fame is a *Virgin and Child* by Cavalier d'Arpino (Caravaggio's teacher). ✪ *Piazza S Maria della Scala • Map K6 • Open 7am–noon, 3:30–7pm daily • Free*

7 Fontana Paola
This wide basin at the end of the Paola aqueduct is a favourite backdrop for wedding photos *(see p60)*. ✪ *Map B5*

8 Villa Doria Pamphilj
Rome's largest public park was established in 1644–52 by Camillo Pamphilj. A great place for picnics. ✪ *Via di S Pancrazio • Map B5 • Open sunrise–sunset daily • Free • DA*

9 Museo di Roma in Trastevere
Housed in a beautifully restored ex-convent, this museum includes life-size dioramas of Ancient Roman rooms and shops. ✪ *Piazza di S Egidio 1b • Map K6 • Open 10am–7pm Tue–Sun • Adm*

10 San Crisogono
The 1626 façade copies the medieval one. Inside are 22 ancient columns and excavations of the 5th-century basilica. ✪ *Piazza S Sonnino 44 • Map L6 • Open 7:30–11:30am, 4–7pm Mon–Sat; 8:30am–1pm, 4:15–7:30pm Sun • Adm*

Stazione di San Pietro

Left **Standa** Right **Stock Market**

TOP 10 Locals' Favourite Shops

1 COIN
This good-value department store is where real Romans shop, for back-to-school clothes, kitchen utensils, stationery, household appliances, and much, much more. There's also a supermarket in the basement, which is great for buying a picnic. ◈ *Via Cola di Rienzo 173* • *Map C2*

2 Franchi
One of the best grocers in the city, extremely popular at lunchtime for its hot dishes and in the evening for its fried and baked *calzone* (stuffed pizza pockets). Locals start queueing up at 5pm. ◈ *Via Cola di Rienzo 204* • *Map C2*

3 Castroni
The gastronomic temple of Rome since 1932, this shop is piled high with packaged and prepared speciality foods from countries the world over, such as Japan, Greece, India, China and the Middle East. ◈ *Via Cola di Rienzo 196* • *Map C2*

4 Energie
Energie provides all that's new in the world of Italian youth fashion. Whether it's jeans, shirts or shoes you're after, all are on offer for both sexes. ◈ *Via Cola di Rienzo 143* • *Map C2*

5 Azi
From kitchenware to furniture, Azi provides slick ideas for the home from top Italian designers. ◈ *Via L Manara 7* • *Map C5*

6 New Fashion
Slightly higher prices than most but better selection and more fashionable wares at this stock house for mostly women's suits and skirts. ◈ *Via Simone de Saint Bon 85–7* • *Map B1*

7 Stock Market
Discount outlet for industrial design objects and various homewares. ◈ *Via Visconti 96* • *Map C2*

8 Polvere di Tempo
Non-mechanical timepieces, including hour glasses, various sundials, candle clocks, astrolabes, all hand crafted by the Argentinian owner. ◈ *Via del Moro 59* • *Map L6*

9 Macallé
A select range of sporting goods, from skis and snowboards to tents and tennis gear. ◈ *Via Pompeo Magno 90* • *Map C2*

10 Costantini
Massive wine cellar; one of the best selections of fine labels in Rome at reasonable prices. ◈ *Piazza Cavour 16* • *Map C2*

Following pages: **St Peter's Basilica and St Peter's Square**

Above **Typical Trastevere café**

🔟 Pubs, Cafés and Bars

1 Ombre Rosse
This laid-back pub is a staple of Trastevere nightlife. The atmosphere is always lively, with tables on the piazza in summer. ◈ *Piazza S Egidio 12–13 • Map K6*

2 Chakra
Located on a quiet street, this charming bar has a relaxed atmosphere and a pretty outdoor terrace that is popular in summer. ◈ *Via dell'Arco di San Calisto 17 • Map K6*

3 Bar Calisto
This quiet neighbourhood bar is the antithesis of the trendy Trastevere scene. Locals come here to play cards, read papers and catch up on the day's gossip. Welcoming atmosphere and drinks at reasonable prices. ◈ *Piazza San Calisto • Map K6*

4 Bar Gelateria Fima
Overpriced and indifferent, sullen service but a prime location smack on Trastevere's public "living room", Piazza Santa Maria. The *spremuta* (freshly squeezed orange juice) is made from a kilo of oranges. ◈ *Piazza S Maria in Trastevere 2 • Map K6*

5 Big Hilda Café
A welcoming joint offering rock 'n' roll, cheap drinks and a range of sand- wiches and salads. ◈ *Vicolo del Cinque 33–4 • Map K6*

6 Friends
The semi-circular bar and restaurant is always packed with Trastevere regulars. The menu includes inventive dishes and excellent bar sandwiches. ◈ *Piazza Trilussa 34 • Map K6*

7 Enoteca Trastevere
A new and positively thriving wine bar, with pleasingly dark wood interior and plenty of seating out front on the cobblestones. Light snacks and cocktails are served too. ◈ *Via della Lungaretta 86 • Map L6*

8 Roma Caput Mundi
One of Rome's most popular Irish pubs with a corner location that most locals pass through for a pint of Kilkenny or Harp during the evening. ◈ *Via Luciano Manara 64 • Map K6*

9 Borgo Antico
A wood-filled, classically styled 16th-century tavern, with coffered ceilings, and offering more than 60 wines by the glass. Typical *osteria* dishes are on offer too. ◈ *Borgo Pio 21 • Map B3*

🔟 Mr Brown
Very popular British-style bar with a vaguely old- fashioned sporting theme and a faithful English ex-pat clientele. ◈ *Vicolo del Cinque 29 • Map K6*

Left **Big Mama** Right **Alexanderplatz**

₁₀ Live Music Venues

Alexanderplatz
A little bit off the beaten track, in Prati, but the best jazz club in Rome bar none – Winton Marsalis, Lionel Hampton, George Coleman and many other international jazz stars have played here *(see p78)*. ⊗ *Via Ostia 9 • Map B1*

Big Mama
Rome's real house of blues, where the big names book and the smaller acts gig. Only open for live performances *(see p78)*. ⊗ *Vicolo S Francesco a Ripa 18 • Map C5*

Stairs Club
A trendy bar with large, comfy sofas on the lower level. Cocktails and bar snacks are available every evening and live accoustic jazz combos are performed once a week. ⊗ *Via della Scala 43 • Map K6*

Stardust
A Parisian-style mini-café (serving American brunches Sundays noon to 5pm) discreetly hides a jazz bar downstairs featuring sporadic live performances and a jam session on Tuesdays *(see p79)*. ⊗ *Vicolo de' Renzi 4 • Map K6*

Four Green Fields
Upstairs there is a vaguely British-style pub, while in the basement live music is played nightly. ⊗ *Via C Morin 42 • Map B1*

Fonclea
Established in 1977, this historic music venue is located close to Piazza del Risorgimento and features a variety of live music including jazz, soul, funk and rock. Punters can either drink at the bar or eat in the buffet restaurant. ⊗ *Via Crescenzio 82 • Map B2*

Birreria Trilussa
Beer and simple dishes are served until the early hours, with live music some nights. Cosy, traditional atmosphere. ⊗ *Via Benedetta 18–20 • Map K6*

The Place
There's always live music on the main stage, be it jazz or soulful singer-songwriters. ⊗ *Via Alberico II 29 • Map B2*

Caffè della Scala
A relaxed bar serving powerful cocktails and a great *grappa* selection. Live music is also on offer from time to time. ⊗ *Via della Scala 4 • Map K6*

Lettere Café
The focus is on books, but a couple of nights a week are devoted to live roots music. ⊗ *Via S. Francesco a Ripa 100 • Map C5*

Stazione di San Pietro

Left **Insalata Ricca** Right **Pizzeria da Ivo**

Cheap Eats

Da Augusto
Die-hard Trastevere *osteria* complete with wooden tables and traditional menu. ✎ *Piazza de' Renzi 15 • Map K6 • 06 580 3798 • Closed Sat D, Sun • No credit cards • €*

Il Duca
A *trattoria* in the heart of the Trastevere action, and serving some of the best lasagne in Italy. There are a few tables outside. ✎ *Vicolo del Cinque 52–6 • Map K6 • 06 581 7706 • Closed L, Mon • €*

La Tana dei Noantri
Lengthy menu promising all the best of Roman cuisine, including *penne arrabbiata* (pasta in a spicy tomato sauce). There are a few tables in the piazza against the church in summer. ✎ *Via della Paglia 1–3, off Piazza Santa Maria in Trastevere • Map K6 • 06 580 6404 • Closed Tue • €*

Pizzeria Da Ivo
A lively football theme and ever-present crowds are the features of Rome's favourite pizzeria *(see p72).* ✎ *Via S Francesco a Ripa 158 • Map C5 • 06 581 7082 • Closed L, Tue • €*

Insalata Ricca
Part of a popular chain of restaurants serving huge salads, pizzas and other light dishes. ✎ *Piazza del Risorgimento 5–6 • Map B2 • 06 3973 0387 • €*

Pizzeria Dar Poeta
Innovative pizza is served here – Roman-style, but with a thick crust *(see p72).* ✎ *Vicolo del Bologna 45–6 • Map K6 • 06 588 0516 • Closed L • €*

Osteria dell'Angelo
Angelo prepares excellent traditional Roman cooking at equally admirable prices. Book ahead. ✎ *Via G Bettolo 24 • Map B1 • 06 372 9470 • Closed L (except Tue & Fri), Sun • €*

Pizzeria Da Vittorio
Good Neapolitan-style pizza, *antipasti*, and a fan-cooled interior plastered with photos of famous patrons make this one of Rome's best pizzerias *(see p72).* ✎ *Via S Cosimato 14A • Map K6 • 06 580 0353 • Closed Sun • €*

Da Giovanni
A tiny *trattoria* that serves good, filling, traditional Roman fare at very low prices. ✎ *Via della Lungara 41A • Map B3 • 06 686 1514 • Closed Sun • €*

Napul'è
Campanian cuisine and more than 40 types of pizza approved by Naples' strict "True Pizza" association. Live Neapolitan music is played most nights. ✎ *Viale Giulio Cesare 89–91 • Map C1 • 06 323 1005 • €*

Price Categories

For a three-course	€ under €30
meal for one with half	€€ €30–40
a bottle of wine (or	€€€ €40–50
equivalent meal), taxes	€€€€ €50–60
and extra charges.	€€€€€ over €60

Above **Il Matriciano**

🔟 Fine Dining

Around Town – Trastevere & Prati

Sabatini
Roman cuisine and seafood in an old Fellini hang-out. Book ahead for a table out on the main square *(see p74)*. ✪ *Piazza S Maria in Trastevere 13 • Map K6 • 06 581 2026 • €€€€€*

Ferrara
Deservedly trendy; decoration is minimalist, with patio seating and the creative menu is based around the remarkable wine selection. ✪ *Via del Moro 1a • Map K6 • 06 5833 3920 • €€€*

Sora Lella
Low wood-beam ceilings and classic Roman cooking define this restaurant on Tiber Island (sadly, no river views). The food is delicious but the portions are small by Italian standards. ✪ *Via Ponte Quattro Capi 16 • Map M6 • 06 686 1601 • Closed Sun • €€€*

Les Etoiles
Not only do you come here for the cuisine, but also for the *al fresco* dining and wonderful panoramas of St Peter's Basilica. ✪ *Via Vitelleschi 34, Hotel Atlante Star • Map B2 • 06 689 3434 • €€€€€€*

Antico Arco
Trendy, pan-Italian, creative eatery in a lovely setting on Gianicolo hill. ✪ *Piazzale Aurelio 7 • Map B5 • 06 581 5274 • Closed Mon–Sat L, Sun D • €€€*

Il Ciak
Excellent game dishes are among the offerings served in this typical Tuscan *trattoria*. ✪ *Vicolo del Cinque 21 • Map K6 • 06 589 4774 • Closed L, Mon • €€*

Alberto Ciarla
Rome's premier seafood restaurant. There's also a well-stocked wine cellar *(see p74)*. ✪ *Piazza di S Cosimato 40 • Map C5 • 06 581 8668 • Closed L, Sun • €€€€€*

Il Matriciano
Businessmen and Cinecittà film directors patronize this Prati restaurant named after the spicy bacon-and-tomato pasta sauce. Try to sit outside in summer. ✪ *Via dei Gracchi 55 • Map C2 • 06 321 3040 • Closed Wed • €€€*

La Pergola
Incredible vistas of the city and food by a top international chef – one of Rome's best dining experiences. ✪ *Rome Cavalieri Hilton Hotel, Via Cadlolo 101 • 06 3509 2211 • Closed Sun–Mon • €€€€€*

Taberna de' Gracchi
Dante Mililli's dining rooms may be large and modern, but the spirit is old-school Roman dining with a few contemporary touches. ✪ *Via dei Gracchi 266–8 • Map C2 • 06 321 3126 • Closed Sun • €€€*

Note: *Unless otherwise stated, all restaurants accept credit cards and serve vegetarian meals*

149

Left **Square Colosseum, EUR** Right **Via Appia Antica**

Beyond the City Walls

THE 3RD-CENTURY AURELIAN WALLS ARE STILL *largely intact and served as the defence of the city for 1,600 years until Italian Unification was achieved in 1870. After that, the walls were pierced in several places so that traffic could bypass the old gates and the modern city quickly sprawled far and wide in every direction. Although it's undeniable that Rome's most dazzling sights are contained within the walls, venturing outside them can have spectacular rewards. Ancient roads and even an entire ancient town, as*

well as some of Rome's oldest churches, the mystical catacombs, and even Benito Mussolini's pretentious contributions to modern architecture are all must-sees if you can draw yourself away from the city centre.

Apse mosaic, Sant'Agnese fuori le Mura

🔟 Sights

1. Ostia Antica
2. San Paolo fuori le Mura
3. EUR
4. Via Appia Antica
5. Catacombs of Domitilla
6. Montemartini Art Centre
7. Catacombs of San Sebastiano
8. Catacombs of San Callisto
9. Foro Italico and Stadio dei Marmi
10. Sant'Agnese fuori le Mura and Santa Costanza

1 Ostia Antica
Ancient Rome's trading heart has a wealth of fascinating ruins that evoke the city's earliest days *(see pp36–7)*.

2 San Paolo fuori le Mura

Façade, San Paolo fuori le Mura

Rome's second largest church has had a history of violent ups and downs. It was built by Constantine in the 4th century, over the spot where St Paul was buried, and for about 400 years it was the largest church in Europe, until it was sacked by the Saracens in 846. It was rebuilt and fortified, but its position outside the walls left it mostly ignored until the mid-11th century, when it underwent a renewal. Then came the 1823 fire, which led to the reworking we see today *(see p45)*. ✆ Via Ostiense 184 • Metro Basilica S Paolo • Open 7am–6:30pm daily • Free

3 EUR
Built by Mussolini as a show-case to the world of the ideal Fascist metropolis, the EUR (l'Esposizione Universale di Roma) is disturbing to many visitors. The critic Robert Hughes described the so-called Square Colosseum as "the most frightening building in the world", yet the aesthetic inspired many postwar architects. Aside from the hard-edged archi-tecture, there's a park with a lake, and a visit to the Museo della Civiltà Romana is instructive. ✆ Metro EUR Palasport and EUR Fermi

4 Via Appia Antica
"The Queen of Roads" was completed in 312 BC by Appius Claudius, also the architect of Rome's first aqueduct. The most pastoral part begins at the circular Tomb of Cecilia Metella, which was made into a fortification in the Middle Ages. Starting here, you'll see more tombs and fragments of tombs, as well as grazing sheep and the private gates to fabulous modern-day villas. As you walk along, look to the east to see the arches of an ancient aqueduct marching towards the city *(see p61)*. ✆ Buses 118, 218

5 Catacombs of Domitilla
This is the largest catacomb network in Rome. Many of the tombs from the 1st and 2nd centuries have no Christian connection; burial of this sort was practised by several religious sects. The chambers have frescoes of both Classical and Christian scenes, including one of the earliest images of Christ as the Good Shepherd *(see p65)*. ✆ Via delle Sette Chiese 282 • Buses 118, 218, 660, 760 • Open Feb–Dec: 9am–noon, 2–5pm Wed–Mon (until 5:30pm in summer) • Adm €5.00

Tomb statue, Via Appia Antica

Statue in the Montemartini Art Centre

Montemartini Art Centre

Rome's very first power station has been transformed into a remarkable showcase for Greek and Roman statues – parts of the Musei Capitolini collection *(see pp24–7)* that, until now, were kept in storage. The effect is extraordinary, playing the monolithic might of modern technology off against the noble, human vulnerability of these ancient masterpieces. ◐ *Via Ostiense 106* • *Metro Piramide, Garbatella* • *Open 9:30am–7pm Tue–Sun* • *Adm* • *DA*

Catacombs of San Sebastiano

Underground cemeteries outside the city walls were created in accordance with laws at the time, not a response to suppression (it was thought

ghosts of the dead could interfere with the living). However, the remains of saints Peter and Paul may have been moved here, further away from the centre, during one of the city's periods of persecution. There are also several 4th-century mausoleums, some with exquisite frescoes. ◐ *Via Appia Antica 136* • *Buses 118, 218* • *Open mid-Dec–mid-Nov: 9am–noon, 2–5pm Mon–Sat (until 5:30pm in summer)* • *Adm*

Catacombs of San Callisto

Rome's first official Christian cemetery, on four levels, features some rooms decorated with stucco and frescoes, and special crypts to early popes and saints that you can also visit. The rooms and connecting passage-ways were hewn out of relatively soft volcanic tufa. The niches, called *loculi*, were designed to hold two or three bodies. ◐ *Via Appia Antica 110* • *Buses 118, 218* • *Open Mar–Jan: 9am–noon, 2– 5pm Thu–Tue (until 5:30pm in summer)* • *Adm*

Foro Italico and Stadio dei Marmi

Originally called the Foro Mussolini, the name was under-standably changed in the late 1940s, even though the 16-m

The Aurelian Wall

This ancient wall was begun by Emperor Aurelian (AD 270–75) and completed by his successor Probus (AD 276–82). It stretches 18 km (11 miles) around the city, with 18 gates and 381 towers, enclosing all seven of Rome's hills. In the 4th century, Emperor Maxentius raised it to almost twice its original height. To this day, most of the wall survives.

Catacombs of San Sebastiano

(55-ft) obelisk still shouts out "Mussolini Dux" ("Mussolini the Leader"). In imitation of every mad Roman emperor, there was even supposed to have been a 75-m (250-ft) statue of Il Duce posing as Hercules. The sculptures of the Stadio dei Marmi, 60 colossal nude young Fascist athletes, are worth a look. ◉ Viale del Foro Italico • Bus 280

10 Sant'Agnese fuori le Mura and Santa Costanza

These 4th-century gems are located in the same Early Christian complex. Both are decorated with sublime mosaic work, the former depicting the martyred St Agnes as she appeared in a vision eight days after her death. The ambulatory around the circular Santa Costanza has truly delightful, richly detailed scenes of an ancient Roman grape harvest.
◉ Via Nomentana 349 • Buses 36, 60, 62, 84, 90 • Open 9am–noon Mon–Sat, 4–6pm Tue–Sun • Free • DA

Santa Costanza

A Morning Walk on the Appia Antica

🕐 Start at the Porta San Sebastiano, the grandest city gate of them all, where you can visit the **Museo delle Mura** (see p55). Climb the stairs for great views. From here, continue straight on along the **Via Appia Antica** (see p153). One of the first sights you'll come to, on the left at a crossroads, is the small church of Domine Quo Vadis? – this marks the spot where Peter, fleeing persecution, encountered Christ and decided to return to Rome and face his martyrdom like a saint. The church contains a replica of footprints in stone, said to be those of Christ, but it is actually an ancient pagan ex voto.

Quite a bit further ahead, you'll come to the **Catacombs of San Sebastiano**. Take the guided tour, and don't miss the curious fresco of a bowl of fruit and a partridge, which, according to some ancient writers, was the most lascivious of all creatures. Continuing on, past a mobile bar where you can buy snacks and drinks, visit the Circus of Maxentius, an ancient racetrack. Note how amphorae were embedded in the bricks to lighten the construction of the upper grandstands. Last stop will be the 1st-century BC Tomb of Cecilia Metella. The frieze of bulls' skulls and garlands is beautiful and the cone-shaped sanctum is peaceful.

🍴 For lunch, walk back to the **Ristorante l'Archeologia** (see p155). After lunch, backtrack a few hundred metres to the bus stop to catch the No. 118 into town.

Left **Mosaic pavement, Hadrian's Villa** Right **Ionic columns, Hadrian's Villa**

🔟 Daytrips from Rome

1 Tivoli

This charming hilltown has world-famous gardens and the villa of Cardinal d'Este, built in the 16th century and boasting 100 fountains. ◈ *COTRAL bus from Ponte Mammolo • Villa d'Este: piazza Trento, 04 2460 0460, Open 8:30am–1hr before sunset Tue–Sun, Adm, DA*

2 Hadrian's Villa

Built as the emperor's summer retreat between AD 118–134, the area was a vast open-air museum of reproductions of Hadrian's favourite buildings.
◈ *Via Tiburtina, 6 km (4 miles) southwest of Tivoli • COTRAL bus from Ponte Mammolo • 06 3996 7900 • Open 9am–1hr before sunset daily • Adm • DA*

3 Tarquinia

A museum of Etruscan artifacts famous for its 4th-century BC terracotta horses. ◈ *Train from Termini or Ostiense or COTRAL bus from Lepanto • Open 8:30am–1 hr before sunset Tue–Sun • Adm*

4 Cerveteri

The necropolis of this 6th-century BC city is still quite intact, complete with streets, houses and frescoes. ◈ *Train from Termini to Cerveteri-Ladispoli • Open 8:30am–1 hr before sunset Tue–Sun • Adm*

5 Castelli Romani

There is much to attract in this area of the Alban Hills. Swim in Lago di Albano, or visit Palazzo Chigi in Ariccia, a Baroque complex designed by Bernini in the 17th century. ◈ *Metro Anagnina, then COTRAL buses • Palazzo Chigi: 06 933 0053, Open 10am–7pm Tue–Sun (gardens open Apr–Sep), Adm*

6 Frascati

From the 16th-century Villa Aldobrandini you can take in magnificent panoramas of Rome. ◈ *Metro Anagnina, then COTRAL bus • Villa Aldobrandini: 06 678 7864, Open 9am–1pm, 3–6pm Mon–Fri (until 5pm in winter)*

7 Palestrina

This town boasts the greatest Hellenistic temple in Italy. Among the treasures unearthed here is a 2nd-century BC mosaic showing the Nile in flood. ◈ *Metro Anagnina, then COTRAL bus • Museum: Open 9am–7pm daily, Adm*

8 Rome's Beaches

The best nearest beach is 115 km (70 miles) to the south at Sperlonga, a medieval town flanked by sandy beaches. ◈ *Train from Termini to Fondi, then local bus*

9 Viterbo

Within this medieval town's walls, visit the Papal Palace, the Archaeological Museum and the Fontana Grande. ◈ *Most sights: Open 8:30am–7pm Tue–Sat, Adm*

10 Pompeii

In AD 79 the volcano Vesuvius erupted, and this city was buried and preserved forever. ◈ *Train from Termini to Naples, then "Circumvesuviana" train • Open 9am–1.5hrs before sunset daily • Adm • DA*

Above **View from La Sibilla**

Price Categories

For a three-course	€	under €30
meal for one with half	€€	€30–40
a bottle of wine (or	€€€	€40–50
equivalent meal), taxes	€€€€	€50–60
and extra charges.	€€€€€	over €60

🔟 Places to Eat

1 Allo Sbarco di Enea, Ostia Antica

Kitsch, but fun. The waiters dress up in Roman gear and the decor is like a low-budget epic movie. The speciality is fish; try the *spaghetti alle vongole* (clams). ◈ *Via dei Romagnoli 675 • Metro Piramide then local train • 06 565 0034 • Closed Mon • €€*

2 Lo Chalet del Lago, EUR

A pleasant surprise in rather flavourless EUR. Huge picture windows rope on the lake make lunch a visual treat. The menu focuses on light fare; the fish dishes are nicely presented. ◈ *Piazza U. E. Terracini • Metro EUR Palasport • 06 591 3743 • €€*

3 Ristorante l'Archeologia, Via Appia Antica

An elegant converted farmhouse, where you dine around the fire-place in winter and in the garden in summer. Rustic regional fare, such as roast lamb and home-made pasta. ◈ *Via Appia Antica 139 • Bus 118 • 06 788 0494 • Closed Tue • €€*

4 La Villetta dal 1940, Piramide

The favourite hangout of 20th-century Surrealist painter Giorgio De Chirico and his crowd of passionately avant-garde artists. The food is hearty and traditional Roman fare, such as *saltimbocca alla romana* (veal and ham). ◈ *Viale della Piramide Cestia 53 • Buses 23, 30, 75, 95, 280, 716, 719 • 06 575 0597 • Closed Wed • €*

5 Coriolano, Porta Pia

The place to eat if you decide to explore Via Nomentana. Try pasta with lobster sauce. ◈ *Via Ancona 14 • Bus 61, 62, 490, 495 • 06 4424 9863 • €€€*

6 La Sibilla, Tivoli

The most spectacular spot in town, overlooking Villa Gregoriana. ◈ *Via della Sibilla 50 • COTRAL bus from Ponte Mammolo • 0774 335 281 • Closed Mon • €€*

7 San Marco, Tarquinia

An old converted monastery. Game and *funghi selvaggi* (wild mushrooms) in season are good. ◈ *Piazza Cavour 18 • Train from Termini or Ostiense or COTRAL bus from Lepanto • 0766 842 234 • Closed Mon • €*

8 Pinocchio, Frascati

Pinocchio (also a hotel) specializes, as does this entire area, in the celebrated *porchetta* (pork roast) ◈ *Piazza del Mercato 21 • Metro Anagnina, then COTRAL bus • 06 941 7883 • Closed Tue L • €*

9 Scylla, Sperlonga

On the beach and great for seafood. ◈ *Via San Rocco 26 • Train from Termini to Fondi, then bus • 0771 549 652 • Closed Tue (winter) • €€*

10 Enoteca La Torre, Viterbo

In addition to great wines, this bar-restaurant offers local dishes, with an emphasis on fish. ◈ *Via della Torre 5 • COTRAL bus from Metro Lepanto • 0 761 226 467 • Closed Sun eve, Mon • €*

Note: *Unless otherwise stated, all restaurants accept credit cards and serve vegetarian meals*

STREETSMART

General Information
158

Tours and Specialist
Holidays
159

Getting to Rome
160

Getting Around Rome
161

Eating and Drinking Tips
162

Accommodation Tips
163

Shopping Tips
164

Things to Avoid
165

Rome on a Budget
166

Special Concerns
167

Banking and
Communications
168

Security and Health
169

Hotel Listings
170–177

ROME'S TOP 10

Left **ENIT logo** Centre **Italian socket** Right **Various newspapers**

General Information

ENIT
ENIT, Italy's national tourist office, is well-intentioned but is often of little help for specific needs. There are branches in most major capital cities. 🕭 www.enit.it

Rome Tourist Offices
Rome has three main tourist offices across the city *(see box)*. There are also 10 privately run information kiosks scattered about the city at prime tourist locations, although their material is less comprehensive than at the tourist offices.

The Internet
Rome's official website is www.roma turismo.com; the Vatican's is www.vaticano.va. Database and search engines such as www. google.com and www. yahoo.com have detailed travel and regional sub-menus linking useful private websites.

Customs and Immigration
Citizens of the UK, Eire, USA, Canada, Australia and New Zealand need only a valid passport to visit Italy for up to 90 days. You may bring into Italy personal items with the following quirky limits: 400 cigarettes (or 550 grams of tobacco), 2 cameras, 10 rolls of film, a pair of skis, two tennis racquets and a litre of alcohol.

Business Hours
Most businesses, churches and some museums open at 8 or 9am, shut for *riposo* from 12:30 or 1pm until 3 or 4pm, and close around 6 or 8pm.

Electricity
Italy is on 220V/50 cycles. To operate a 110V device you need an adaptor (most laptops and camcorders have this built in). You will also need an adaptor if your equipment has pronged plugs rather than Europe's two round pins.

TV and Newspapers
Most 3-star hotels and above have satellite TV with CNN and BBC news. English-language newspapers such as the *International Herald Tribune*, *USA Today*, *New York Times* and magazines are sold at most newsstands. The weekly *Roma C'è* ("This is Rome") beats the tourist office's handout for events, entertainment listings, plus sightseeing information and special tours (section in English).

When to Go
Rome has a temperate climate. August heat is oppressive; February snow flurries are possible. Spring's middle ground keeps hotels booked; autumn is less crowded, but prone to downpours.

High season is Easter to July and September to October. Rome is deserted much of August as residents head to the beaches or mountains to escape the heat and most of the city's shops and restaurants are closed.

Public Holidays
Public holidays include 1 and 6 January, Easter Sunday and Monday, 25 April, 1 May, 15 August, 1 November and 8, 25 and 26 December.

What to Pack
Italians dress well so try to bring one nice outfit. Few restaurants, however, require jacket and tie. Many churches do not allow you to enter with bare knees or shoulders (no shorts, miniskirts or vests) so make sure you have something to cover yourself up.

Rome Tourist Offices

Via Parigi 5
Map E3
• *06 4889 91*
• *Open 9am–7pm Mon–Sat*

Termini Railway Station
Map F3
• *Open 8am–9pm daily*

Fiumicino Airport
06 8205 9127
• *Open 8:15am–7pm daily*

Left **Tourist horse and carriage** Right **Bus tour**

🔟 Tours and Specialist Holidays

1 Package Tours
Airlines, large travel agencies and tour companies offer discount packages combining airfare and hotels. Many, however, stick to large international hotel chains, usually in uninteresting neighbourhoods. You can often do better at a small hotel in the centre.

2 Standard Guided Tours
Tours, booked by your travel agent, leave the driving, hotels, language barriers, and all decisions to the tour company, but they often take out much of the fun in the process. You see the company's neatly packaged idea of Rome, not the Rome you can find travelling on your own. It's also hard to meet the locals when surrounded by a large group of compatriots.

3 Study Holidays
Art history is so much better when the teacher can show you real paintings. History, culture, painting, cookery and language courses are all available. The following websites have more information: www.specialtytravel.com, www.shawguides.com, and www.infohub.com.

4 Rome Bus Tours
City-run ATAC bus No. 110 makes a three-hour circuit around 80 sights with no guide. It leaves daily from outside Termini every 25 minutes from 8:35am to 8:15pm Mon–Fri, every 20 minutes from 8:40am to 8:20pm Sat–Sun. The €13 ticket allows you to hop on and off. If you want a guide's commentary, take a ride with Green Line Tours, American Express or Carrani Tours. ⊗ *ATAC bus: 800-431784, www. atac.it • Green Line Tours: via Farini 5A, 06 4815764, www.greenline tours.com • American Express: piazza di Spagna 38, 06 72282 • Carrani Tours: Via Vittorio E. Orlando 95, 06 474 2501*

5 Walking Tours
Enjoy Rome runs three-hour walks of Ancient Rome, Rome at Night (both daily), the Vatican and Trastevere and the Jewish Ghetto (both thrice weekly). The tourist office has recently been sponsoring free guided walks, usually at weekends. ⊗ *Enjoy Rome: via Margherita 8a, 06 445 1843, www.enjoyrome.com*

6 Bicycle Tours
Enjoy Rome also runs very cheap, four-hour bike tours of Rome, including bike and helmet rental. Or rent a mountain bike (the ancient cobbles are very rough) to ride down Via Appia Antica on a Sunday *(see p61).*

7 Italian Lessons
A company geared toward holiday-makers is Italiaidea, offering courses lasting two to eight weeks, a 15-hour "survival Italian" crash course, and walking tours, weekend trips, and cooking classes geared towards language skills. ⊗ *Italiaidea: 06 6830 7620, www.italiaidea.com*

8 Art Lessons
Rome certainly doesn't lack for inspiration. To bring out the Michelangelo in you contact Atelier Alupi who run week-long workshops three times a year in drawing, oil and watercolour painting. The Istituto Italiano Arte Artigiania e Restauro will teach you about art restoration in a weekend course, or the techniques of fresco or stained glass in two-week courses. ⊗ *Atelier Alupi: 01 4321 3172, www.atelieralupi.com • Istituto Italiano Arte Artigiania e Restauro: 06 575 7185, www. scuolarestauro.it*

9 On-Site Tours
Some churches, museums and ancient sites offer guided visits, often for free. Many museums also feature self-guided tours on portable tape players for a nominal fee.

10 Private Guides
The tourist office *(see p158)* keeps lists of licensed private guides available for hire. Rates vary widely; expect to pay at least €15–20 an hour.

Left **Fiumicino Airport** Right **Termini Railway Station**

Getting to Rome

1 By Air from Great Britain

British Airways (www. britishairways.com), Ryanair (www.ryanair. com), easyJet (www.easy jet.com) and Alitalia (www.alitalia.com) all fly direct from London to Rome. Jet2 (www. jet2.com) fly from Leeds and Manchester, while FlyGlobespan (www. flyglobespan.com) fly from Edinburgh. From Ireland, Aer Lingus (www.aerlingus.ie) flies direct from Dublin.

2 By Air from North America

There are several direct flights on US carriers, plus Italy's Alitalia.

3 By Air from Australasia

Alitalia flies from Melbourne to Rome twice weekly. Qantas (www. qantas.com) flies thrice weekly from Sydney, Melbourne, Brisbane and Cairns (plus Auckland, Wellington and Christchurch in New Zealand) to Rome, via Milan. All flights have a least one stopover.

4 By Air from Europe

Most major European carriers fly to Rome from their main hub cities.

5 Internet Bargains

Most airlines now use websites to promote last-minute bargains and internet-only fares. Most have banded together on www.orbitz.com and collate the best regular fares offered, but only from the US, UK or Canada. Flexible schedules can take advantage of E-savers fares (weekly emails of bargain rates for trips over the coming weekend) and sites such as www.lastminute.com.

6 Fiumicino (Leonardo da Vinci) Airport

Rome's international airport is 30 km (18 miles) west of the city. Taxis cost about €45 to the centre, with bags. Hourly express trains to the city take 30 minutes, but arrive at Termini's track 22, a 15-minute hike from the ticket area (thankfully there are now moving walkways downstairs to help). Or you can catch a local train, getting off at Trastevere station and riding the No. 8 tram to central Trastevere or across the bridge to Largo Argentina (see p99). ✆ Fiumicino Airport: 06 65951

7 Ciampino Airport

Ciampino, Rome's smaller airport which is used mainly for domestic and European charter flights, is 15 km (9 miles) south of town. CO.TRA.L buses leave every half an hour for Anagnina, a stop on metro line A. Taxis cost €40 into the centre, with bags. ✆ Ciampino Airport: 06 794 941, www.adr.it

8 By Train

From London, you can take the Channel tunnel to Paris and pick up a daily or overnight train to Rome (13 hours). The Eurostar (ES) bullet train speeds in 3.5 hours from Milan to Rome via Florence. Regular Italian trains range from express EC/IC/EN (all require high-speed supplements), to the speedy IR, to stop-everywhere diretto and espresso trains.

9 Termini Railway Station

Rome's main railway station has ticket windows and automated machines in the outer hall, shops, restaurants and travel agents in the inner hall and a shopping centre in the basement. The tourist office is in the inner hall (see p158). It also has a left-luggage office and 24-hour pharmacy.

10 By Car

Italy's trunk road, the A1 autostrada, travels from Milan in the north through Bologna and Florence to Rome, then continues on to Naples. The A12 skirts Italy's west coast from Genova (where it links to the A10 from southern France) via Pisa to Fiumicino Airport. They all intersect Rome's G.R.A. (Grande Raccordo Anulare) ring highway, which allows you to circle the city or enter it from any direction you wish.

Left **City centre bus** Centre **Pedestrian signs** Right **Roman taxis**

🔟 Getting around Rome

1 City Buses
Rome's ATAC bus network has central hubs at Termini, Piazza Venezia, Largo Argentina, and Piazza San Silvestro. Newsagents sell maps; *fermata* (bus stop) signs list the routes of the lines which stop there. Buy tickets at newsstands, tobacconists or machines at major stops. Stamp the ticket in the machine on the bus; they are valid for 75 minutes with unlimited transfers.

2 Metro
Two lines intersect at Termini, mainly serving the suburbs. Good tourist stops include Spagna (Spanish Steps), Colosseo, San Paolo (basilica), Ottaviano (six blocks from St Peter's), and Cipro (six blocks from Vatican Museums). Tickets for bus and metro are the same. The metro is currently receiving an upgrade and delays are possible.

3 Walking
The historic centre is increasingly pedestrianized, but many streets are narrow, clogged with traffic and lack pavements. The cobblestones are hard on your feet, so wear sturdy shoes.

4 Taxis
Taxi ranks are found at the airports, train stations, major squares and tourist sights. Base rate is €2, plus 50 cents per kilometre in 1-cent increments. Extra fees are charged for luggage, from 10pm to 7am, on Sundays and airport runs. Tip the driver about 10 per cent of the final fare.

5 Rental Cars
Traffic is bad in Rome, and parking expensive and rare – if you are on a longer trip, pick up the car on your last day in Rome. Local outfits are rarely cheaper than international ones. Most companies require theft protection; check if your credit card covers this insurance. Petrol is expensive but diesel is available everywhere. Most petrol stations close on Sunday but many have automated machines.

6 Road Rules
Official speed limits are 30–50 kmph (18–30 mph) in town, 80–110 kmph (50– 70 mph) on two-lane roads outside town, and 130 kmph (90 mph) on highways, where left lanes are for passing only or heavy goods vehicles.

7 Parking
Few hotels have garages, although many have agreements with local ones or a few free spaces on the street. Round blue signs with a red slash mean no parking; white-lined spaces are free (though often restricted to residents); yellow spaces off-limits; blue spaces available for an hourly fee (pay at meter). Parking rates are best at Parcheggio Borghese under Villa Borghese park and Gianicolo under that hill.

8 Bicycles and Scooters
Roman traffic makes cycling or scootering dangerous. Sundays are calmest and several roads close to traffic for bikers. Rental outfits include Roma in Scooter and, offering discounts to those with train tickets, Treno e Scooter. ✆ *Roma in Scooter: Via Cavour 80, 06 481 5669, www.scooterhire. it • Treno e Scooter: Termini's Piazza dei Cinquecento exit, 06 4890 5823, www. trenoescooter.191.it*

9 Daytrips
Although for far-flung sights you catch trains at Termini, some sights within in Lazio are serviced by local train lines including Ostia Antica *(see pp36–7)* from Porta San Paolo station, near Piramide Metro stop. Many are also accessible by CO. TRA.L coaches, including Tivoli *(see p154)*.

10 Maps
TCI (Touring Club Italiano) maps are best and widely available. Road signs (green for motorways, blue for state roads) indicate destinations more often than route numbers; know the name of the first village, town and city on your route.

Left **Italian white wine** Right **Italian dessert**

Eating and Drinking Tips

1 Restaurant Types

Traditionally, a *ristorante* is the most formal and expensive eatery; a *trattoria* is a family-run, moderately priced place; an *osteria* anything from a simple *trattoria* to the equivalent of a pub with a few dishes of mixed meats and cheeses along with wine.

2 The Italian Meal

Italian meals, especially dinner, are drawn-out affairs of two to four hours, followed by an *espresso* (small, strong coffee) and liqueur (*digestivo*) such as *grappa* (see p77). Breakfast is traditionally just an *espresso* or *cappuccino* (coffee with steamed milk) with a sweetened croissant (*cornetto*). Many hotels lay out a large breakfast buffet.

3 Antipasto

The appetizer course is traditionally *bruschetta* in pizzerias (toasted bread rubbed with garlic, olive oil, salt and often topped with tomatoes) and/or cured meats such as *prosciutto* and *salami*. And most places have a buffet table of vegetables where you can help yourself.

4 Primo

The first course. Pastas include *bucatini all'amatriciana*, *spaghetti alla carbonara*, *gnocchi di patate* and *cacio e pepe* (see p76). Soups (*minestre*) include *minestrone*

(vegetable) and *straciatella* (egg with Parmesan in chicken broth). *Risotto* (creamy rice) is usually cooked with vegetables.

5 Secondo

The main course. Meats include *bistecca* or *manzo* (beef), *vitello* (veal), *agnello/abbacchio* (mutton/lamb), *pollo* (chicken), *maiale* (pork), *cinghiale* (boar), *coniglio* (rabbit) and *anatra* (duck). They are usually grilled (*alla griglia*) or roasted (*arrosto*). Fish include *branzino* (bass), *acciughe* (anchovies), *baccalà* (cod), *sogliola* (sole), *orata* (bream) and *rombo* (turbot), usually grilled, roasted, or *all'acqua pazza* (simmered in white wine and seasonings).

6 Dolce

The dessert. Most popular are simple *cantucci con vin santo* (biscuits with dessert wine) or ice cream such as the *tartufo* ice cream ball. Custards of milk (*panna cotta*, *latte portugese*) and egg (*crème caramel*) are also favourites, as is *tiramisù* (trifle of sponge fingers soaked in *espresso* and perhaps alcohol and layered with mascarpone cheese and dusted with cocoa).

7 Wine and Water

No Italian meal is complete without red (*rosso*) or white (*bianco*) wine (*vino*), either a

carafe (*un litro*) or a half-carafe (*mezzo litro*) of the house wine (*vino della casa*), or a labelled bottle (see p77). Italians temper their wine with water, either fizzy (*gassata*) or still (*non-gassata*).

8 Cover Charges and Tipping

The *pane* (bread) charge of €1–€4 per person can be avoided, but this won't endear you to the waiters. If the menu says "*servizio incluso*" service charge is built in, although it is customary to round up by a few coins each. If not, tip a discretionary 10 per cent.

9 Restaurant Etiquette

Jacket and tie are almost never required, although in more up-market places reservations often are. Waiters expect you to linger over your meal, and won't rush you (some mistake this for slow service).

10 Bars, Pizza Rustica and Tavole Calde

Most Italian bars serve morning *cappuccino* and *cornetto*, *espresso* all day, and apéritifs (*aperitivi*) in the evening, along with sandwiches (*panini*), pastries and ice cream (*gelato*). A *tavola calda* is a glorified bar/cafeteria with prepared dishes behind a counter. A *pizza rustica* or *pizza a taglio* sells pizza by the slice, priced by the *etto* (100 grams).

Left **Hotel doorman** Right **Hotel garden**

🔟 Accommodation Tips

1 Hotels
Italian hotels are categorized from 1-star (basic) to 5-star (deluxe), based largely on the amenities offered rather than location. At 3 stars and above, all rooms have at least private bathroom, TV and telephone.

2 Rental Rooms
The tourist office (see p158) has a list of these invariably cheap options which can range from a lovely room with semi-private access or a cramped spare bedroom in someone's modern apartment. Amount of contact with the family varies, but it can be a great way to meet locals.

3 Apartments
The best sources to help you find an apartment (for a week, a month, or a year) are the English-language twice-monthly *Wanted in Rome* (www.wantedinrome.com) and the twice-weekly *Porta Portese* (www. porta-portese.it) want-ad magazine. People also post apartment notices on message boards at English-language bookshops and Trastevere's Pasquino cinema.

4 Residences
These self-catering apartments, with limited maid service, are popular with long-term tourists (two weeks or more) and those who prefer more privacy. Rome's official

website (www.roma turismo.com) lists several residential options.

5 Camping and Caravaning
Rome has several camp sites *(campeggi)* ringed around the periphery, including Camping Flaminio, Seven Hills, Camping Tiber and Roma Camping. Italians tend to eschew tents for camper vans. You end up paying almost as much as for a cheap hotel: a fee per person and for the camp site itself. ✆ *Flaminio Village: via Flaminia Nuova 821, 06 333 2604, www.villageflaminio.com • Seven Hills: Via Cassia 1216, 06 3031 0826, www.sevenhills.it • Camping Tiber: Via Tiberina km 1400, 06 3361 0733, www.campingtiber. com • Roma Camping: Via Aurelia 831, 06 662 3018, www.ecvacanze.it*

6 Hostels
Cheap beds in single-sex, shared dorms cost about €18 per night. They are full of students, and usually impose a curfew of midnight. The official IYH hostel is in the bleak Foro Italico (see p152). There are better, smaller, private hostels listed at www.hostels.com and www.hiayh.org. ✆ *IYH hostel: Viale delle Olimpiadi 61, 06 323 6267*

7 Bed-and-Breakfast
The newest category of Italian lodging falls

somewhere between rental rooms and hotels, a sort of reincarnation of the old *pensione*, offering a handful of rooms along with breakfast and, usually, a friendly family reception.

8 Should You Reserve?
Reserving the first and last nights of a trip is always wise. The best-known hotels can fill up months in advance, so book ahead. Rome tends to be very crowded in May and June, but you should have no problem finding a room when you arrive, either calling around from the train station payphone or asking the tourist office.

9 Booking Services
The HR hotel consortium at Fiumicino airport and Termini railway station (see p158) will book you rooms for free, as will the private agency Enjoy Rome (see p159). As yet, internet booking services have highly erratic stables of hotels in their databases.

10 Hidden Charges
Rooms with private bath, a view or for stays less than three days are more costly. An extra bed is usually 30–35 per cent more. Breakfast may not be included, parking almost always extra, and prices on minibar items and phone calls shockingly high.

Streetsmart

Left **Leather designer gloves** Right **Antiques shop**

Shopping Tips

Shop Hours
Most shops follow normal business hours *(see p158)* and open at 8–9am, shut for lunch until 3–4pm, and close around 6–8pm. In tourist areas and at larger stores, the lunch break *(riposo)* is slowly disappearing in favour of *orario continuato* (open all day).

Haggling
Expected in markets *(see p69)*, but hardly ever in shops. Many market stall-holders now hail from Middle Eastern countries where bargaining is an art form, so be ready to do the full ritual, including acting less and less interested, while the merchant acts ever more offended and claims he can go no lower. He will not sell it for less than a profit, so any price agreed upon is acceptable.

VAT Refunds
Italy's Value Added Tax (IVA) is a sales tax already added on to the sticker price of every item. If you are a non-EU resident and spend more than €155 in a single shop, you can get the tax refunded. Ask the store to help you fill out the forms; then take these and the receipts to the customs office at the airport of the last EU country you'll be visiting to complete the paperwork. Your refund will be posted but it may take months. Stores marked

"Tax-Free Shopping for Tourists" speed up the process, giving you a cheque for the customs office to stamp, then you redeem it at the airport's Tax-Free Shopping desk.

Customs Limits
UK and Irish citizens can bring home virtually anything duty-free (although theoretical amounts such as 90 litres of wine apply). US citizens are limited to $400 worth of goods duty-free, including 200 cigarettes and 100 cigars. Canadian, Australian and New Zealand limitations are similar. Only British and EU residents may export flowers, fruits, vegetables, meats (unless tinned) and soft cheeses.

Wine
New anti-terrorism legislation means that you can no longer take on board wine that is purchased outside the airport. Shipping wine home is a good alternative but can be expensive.

Fashion and Stock Houses
Designer fashion is rarely cheaper than back home, but there is the cachet of having found those great shoes in Rome. Stock houses sell last year's styles, overstock, slight irregulars or items that won't sell in boutiques, offering a variety of labels at prices from 40–80 per cent lower than normal.

Art and Antiques
As the heart of the Roman Empire and an epicentre of the Renaissance and Baroque, Rome is full of antiquities, paintings and sculpture from the Middle Ages to today. There's also a good market in furnishings from Renaissance-era to Art Nouveau to simple, country-style pieces. Note that exporting goods requires correct paperwork.

Design Objects
Italians are masters of industrial design, from Ferraris to Alessi kettles. If the Ferrari doesn't fit your budget, consider shopping for kitchen implements, homewares or lighting systems, many sketched out by top international designers.

Religious Objects
Religious mementos, from kitsch, to solemn, to the classy, are hawked from stands and shops around the Vatican and, to some extent, across Rome. You can bring your purchase to the Wednesday Papal audience, during which he issues a mass blessing.

Crafts
Italy is renowned for hand-painted ceramics – a souvenir with a practical use. Rome is also home to many fine jewellers, from big names such as Bulgari to artisans labouring in small boutiques.

Left **Termini** railway station Right **No. 64** bus

TOP 10 Things to Avoid

1 Rome in August
Rome is a ghost town in August and unbearably hot. Most Italians go on holiday for the month and while most sights are open and hotels are emptier, many shops and restaurants are closed, and you're only seeing the tourist side of the city, not its true nature *(see p158)*.

2 Pickpocket Bottlenecks
Pickpockets infest many of Rome's streets, squares and metro stations but are worst and at their most aggressive at a few prime tourist bottlenecks: the narrow pavement around the Vatican walls from the museums to St Peter's; around the Forum, especially the road from the back of the Capitoline; and the pedestrianized via dei Pastini and via di Pietra from the Pantheon to the Trevi Fountain.

3 Vatican Museums when they're Free
Yes, you get in for free the last Sunday of each month, but the trade-off is that the museums – often claustrophobic even on a good day – become a crush of bodies.

4 Restaurants around the Vatican and Forum
With rare exceptions, the restaurants that cluster around Rome's two prime tourist spots, advertising menus in six languages and often planted with a waiter waving you over, put the Roman dining experience to shame. No self-respecting Italian patronizes them, and you would be wise to avoid them.

5 Termini Area after Dark
The homeless and dispossessed congregating in the dull train station neighbourhood, home to a glut of budget hotels, make it unsavoury after dark. Generally, the streets south of the station are darker and more dangerous than those to the north.

6 The No. 64 Bus
The "Pickpocket Express" or "Wallet Eater" trundling from Termini to St Peter's has long held the title for the worst pickpocketing bus in Rome. It now faces competition from the No. 40, an express bus on the same route. Keep your wits about you, and one hand on your wallet or purse.

7 Wearing Belt Packs
The worst travel accessory ever invented. Nothing has pleased the world's pickpockets more than the popularity of these pouches, which place all of your most important belongings discreetly below eye-level and at the perfect height for a light-fingered thief to rifle through at his leisure.

8 Driving in Rome
A car is utterly unnecessary in Rome: many of its sights are on pedestrian roads so you can't drive to them anyway, and parking spaces at those accessible by car are almost impossible to find. All parking in the city is limited and preposterously expensive, and to the uninitiated, Italians seem to drive like maniacs *(see p161)*. Save renting a car until the last day of your stay in Rome and use it only to drive out of town.

9 Piazza Navona and Pantheon Areas on Thursdays
Save these areas for a different day as two of the more important sights on the Tiber Bend are closed on Thursday: Sant' Agostino with its unmissable Caravaggio works *(see p83)* and the painting collection of the Galleria Doria Pamphilj *(see p91)*.

10 The Catacombs at Weekends
Two words: tour buses. These are actually worse on Saturday, now that all vehicular traffic save a public minibus is diverted off the Via Appia Antica (the catacombs' main access road) on Sundays *(see p151)*.

Left **Street chestnut seller** Right **Roman market**

Rome on a Budget

The Vatican for Free

The Vatican Museums *(see pp8–9)* are free the last Sunday of each month but do get very crowded *(see p165)*. However the free day is useful if you want to return to tour some of the less popular museums and collections.

Sightseeing for Free

The Roman Forum *(see pp16–19)* is one of the top free sights in the world. Churches are free and hold some of Rome's greatest art and architecture, however you often pay for entry into crypts, archaeological excavations and treasuries. Rome's squares are free theatres of life for the price of a *cappuccino*.

Sightseeing Discounts

Sights and museums are run by a variety of agencies, from national to municipal to private, so prices vary. National museums are free under 18 and over 60 to almost everyone save Americans (a complicated rule connected with reciprocity agreements). One of the best deals is the *Roma Archeologia* Card, a €20 7-day ticket that is valid for sites such as the Colosseum, the Palatine, monuments along the Via Appia and the various museums of the Museo Nazionale.

Travel Discounts

Those under 26 can buy a *Carta Verde* for about €40 that offers 30 per cent discount on any train ticket; the same deal for over 60s is called *Carta Argento*. Available from railway stations.

Accommodation

Generally, prices get higher as you move towards the centre of the city and the hotel has more stars to its rating. A 1- or 2-star hotel (fewer amenities) or taking a room without a private bathroom will save you money, and is preferable to looking outside the centre or in the Termini neighbourhood where cheap hotels congregate *(see p174)*. If you can get out of paying for the hotel's breakfast, the same thing at a café costs a quarter of the price. Avoid making phone calls or using the mini-bar; both are overpriced.

Cheap Eats

In food-loving Italy, price or category of restaurant has little to do with how good the food is, so a cheaper *osteria* or *trattoria* is just as tasty as a fancy *ristorante*. Appetizers cost almost as much as first courses for less food. House wine is cheaper than bottled; tap water *(acqua dal rubinetto)* is free. *Tavole calde* and bars offer cheap meals for those in a hurry *(see p162)*.

Picnics

You can visit a string of small grocery stores *(alimentari)*, greengrocers *(fruttivendolo)*, bread and pastry shops *(panetteria* or *pasticceria)*, wine stores *(vini olii, enoteca* or *fiaschetteria)* or simple street stalls and create your own picnic to eat on a square, take on a daytrip, or enjoy back in your hotel room.

Pay in Cash

Cash is sometimes preferable to credit, and will often secure you a discount in shops and smaller hotels. Just make sure you leave with some kind of receipt.

Travel Off-Season

Roughly, late October to before Easter is low season in Rome, when rates on airfares and hotels can drop considerably, plus you visit without the crowds and long queues *(see p158)*.

Shop Wisely

Some fashion items are no cheaper in Italy than abroad. When possible, save your purchasing for one store so you can gather up the VAT limit and get a refund *(see p164)*. Go for artisan products rather than souvenirs, and purchase from the craftspeople themselves to avoid resale mark-ups. Or take advantage of the city's many markets for more bargains *(see p69)*.

Left **Disabled access** Right **Students**

🔟 Special Concerns

1 Disabled Travellers

Rome isn't fully accessible to disabled travellers, largely because many of its buildings are hundreds of years old and preservation laws prevent alteration to accommodate wheelchairs. However, most major museums have added facilities and many hotels (especially 4- and 5-star properties) have converted a few rooms. Several metro stops (but not the important Colosseo one) are wheelchair accessible. You'll have the best luck at restaurants during warm months, when many have tables outdoors (though bathrooms may not be accessible).

2 Resources for the Disabled

RADAR (Royal Association for Disability and Rehabilitation), based in London, publishes a series of useful pamphlets. Holiday Care Service in England offers advice on disabled-friendly accommodation. In Rome, contact CO.IN or browse their useful website. ✆ *RADAR: 020 7250 3222, www.radar.org.uk • Holiday Care Service: 01293 774 535 • CO.IN: 06 71 29 011, 800 271 027 (freephone), www.coinsociale.it*

3 Senior Citizens

Older travellers are treated as respected elders in a traditional society such as Italy's.

Discounts for *anziani* are often available at sights and for some transport from age 60 or 65.

4 Women Travellers

The Latin lover is alive and well and women can expect to receive much more attention than at home. Open staring, verbal flirtation, bottom-pinching and even inappropriate rubbing on buses are all common. Be firm. Most of this is harmless, but can be annoying and unwelcome.

5 Resources for Women

There is little in the way of official resources for women, but there is a women's bookshop, Libreria delle Donne, which acts as a reference point and resource centre for women. ✆ *Libreria delle Donne: via dei Fienaroli 31, Map K6 • 06 581 7724*

6 Student Travellers

Rome has dozens of study abroad programmes, a huge university and tens of thousands of international students. Ask for a *"studente"* ticket to get reduced admissions on sights. Students tend to hang out in the bars of Trastevere *(see p147)* and Campo de' Fiori *(see p106)* and the clubs of Testaccio *(see p124)*, as well as around the Trevi Fountain and Spanish Steps *(see pp108–11)* after dark.

7 Resources for Students

While student ID cards are useful, the only one widely accepted is the ISIC (International Student Identity Card).

8 Families

Italians love families and will welcome your clan warmly. Most hotels will add a cot to your room for 30–35 per cent extra and restaurants often offer children's half-portions *(mezza porzione)* for 50–75 per cent less than the adult price.

9 Gay and Lesbian Travellers

Homosexuality is legal in Italy and quite broadly accepted in as cosmopolitan a city as Rome, which hosted the World Pride festival in 2000.

10 Resources for Gays and Lesbians

The national ARCI-Gay organization has offices in Rome, as does the lesbian branch, ARCI-Lesbica. However, the locally based Mario Mieli and Di' Gay Project groups are the most important. Useful websites include www.gay.it and www.mariomieli.org. ✆ *ARCI-Gay: via Goito 35B, 06 6450 1102, www.arcigay. it • ARCI-Lesbica: Via Stefanini 15, 06 418 0211, www. arcilesbica.it • Di' Gay Project: Via Costantina 82, 06 513 4741, www.digay project. org • Mario Mieli: Via Efeso 2a, 06 541 3985*

Left **Automated teller machine** Centre **Postboxes** Right **Italian bank**

Banking and Communications

1 Changing Money

Always change money at a bank (or, for American Express card-holders, at an Amex office) for the best rates and lowest commission charges. Bring your passport as ID. Exchange booths *(cambio)* are good at a pinch, but have worse rates and/or higher commission. Never exchange a travellers' cheque (or use one to pay) at a shop or hotel unless you have to; the rates are awful.

2 Automated Teller Machines

The fastest, easiest and cheapest way to get local currency is via an ATM *(bancomat)*, drawing money directly from your home account. No ID checks, no queues, and you get a better rate than inside the bank. Also no commission charge, unless your home bank charges you for out-of-network ATM use.

3 Credit Cards

MasterCard and Visa are accepted everywhere except the smallest shops, *trattorie* or hotels. American Express is also accepted in many places. Diner's Club tends to be valid only at pricier places. You can get credit card cash advances from ATMs, but interest starts accruing immediately and both credit card companies and issuing banks charge small percentage fees for the service.

4 Travellers' Cheques

While still the safest way to carry money (if you lose them and have kept a list of their numbers separate, you can have them speedily replaced), travellers' cheques are doomed by the evolution of ATMs. A few cheques are good for emergencies, however. Buy them in dollars, pounds sterling or euros. Personal cheques are useless, unless you're an Amex card-holder, in which case you can cash them at American Express offices.

5 Currency

In 2002, Italy joined most of Europe in adopting the euro (€) to replace the lira. Euro coins come in 1, 2, 5, 10, 20 and 50 euro cents and €1 and €2. Notes come in €5, €10, €20, €50, €100, €200 and €500 denominations.

6 Public Phones

Most payphones in Italy now accept only pre-paid phonecards *(scheda telefonica)* which you can buy in several denominations at newsstands and tobacconists *(tabacchi)*. Break off the corner before use.

7 Calling Home

There are international phone booths in major railway stations and a range of pre-paid *carta telefonica internazionale* for making international calls, but the cheapest way is with a calling card with an international plan tied to your home phone account. To reverse the charges from any phone, dial the international operator on 170. Never call from hotels, which charge very high rates. To call Italy from abroad, dial your international prefix then Italy's country code (39), then the number, including the zero.

8 Internet Access

Internet parlours and cafés are popping up constantly (ask at the tourist office; they tend to appear and disappear frequently). Increasingly, hotels are installing a common-use computer with web access.

9 Postal Services

Italy's post can be slow – letters might arrive home in three days or three months. You don't need to visit a post office *(ufficio postale)*; just ask any tobacconist or newsagent for stamps *(francobolli)* for the country to which you are mailing. Then drop it in the slot of the postbox (usually red) labelled *"per tutte le altre destinazioni"*.

10 Receiving Mail

Mail addressed to you at "FERMO POSTA/ Piazza San Silvestro 19/ 00187 Roma, Italia/ ITALY" will make it to the main post office on Piazza San Silvestro. There's a small fee to pick it up.

Left **Pharmacy sign** Centre **Roman police station** Right **Roman ambulance**

TOP 10 Security and Health

1 Emergency Numbers

Dial 113 for general emergencies. Dial 112 for the *carabinieri* police, 118 for an ambulance, 115 for the fire department, and 803-116 for car breakdowns (a pay towing service).

2 Safety

Italy is a remarkably safe country. Aside from pickpockets, there is little to fear. Violent crime is rare, and although women (especially young foreign women) may get a lot of attention, it's mostly harmless. Italians do tend to drive aggressively, so be attentive behind the wheel.

3 Pickpockets

On crowded buses, especially the No. 64 *(see p165)*, the metro, and around train stations and other areas tourists congregate, pickpockets work the crowds. Keep your wits about you and keep your passport, credit cards, plane or train tickets, and all money except for a day's worth of cash in a money belt worn under your clothes, either around the waist or on a string around the neck.

4 Young Muggers

Women dressed in colourful but dirty clothes, usually with swaddled babe in arms, tend to stick to forceful begging, but packs of small children will lift your valuables in a flash, and have been known to use force. A common ruse is to swarm you holding up pieces of cardboard with words scrawled on them while the pickpocketing happens underneath.

5 Scams

Scams, while not particularly rampant, are attempted on tourists. Act attentive and in charge and the unscrupulous are unlikely to try. Look out for taxis who might try to set the meter for "out of town" rates rather than local, and restaurants that try to pad the bill with items not ordered. They are also the most likely to try and double-charge your credit card.

6 Police

There are two main police branches you might deal with, the regular *polizia* and the more military-trained, national *carabinieri* force. A police station is called *una questura*.

7 Health Insurance

Check your personal insurance to see if it covers you abroad. Usually you must pay any hospital charges up front and file for reimbursement when you get home, although Blue Cross/Blue Shield members can visit affiliated hospitals in Rome using their card as they do at home.

8 Hospitals

Roman hospitals *(ospedale)* are efficient and semi-privatized. The emergency room is called *pronto soccorso*. For uncomplicated visits not requiring hospital admission, they'll usually give you a check-up, write a prescription if necessary and send you off with a smile, with no paperwork involved.

9 Pharmacies

Italian pharmacies *(farmacie)* are usually very well equipped and knowledgeable in helping you with minor ailments. At night and on Sundays, a sign is posted at each pharmacy listing those that are open all hours. Full-time 24-hour pharmacies include the ones at Piazza Barberini 49, Via Arenula 73 and outside Termini railway station where Via Cavour meets Piazza dei Cinquecento.

10 Food and Water Safety

Italian water is safe to drink everywhere except on trains and any source signposted *"aqua non potabile."* Food is largely safe although uncooked seafood is always chancy. The BSE (Mad Cow Disease) scare which led to a temporary ban of all beef on the bone is over, which means that the popular dish *bistecca fiorentina* can once again be made from the usual T-bone cut.

Left **Majestic** Centre **Raphael** Right **Regina Baglioni**

Bastions of Luxury

1 Eden
Perhaps Rome's most illustrious defender of the grand tradition, this historic hotel has been the choice of celebrities for years. Not only because every detail speaks of refinement, but also because of the superb restaurant/bar that tops the edifice dominating the entire city *(see p136)*. ✪ *Via Ludovisi 49 • Map E2 • 06 478 121 • www.hotel-eden.it • DA • €€€€€*

2 Hassler
In one of the few genteel giants that's not yet part of a luxury chain, the honey-coloured tones of the public rooms set the mood of timeless luxury. The suites and the famous roof terrace restaurant offer some of Rome's most magnificent views. ✪ *Piazza Trinità dei Monti 6 • Map D2 • 06 699 340 • www.hotelhasslerroma.com • DA • €€€€€*

3 De Russie
This historic hotel, a favourite with Picasso, has been refurbished in a sumptuous yet understated style. Delights include terraced garden cafés, an excellent restaurant, a spa and gym and a secret garden on the Pincio. Rooms are spacious and elegant – muted colours and sheer comfort. ✪ *Via del Babuino 9 • Map D2 • 06 328 881 • www.roccofortehotels.com • DA • €€€€€*

4 St Regis Grand
Extravagant opulence, recently restored to its full glory. Originated by César Ritz in 1894, it continues to live up to the illustrious hotelier's name. A world-class restaurant, Vivendo, a business centre and a fitness club complete the offerings. ✪ *Via V E Orlando 3 • Map E3 • 06 47 091 • www.stregis.com/grandrome • DA • €€€€€*

5 Majestic
Magnificence is the keynote in the oldest of the Via Veneto hotels, founded in 1889. Rich decor is everywhere, as well as antiques and bathrooms with Jacuzzis. ✪ *Via Veneto 50 • Map E2 • 06 421 441 • www.hotelmajestic.com • DA • €€€€€*

6 Regina Baglioni
A setting fit for a king, which it has been more than once. Wall silks, Oriental carpets, paintings, marble floors, antiques – this beautiful hotel is truly a palace inside and out. Seventh-floor suites have panoramic views. ✪ *Via Veneto 72 • Map E2 • 06 421 111 • www.baglionihotels.com • DA • €€€€€*

7 De la Ville Inter-Continental
Certainly one of Rome's prettiest hotels, graced with fine art, marble and antiques, all lit by Venetian glass chandeliers. Each room is different in theme. Situated at the top of the Spanish Steps, it could hardly be more central. ✪ *Via Sistina 69 • Map D2 • 06 673 31 • www.rome.intercontinental.com • DA • €€€€€*

8 Grand Hotel Flora
Part of the Marriott chain, this hotel has the air of refinement you expect on Via Veneto, combined with efficiency. The decor features marble, antiques and soft colours. Extras include a roof garden restaurant and a piano bar. ✪ *Via Veneto 191 • Map E2 • 06 489 929 • www.hotelfloraroma.com • DA • €€€€€*

9 Giulio Cesare
Formerly the villa of a countess, the atmosphere is still decidedly aristocratic. Chandeliers, antiques, paintings, Oriental carpets and a grand piano typify the public rooms. Mirror-lined hallways lead to elegant bedrooms with marble baths. ✪ *Via degli Scipioni 287 • Map B2 • 06 321 0751 • www.hotelgiuliocesare.com • €€€€*

10 Atlante Star
Attentive service and a host of extras, such as free airport pick-up and Jacuzzis. The rooftop restaurant is famous for its panorama of St Peter's. ✪ *Via Vitelleschi 34 • Map B2 • 06 687 3233 • www.atlantehotels.com • €€€€€*

Note: *Unless otherwise stated, all hotels accept credit cards, have en-suite bathrooms and air conditioning*

Above **Locarno**

Price Categories	
For a standard, double room per night (with breakfast if included), taxes and extra charges.	€ under €100
	€€ €100–150
	€€€ €150–250
	€€€€ €250–350
	€€€€€ over €350

Romantic Charmers

Westin Excelsior

The grande dame of Rome's hotels, noted for its *belle époque* architecture and commanding location. Notes of grandeur abound everywhere you look, with a choice of several fine restaurants, too. ✪ *Via Veneto 125 • Map E2 • 06 470 81 • www.westin.com/excelsior rome • DA • €€€€€*

Lord Byron

This refined boutique hotel was originally a monastery, but there's nothing ascetic about it nowadays. The decor is an eclectic mix of styles and periods, but all of it evokes opulence. Its location provides serene solitude that makes a perfect antidote to the hectic life of the centre. ✪ *Via G de Notaris 5 • Map B2 • 06 322 0404 • www.lordbyronhotel.com • €€€€*

Raphael

Certainly one of Rome's most appealing hotels. Situated just behind Piazza Navona, the location is perfect, and the ivy-covered façade suggests timeless charm and cosiness. The foyer is full of unusual art treasures and most of the rooms are originally decorated, some with parquet floors and marble accents. Great views from the terraces. ✪ *Largo Febo 2 • Map L3 • 06 682 831 • www. raphaelhotel.com • €€€€€*

D'Inghilterra

Hemingway and Liszt are among the distinguished past guests of this 17th-century edifice, right in the heart of the designer boutique district *(see p114)*. The lavish rooms have antiques and the marble bathrooms provided with fresh orchids. ✪ *Via Bocca di Leone 14 • Map D2 • 06 699 811 • www.royaldemeure.com • DA • €€€€€*

Farnese

This renovated *belle époque* mansion is furnished with period authenticity. Captivating *trompe-l'oeil* fresco decorations, wonderful modern bathrooms and a roof garden are just a few of its attractions. Rich fabrics and high ceilings are typical of the rooms. ✪ *Via Alessandro Farnese 30 • Map C1 • 06 321 2553 • www.hotel farnese.com • €€€€*

Grand Hotel del Gianicolo

Located on the hill above Trastevere, this former convent offers every amenity, including beautiful gardens with a swimming pool, and roof gardens. The location is serene, despite nearby traffic. Public rooms feature Venetian glass fixtures. ✪ *Viale delle Mura Gianicolensi 107 • Map B4 • 06 5833 3405 • www.grandhotelgianicolo. it • DA • €€€€€*

Hotel Piranesi

A romantic boutique hotel run by a charming family. The bedrooms have wooden floors and are beautifully decorated with brocade. Fine views from the roof terrace. ✪ *Via del Babuino 196 • Map D2 • 06 328 047 • www.hotel piranesi.com • DA • €€€€*

La Residenza

Occupying an elegant villa this is one of Rome's special secrets. Great atmosphere, created by a canopied entrance and the deluxe bar and terrace. Some rooms have balconies. ✪ *Via Emilia 22–4 • Map E2 • 06 488 0789 • www.thegianetti hotelsgroup.com • €€€*

Locarno

An Art Nouveau hotel near Piazza del Popolo. The patio has a small fountain, and antiques punctuate the decor. Rooms have high ceilings and wooden floors, and breakfast is served on the roof terrace. ✪ *Via della Penna 22 • Map D2 • 06 361 0841 • www.hotel locarno.com • €€€*

St Anselmo and Villa San Pio

Nestled on a tranquil hill, these adjacent establishments are both spacious and pleasant. Rococo decor predominates, including tapestries and chandeliers. ✪ *Piazza Sant' Anselmo 2 • Map D5 • 06 574 3547 • www. aventinohotels.com • €€€*

Left **Pantheon** Right **Bedroom, Pantheon**

🔟 Comfort, Style and Value Hotels

1 Pantheon
This small, tasteful establishment is less than a block from the eponymous temple *(see pp14–15)*. Public areas boast stained glass, mosaics, beamed ceilings and an imposing crystal chandelier. The door to each room sports an antique print of one of Rome's obelisks, and inside you'll find fresh flowers. ◈ *Via dei Pastini 131 • Map M3 • 06 678 7746 • www.hotelpantheon. com • DA • €€€*

2 Dei Borgognoni
Although just around the corner from the bustling historic centre, this thoroughly up-to-date period building feels removed from it all. Subdued lighting and colours enhance the antique accents, and the hushed garden is most inviting. Some rooms have private patios. ◈ *Via del Bufalo 126 • Map P1 • 06-6994 1505 • www.hotel borgognoni.it • DA • €€€€*

3 Condotti
Amid the designer boutiques along this street *(see p111)*, the hotel offers comfort and period furnishings. All rooms are soundproofed, and many feature views over the rooftops; one has a terrace. The staff are unfailingly attentive. ◈ *Via Mario de' Fiori 37 • Map N1 • 06 679 4661 • www.hotelcondotti.com • €€€*

4 Cesàri
This little gem was famous in the 1800s, when the French writer Stendhal stayed here, and the exterior is little changed. The interior, however, has been kept up-to-date, set off with antiques and old prints. All rooms have blue marble bathrooms. ◈ *Via di Pietra 89A • Map N2 • 06 674 9701 • www. albergocesari.it • €€€*

5 Fori Imperiali Cavalieri
Just steps away from all the sights of the ancient centre. Serenity reigns supreme, with decor and service to match. The historic building has been renovated and every room is equipped with a dataport. ◈ *Via Frangipane 34 • Map Q5 • 06 679 6246 • www.cavalieri.it • €€€*

6 Tritone
Recently done-up, this hotel is located very near the Trevi Fountain and many other sights. The emphasis is tranquillity, ensured by double-glazing and wall-to-wall carpeting throughout. The buffet breakfast in the roof garden is a joy. ◈ *Via del Tritone 210 • Map P1 • 06 6992 2575 • www. travelroma.com • €€€€*

7 Teatropace 33
In a quiet street just a few minutes from Piazza Navona, Teatropace 33 occupies a beautifully restored cardinal's palazzo. Every room in the stylish interior is different. No lift. ◈ *Via del Teatro Pace 33 • Map L2 • 06 687 9075 • www. hotelteatropace.com • €€€*

8 Santa Chiara
Housed in three historic buildings and run by the same family for 200 years. Situated behind the Pantheon, all rooms are spacious and full of character. Features include marble-topped desks, oak headboards and travertine bathrooms. ◈ *Via Santa Chiara 21 • Map M3 • 06 687 2979 • www.albergo santachiara.com • €€€*

9 Isa
Style and friendly service near St Peter's. Don't let the plain exterior dismay you; inside is a touch of Classical fantasy, so you know you're in Rome – murals, wall silks and marble bathrooms, and most rooms have balconies. ◈ *Via Cicerone 39 • Map B3 • 06 6616 3224 • www. boutiquehotelisa.com • €€€*

10 Des Artistes
A comfortable, no-smoking hotel. Pleasing fabrics, paintings and marble bathrooms create an air of luxury. Rooms also equipped with dataports. One of the best choices in the Termini area, there's a floor set aside for budget travellers. ◈ *Via Villafranca 20 • Map F3 • 06 445 4365 • www. hoteldesartistes.com • €€*

Note: Unless otherwise stated, all hotels accept credit cards, have en-suite bathrooms and air conditioning

Price Categories

For a standard, double room per night (with breakfast if included), taxes and extra charges.

€	under €100
€€	€100–150
€€€	€150–250
€€€€	€250–350
€€€€€	over €350

Above **Sole al Pantheon**

Rooms with a View

1 Sole al Pantheon

Noted as an inn since 1467, this distinguished hotel was the choice of Renaissance writer Ariosto. Facing the Pantheon, it has painted period decoration in many of the rooms and modern touches such as Jacuzzis and double-glazing. ◊ *Piazza della Rotonda 63 • Map M3 • 06 678 0441 • www.hotelsole alpantheon.com • €€€€€*

2 Victoria

Round the corner from its extravagant neighbours *(see p170)*, this hotel provides a modest alternative if you want to be near Via Veneto. However, by no means is it without its charms. A terrace bar has spectacular views of the ancient Aurelian Wall and Villa Borghese. Service is excellent. ◊ *Via Campania 41 • Map E2 • 06 473 931 • www.hotelvictoriaroma. com • DA • €€€*

3 Scalinata di Spagna

With its coveted location in an 18th-century villa at the top of the Spanish Steps, this intimate jewel boasts marvellous views from many of its rooms and from the trellis-covered terrace. The rooms are not large but are beautifully appointed. Book well in advance. ◊ *Piazza Trinità dei Monti 17 • Map D2 • 06 679 3006 • www.hotelscalinata. com • DA • €€€*

4 Domus Aventina

A former 14th-century convent with a 17th-century façade, this serene hotel has large, softly coloured rooms. From the balconies and terrace there are great views, and prints, murals and Classical artifacts lend elegance. ◊ *Via di Santa Prisca 11B • Map D5 • 06 574 6135 • www. hoteldomusaventina.com • €€€*

5 Teatro di Pompeo

Have breakfast under the arches of the first theatre in Rome, built by Pompey the Great in 55 BC. Rooms have beamed ceilings, marble-topped furniture and some have great views. The style and many of the amenities of bigger hotels. ◊ *Largo del Pallaro 8 • Map N6 • 06 687 2566 • www.hotel teatrodipompeo.it • €€€*

6 Coronet

This small hotel occupies a part of the Palazzo Doria-Pamphilj *(see p93)*. Request an interior room with garden views. ◊ *Piazza Grazioli 5 • Map N3 • 06 679 2341 • www.hotelcoronet.com • €€€*

7 Homs

On a quiet shopping street, this mid-size hotel is a bit plain, but antiques here and there give it a gracious feel. There are two roof terraces, one enclosed for year-round breakfasts, from which you can enjoy the panorama of Rome's skyline. ◊ *Via della Vite 71–2 • Map D2 • 06 679 2976 • www. hotelhoms.it • €€€*

8 Inn at the Spanish Steps

This up-market hotel is in a 17th-century building – once lived in by Hans Christian Andersen. It has great views of the Spanish Steps from its attractive rooftop garden. Well-equipped rooms include satellite TV and internet access. ◊ *Via dei Condotti 85 • Map D2 • 06 699 25657 • www. atspanishsteps.com • €€€€€*

9 Albergo del Sole al Biscione

What some claim is Rome's very first hotel. Its best feature is the roof terrace, affording the fine views. Rooms are basic, but the atmosphere is cosy. No breakfast. ◊ *Via del Biscione 76 • Map L4 • 06 6880 6873 • www.solealbiscione.it • No credit cards • €€*

10 Abruzzi

Old-fashioned *pensione*-style relic. The rooms are large and clean and each has its own washbasin. Ask for a room that opens onto the dazzling view. ◊ *Piazza della Rotonda 69 • Map M3 • 06 679 2021 • www.hotelabruzzi.it • No credit cards • No en-suite bathrooms • €€€*

Above **Cavalieri Hilton**

TOP 10 Business Hotels

1 Grand Hotel de la Minerve

Occupying the 17th-century Palazzo Fonseca behind the Pantheon, services and quality here live up to the highest international standards. The *pièce de résistance* is the Venetian-glass-canopied lounge. Rooms are large and the view from the roof terrace encompasses all of Rome. ⊗ *Piazza della Minerva 69* • *Map M3* • *06 695 201* • *www.grandhotel delaminerve.it* • €€€€€

2 Parco dei Principi

Just at the edge of Villa Borghese stands this modern high-rise, yet inside all is over-the-top Italian court decor. Panoramas from every room take in greenery and the city's domes. There's a gym, pool, patios, lounges and a well-quipped business centre, as well. ⊗ *Via G Frescobaldi 5* • *Map E2* • *06 854 421* • *www.parcodeiprincipi. com* • €€€€€

3 Grand Hotel Plaza

Dating from 1860, this is one of Rome's oldest hotels, and is replete with Edwardian lavishness. Grand salons with stained-glass skylights, chandeliers, frescoes and antiques combined with modern amenities produce a comfortable ambience. Large rooftop terraces offer stunning views.

⊗ *Via del Corso 126* • *Map D2* • *06 67495* • *www.grand hotelplaza.com* • €€€€€

4 Cavalieri Hilton

High on a hill across the river, outside the centre, this hotel has two restaurants (one is Michelin-starred), four bars, indoor and outdoor pools, a beauty salon, spa, fitness centre, tennis courts and parks make this possibly the best place in Rome for doing business on a grand scale. ⊗ *Via Cadlolo 101* • *Map B1* • *06 350 91* • *www.cavalieri-hilton.it* • *DA* • €€€€€

5 Mecenate Palace

With views of Santa Maria Maggiore *(see p127)*, this comfortable hotel is named after a great patron of the arts under Augustus Caesar. The terrace café is ideal for small conferences and there's a meeting hall that holds up to 40 people. ⊗ *Via Carlo Alberto 3* • *Map F3* • *06 4470 2024* • *www.mecenate palace.com* • *DA* • €€€€

6 Nazionale a Montecitorio

Right next to the Italian Parliament, this 16th-century palace has hosted many politicos. A regal atmosphere, especially in the restaurant with its marble floor. ⊗ *Piazza Montecitorio 131* • *Map M1* • *06 695 001* • *www.nazionaleroma.it* • *DA* • €€€€

7 Bernini Bristol

This unprepossessing brick building faces Bernini's Triton fountain *(see p133)*. The decor is also uninspiring, but this marble-laden hotel is comfortable and has secretarial and other facilities. There's a roof garden, and top rooms have fine views. ⊗ *Piazza Barberini 23* • *Map Q1* • *06 488 3051* • *www.bernini bristol.com* • *DA* • €€€€€

8 Dei Consoli

Elegant and refined, with all conveniences, including internet access, hydromassage and meeting rooms. ⊗ *Via Varrone 2D* • *Map B2* • *06 6889 2972* • *www.hotel deiconsoli.com* • *DA* • €€€€

9 Forum

This converted convent has a roof garden restaurant overlooking the Imperial Fora. Walnut-panelled interiors create warmth, while painted tiles decorate the bathrooms. The meeting room seats 15–80 people and is equipped with all facilities. ⊗ *Via Tor de' Conti 25–30* • *Map P4* • *06 679 2446* • *www. hotelforumrome.com* • €€€

10 Santa Maria

One of Trastevere's newest hotels is a refurbished cloister, offering all the amenities, such as conference facilities. ⊗ *Vicolo del Piede 2* • *Map K6* • *06 589 4626* • *www.hotel santamaria.info* • *DA* • €€€

Note: *Unless otherwise stated, all hotels accept credit cards, have en-suite bathrooms and air conditioning*

Price Categories

For a standard, double room per night (with breakfast if included), taxes and extra charges.

€	under €100
€€	€100–150
€€€	€150–250
€€€€	€250–350
€€€€€	over €350

Above **Roof terrace, Campo de' Fiori**

🔟 Budget Gems

Sant'Anna
This fashionable small hotel in the medieval Borgo next to St Peter's has frescoes in the breakfast room and a fountain in the courtyard. The rooms are spacious and those at the top have their own tiny terraces. The area is quiet and still has very much the feel of old Rome. ◎ *Borgo Pio 134 • Map B3 • 06 6880 1602 • www.hotelsantanna. com • €€€*

San Carlo
The overall decor echoes a Classical influence, with marble touches placed here and there. Situated on one of the quieter streets near the Spanish Steps, the rooms are light and commodious, and some have rooftop views and private terraces. Breakfast is offered in the top-floor garden. ◎ *Via delle Carrozze 93 • Map D2 • 06 678 4548 • www.hotel sancarloroma.com • €€€*

Alimandi
Close to the Vatican, recently remodelled with an attractive foyer and large rooms. Terraces and a roof garden are outstanding features for this price range. The staff are committed to quality service. On a fairly quiet shopping street, handy to public transport. Free cable TV and airport shuttle. ◎ *Via Tunisi 8 • Map B2 • 06 3972 3941 • www.alimandi.org • €€*

La Cisterna
The medieval heart of Trastevere at its best: comfortable, recently spruced-up rooms and a quiet position on an out-of-the-way street. Out back there's a small courtyard with a fountain, where guests can have their breakfast, or just relax. ◎ *Via della Cisterna 8 • Map K6 • 06 581 7212 • www.cisternahotel.it • €€*

Santa Prisca
A converted modern convent structure, there is a slight institutional feel to this place, but it is surrounded by its own park and leafy terraces, plus ample free parking. There's also a restaurant and an American bar. ◎ *Largo M Gelsomini 25 • Map D6 • 06 575 0009 • www.hotelsantaprisca.it • DA • €€*

Margutta
An outstanding choice for location and value. The façade and public areas are low-key, but the rooms are clean and airy with wrought-iron beds. Several rooms share a roof terrace. ◎ *Via Laurina 34 • Map D2 • 06 322 3674 • www.hotelmargutta.it • €€*

Campo de' Fiori
Friendly, clean and in a great location. The roof terrace has views of the rooftops, spires and domes of this ancient quarter. Inside, the decor is replete with touches to remind you that you are in a medieval building: mirrors, frescoes and an exposed ancient wall. ◎ *Via del Biscione 6 • Map L4 • 06 6880 6865 • www. hotelcampodefiori.com • No air conditioning • €€*

Carmel
Old-fashioned *pensione*. The decor is spartan, but there's a vine-covered terrace and most rooms have double-glazing. A unique touch is the kosher kitchen for use by Jewish guests. ◎ *Via Goffredo Mameli 11 • Map K6 • 06 580 9921 • www. hotelcarmel.hotmail.com • €€*

Smeraldo
An excellent choice for both location and quality. The name is evoked by the emerald-green marble entrance, and throughout there are marble accents. Rooms are clean and simple and there are two terraces. Some rooms have private balconies. ◎ *Vicolo dei Chiodaroli 9 • Map M4 • 06 687 5929 • www. smeraldoroma.com • €€*

Trastevere
This unassuming establishment captures the medieval charm of Trastevere. Open brickwork is an accent throughout and stencils decorate the walls. Rooms have views of the local market. ◎ *Via L Manara 24A–25 • Map K6 • 06 581 4713 • www.hotel trastevere.com • €€*

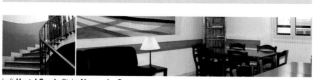

Left **Hostel Sandy** Right **Alessandro Downtown**

Hostels and Religious Institutions

1 Colors

Run by the highly experienced Enjoy Rome team and handily located in a quiet street near St Peter's. Rooms are clean, staff are friendly and multilingual. Internet access and free use of the kitchen and the terrace. No curfew. No breakfast served. Self catering apartments are available. ⬡ *Via Boezio 31 • Map B2 • 06 687 4030 • www.colorshotel.com • No credit cards • €€*

2 Fawlty Towers

On the pleasanter, north side of Termini Station, efficient, clean, with internet access, kitchen, satellite TV and terrace. Helpful English-speaking staff. No curfew, no lockout. Bookings accepted for private rooms only; otherwise first come, first served. Breakfast included. ⬡ *Via Magenta 39 • Map E2 • 06 445 4802 • www.fawlty towers.org • No credit cards • No air conditioning • €–€€*

3 M & J Place Hostel

Just to the right of Termini Station; kitchen use, internet access, no curfew. Multilingual staff, 24-hour reception; lockers and left luggage service. Tourist information, plus discount coupons. Dormitories and private rooms available. Breakfast included. ⬡ *Via Solferino 9 • Map E2 • 06 446 2802 • www.mejplacehostel.com • No credit cards • €*

4 Hostel Alessandro & Alessandro Downtown

Friendly, international staff, 24-hour reception, no curfew, kitchen, internet access, free coffee, tea and pastries. Lockers, free maps and tourist information. Hostel Alessandro is situated to the north of Termini, Alessandro Downtown on the other side, near Via Cavour. ⬡ *Via Vicenza 42 & Via Carlo Cattaneo 23 • Map E2 • 06 446 1958/434 0147 • www.hostelalessandro. com • Air conditioning (Downtown only) • DA (Downtown only) • €*

5 Hotel Ottaviano

Private hotel/hostel, just outside the Vatican walls. Friendly, English-speaking staff and no curfew. Satellite TV, internet access, lockers, tourist information and maps, but no breakfast served. Run by the same people as Hotel Sandy. ⬡ *Via Ottaviano 6 • Map B3 • 06 3973 7253 • www. pensioneottaviano.com • No credit cards • No air conditioning • €*

6 Hostel Sandy

All-dormitory hostel. Rooms sleep from three to eight; many have fridges. No curfew. Lockers, tourist info, maps, free internet access. ⬡ *Via Cavour 136 • Map E3 • 06 488 4585 • www.sandyhostel.com • No credit cards • No air conditioning • €*

7 Bed & Breakfast Cicerone 28

This simple apartment near the Vatican is clean and quiet, since it's on the top floor. The basic rooms come with en suite or shared baths, and there's a breakfast room with a TV. ⬡ *Via Cicerone 28 • Map B2 • 06 320 8195 • www.cicerone 28.it • No credit cards • €*

8 B&B Agencies

For bed-and-breakfast accommodation in Rome, contact the B&B Association of Rome. ⬡ *B&B Association of Rome: Via A Pacinotti 73, 06 5530 2248, www.b-b.rm.it*

9 The Beehive

Run by an American couple, this contemporary part hotel and part hostel (it has one dormitory room) is near Roma Termini but is quiet with a secluded walled garden. Offers free Internet access and national phone calls. ⬡ *Via Marghera 8 • Map K4 • 06 4470 4553 • www. the-beehive.com • No credit cards • €*

10 Centro Diffusione Spiritualità

This religious house, next to the botanical gardens in Trastevere, is a bit charecterless but clean and well organized, and there's a lovely garden. Curfew 11pm. ⬡ *Via dei Riari 43–4 • Map J5 • 06 6880 6122 (06 8530 1758 for bookings) • No credit cards • No air conditioning • €*

Note: *Unless otherwise stated, all hotels accept credit cards, have en-suite bathrooms and air conditioning*

Streetsmart

Price Categories

For a standard, double room per night (with breakfast if included), taxes and extra charges.

€	under €100
€€	€100–150
€€€	€150–250
€€€€	€250–350
€€€€€	over €350

Above **View from Residence Palazzo al Velabro**

🔟 Residences and Apartments

1 Santa Chiara
The perfect location for experiencing the very heart of the city, just behind the Pantheon. It offers three apartments for two to five people. The topmost is graced by beamed ceilings, a fireplace and a terrace with an unforgettable view of the ancient dome. *Via S Chiara 21 • Map M3 • 06 687 2979 • www.albergosantachiara. com • €€*

2 Residence Palazzo al Velabro
An elegant establishment just around the corner from Piazza Venezia. The setting offers understated luxury, privacy and convenience. Guests stay in apartments named after a Roman emperor, god, king or poet. The staff are helpful. Minimum three-day stay. *Via del Velabro 16 • Map N4 • 06 679 2758 • www.velabro.it • DA • €€€*

3 Aldrovandi Residence
Outside the city centre, just beyond Villa Borghese in the Parioli district, full of greenery. The furnishings are handsome and the service deferential. Guests are welcome to use the pool of the Hotel Aldrovandi next door. Minimum one-week stay. *Via Aldrovandi 11 • Tram No. 8 • 06 322 1430 • www.aldrovandiresidence.it • DA • €*

4 Residenza Farnese
A great find. Just around the corner from the Piazza Farnese and offering space and comfort. The building is a restructured 15th-century palazzo in an area loaded with history. *Via del Mascherone 59 • Map K4 • 06 6889 1388 • www. residenzafarneseroma.it • €€€*

5 Residence Ripetta
Located very near Piazza del Popolo, this 17th-century convent has been refurbished and offers a large range of apartment options for both short- and long-term visitors. The style of the furnishings is fairly basic but clean, and staff make every effort to see to your needs. Minimum one-week stay. *Via di Ripetta 231 • Map D2 • 06 323 1144 • www.ripetta.it • DA • €€€*

6 Trastevere
In the heart of this medieval district, just a block away from the main piazza. This modest hotel also offers small, clean apartments with kitchens. *Via L Manara 24A–25 • Map K6 • 06 581 4713 • www. hoteltrastevere.com • €€*

7 Residence Babuino
On one of Rome's chicest streets, this residence has a few small apartments. Decor is a mix of medieval and modern: wood-beam ceilings with contemporary furnishings. Rooms are spacious and some have terraces. Minimum one-month stay. *Via del Babuino 172 • Map D2 • 06 361 1663 • No credit cards • €€€€*

8 Residence In Trastevere
This small 17th-century mansion has been transformed into suites. Open beams, painted decorations and other nice touches. The roof terrace offers views of the Gianicolo and the river. Minimum one-week stay. *Vicolo Moroni 35–6 • Map K6 • 06 581 2768 • www.romerenting.com • No credit cards • No air conditioning • €*

9 Residence Vittoria
In Rome's most fashionable shopping district, this residence emphasizes luxury. The building has a range of accommodation, from studios to penthouses. Minimum one-month stay. *Via Vittoria 60–64 • Map D2 • 06 679 7533 • www. residencevittoria.com • No credit cards • €€€€€*

10 Apartment Rentals
Numerous services offer apartment rental. Prices vary depending on type, length of stay and number of people. *AT@ HOME: Via del Babuino 56, 06 321 0102, www.at-home-italy.com • Rome Sweet Home: Via della Vite 32, 06 6992 4833, www. romesweethome.it, €*

General Index

A

abbacchio 162
abbacchio scottadito 76
Abbey Theatre Irish Pub 88
Abruzzi (hotel) 173
Abruzzi (restaurant) 117
Acattolica Cemetery 121
Acchiappafantasmi 73
acciughe 162
accommodation tips 163
  on a budget 166
Acqua e Farina? 125
Acqua Vergine aqueduct 46, 109
Adoration (Pinturicchio) 33
Adoration of the Shepherds (da
  Cortona) 86
Aeneas and Anchises (Bernini) 21
Africa 137
Afro 43
Agata e Romeo 74, 131
agnello 162
Agrippa 46
Ai Monasteri 85, 87
airports 160
air travel 160
Al 34 117
Alban Hills 154
Albergo del Sole al Biscione 173
Alberto Ciarla 74, 149
Alberto di Castro 113
Aldrovandi Residence 177
Alessandro Downtown 176
Alexander VI 39
Alexander VII 99
Alexanderplatz 78, 147
Alimandi (hotel) 175
L'Alibi 124
all'acqua pazza 162
alla griglia 162
Allo Sbarco di Enea (Ostia
  Antica) 155
All Saints' Day 67
Alpheus 124
Amarena Chic 95
American Express tours 159
Ammannati, Bartolomeo 51
anatra 162
ancient art collections 31
ancient Roman art 31
Ancient Rome 118–25
  itinerary 121
  map 118
  Rome's trendiest niglife 124
  top 10 sights 118–21
  traditional Roman
    restaurants 125

ancient sights 40–41
Andrea 137
Angel and St Matthew
  (Caravaggio) 83
Angelico, Fra 42
L'Angolo di Napoli 129, 131
L'Antica Cantina 116
Antica Cappelleria Troncarelli
  87
Antica Taverna 89
Antichità 105
Antico Arco 149
Antico Caffè Greco 70, 116
antipasto 162
Antiqua Domus 87
antiques, buying 164
Antonioni, Michelangelo 59
apartments 163, 177
aperitivi 162
Apollo and Daphne (Bernini) 20,
  49
Apollo Belvedere 8
Apollodorus of Damascus 22
Appian Way 61, 150, 151, 153
Ara Pacis 90, 91, 93
Arch of Constantine 23
Arch of Septimius Severus 16
Arch of Titus 17
L'Archetto 117
ARCI-Gay 167
ARCI-Lesbica 167
Arezzo, Margaritone d'
  St Francis portrait 141
Arion 136
Arnaldo ai Satiri 60
Arpino, Cavalier d'
  Virgin and Child 142
Arricia 154
arrosto 162
art and antiques, buying 164
art and art history courses 159
L'Art Nouveau 87
Des Artistes (hotel) 172
artistic masterpieces 48–9
ATAC
  buses 161
  bus tours 159
Atelier Alupi 159
Atlante Star (hotel) 170
Augustarello 125
Augustus 41
  Mausoleum 92, 93
Aula Ottagona 28, 133, 135
Aurelian Wall 121, 152
automated teller machines
  (ATMs) 168

autostrade 160
AZI 143

B

Babington's Tea Rooms 110,
  116
Il Bacaro 97
baccalà 162
Baia Chia 131
banking 168
Bar Calisto 146
Bar del Fico 88
Bar della Pace 79
Bar Gelateria Fima 146
bars and pubs
  around the Pantheon 96
  best 78–9
  eating and drinking tips 162
  Spanish Steps and Villa
    Borghese 116
  Trastevere and Prati 146
Barberini, Maffei *see* Urban VIII
The Barber of Seville (Rossini) 99
Barbo, Pietro 51
La Barcaccia 110
Barrita Boutique 130
Basilica of Maxentius and
  Constantine 17
Basilica of Neptune 15
bathhouses, ancient Roman 19
Bath of Venus 50
Baths of Caracalla 118, 119–20
  opera season 66
Baths of Diocletian 28, 40, 132,
  133
Baths of Trajan 63
beaches 154
Beata Ludovica Albertoni
  (Bernini) 49
bed and breakfast
  accommodation 163
  agencies 176
Bed & Breakfast Cicerone 28,
  176
Beehive (hotel) 176
belief systems 19
Belvedere Torso 9
Ben Hur 58
Benigni, Roberto 59
Benucci 113
Bernasconi 101
Bernini Bristol (hotel) 174
Bernini, Giovanni 20, 46, 47, 51,
  82
  Aeneas and Anchises 21
  Apollo and Daphne 20, 49

Bernini, Giovanni (cont.)
La Barcaccia 110
Beata Ludovica Albertoni 141
Chigi Chapel 33
David 20
Ecstasy of St Teresa 49, 133
Elephant obelisk 93
Four Rivers Fountain 83
Innocent X bust 91
Palazzo Chigi 154
Palazzo di Montecitorio 94
Piazza Barberini fountains 134
Piazza San Pietro 12
Ponte Sant'Angelo statues 141
Rape of Persephone 20
San Lorenzo in Lucina chapel 94
Santa Maria della Vittoria 133
Santa Maria in Via Lata altar 94
Sant'Andrea al Quirinale 134–5
St Peter's Basilica 12–13
Bertolucci, Bernardo 59
The Bicycle Thieves (de Sica) 58
Beyond the City Walls 150–55
day trips from Rome 154
itinerary 153
map 150
places to eat 155
top 10 sights 151–3
bicycles
rental 161
tours 159
Big Hilda Café 146
Big Mama 78, 147
Bioparco (zoo) 64
Birreria Peroni 75, 117
Birreria Trilussa 147
bistecca 162
bistecca fiorentina 169
Black Duke 96
Bloom 88
Bocca della Verità 100
Boniface VIII 39
Borghese, Cardinal Scipione 20, 21, 111
Borgia Apartments (Vatican City) 9
Borgo 138
Borgo Antico 146
Dei Borgogni (hotel) 172
Borromini, Francesco
Palazzo Barberini 51
Palazzo Spada 43

Borromini, Francesco (cont.)
Sant'Agnese in Agone façade 86
Sant'Ivo façade 83
San Carlo alle Quattro Fontane 135
La Bottega del Marmoraro 113
La Botticella 88
Botticelli, Sandro 11
Burning Bush 10
Cleansing of the Leper 10
Punishment of the Rebels 10
Bramante (café/bar) 88
Bramante, Donato 84
Santa Maria del Popolo apse 33
Via Giulia 104
branzino 162
breakfast 162
Breughel the Elder, Jan 43
Il Brillo Parlante 117
Brioni 136
Brooks 105
Bruno, Giordano 46, 99
bruschetta 162
bucatini all'amatriciana 76, 162
Buccone 115
budget travel 166
Bull Dog Pub 88
Burial of St Petronilla (Guercino) 26
Burning Bush (Ghirlandaio) 10
bus, travelling by 161
bus tours 159
business hours 158
Byron, Lord 56

C
cacio e pepe 77, 162
Café de Oriente 124
Café de Paris 136
Café Rosati 116
cafés and *gelaterie*
around the Pantheon 96
best 70–71
Quirinal & Via Veneto 136
Spanish Steps and Villa Borghese 116
Trastevere and Prati 146
Café Sant'Eustachio 70, 93, 96
Café Veneto 137
Caffè Canova 111, 116
Caffè della Scala 147
Caffè delle Arti 20
Caffè Farnese 106
Caffè Latino Jazz Club 124

Caffè Rosati 71
Caffè Valorani 22
Calixtus I 45
Calling of Peter and Andrew (Ghirlandaio) 10
Calling of St Matthew (Caravaggio) 45, 49, 83
Calzoleria Petrocchi 87
Cambio, Arnolfo di0
statue of St Peter 12
St Peter's *baldacchino* 12 140
Campari 77
Campidoglio 61
view from 53
Campidoglio Palazzi 50
camping 163
Camping Flaminio 163
Camping Tiber 163
Campo de' Fiori 46, 99, 101
market 69, 98
Campo de' Fiori (hotel) 175
Campo de' Fiori to the Capitoline 98–107
best of the rest 104
itinerary 101
map 98
nightspots 106
shops 105
top 10 sights 98–101
Campo Marzio Roma 95
Cannavota 34, 129, 131
Canova, Antonio 43
Pauline Bonaparte 21
studio 112
cantucci con vin santo 162
Capitoline Hill 99
cappuccino 162
Capranica Wine Bar 96
Capuchin crypt 54, 64, 134, 135
car
rental 161
travelling by 160
carabinieri 169
Caravaggio 20, 42, 82
Angel and St Matthew 83
Calling of St Matthew 45, 49, 83
Conversion of St Paul 32
Crucifixion of St Peter 32
Deposition 9, 48
Gypsy Fortune-Teller 26–7
Judith and Holofernes 133
Madonna del Loreto 84
Madonna of the Serpent 20
Martyrdom of St Matthew 83
Mary Magdalene 91

Caravaggio (cont.)
  Rest on the Flight into Egypt
    91
  *Self-Portrait as a Sick
    Bacchus* 21
  Young St John the Baptist
    26, 91
caravanning 163
carciofi alla giudia 76, 162
carciofi alla romana 76, 162
Carmel (hotel/*pensione*) 175
Carnival 67
Caro Diario (Moretti) 59
Carrani Tours 159
Carta Argento 166
Carta Verde 166
Casa di Goethe 112
Casa di SS Giovanni e Paolo
  (Celian) 53
Casina di Pius IV 140
Casina Valadier 60
Castel Sant'Angelo 138, 140
  view from 53
Castelli Romani 77, 154
Castroni 68, 143
Cat Sanctuary at Largo
  Argentina 54
Catacombs 52, 65
  Catacombs of Domitilla
    151
  Catacombs of San Callixtus
    152
  Catacombs of San
    Sebastiano 152, 153
  things to avoid 165
Cavalieri Hilton 174
Cavallini, Pietro
  Last Judgment 140
  Life of the Virgin mosaics
    139
Cecilia, St 140
Cecilia Metella, tomb of 151,
  153
The Cenci (Shelley) 57
CentroDiffusione Spiritualità
  176
Cerveteri 154
Cesàri (hotel) 172
Cézanne, Paul 43
Chakra 146
Lo Chalet del Lago (EUR) 61,
  155
Chapel of Nicholas V (Vatican
  City) 9
Chapel of St John 23
Chapel of St Matthew 45
Chapel of St Zeno 128
Charles V 39, 50

Checchino dal 1887 74, 124
Chianti 77
Chiesa Nuova 86
Chigi Chapel (Bernini/Raphael)
  32–3
Childe Harold's Pilgrimage
  (Byron) 56
children, sights for 64
Chirico, Giorgio de 43
Christianity, establishment of
  128
Christmas Eve midnight mass
  67
Christmas market 67
churches 44–5
Il Ciak 149
Ciampino Airport 160
Cicero 57
Cinecittà films 58–9
cinghiale 162
La Ciociara (Moravia) 56
Circus Maximus 121
Circus of Maxentius 153
La Cisterna 175
Città del Sole 95
Clamur 124
Classical writers in Rome 57
Cleansing of the Leper
  (Botticelli) 10
Clement VII 39, 91
Cleopatra (Mankiewicz) 59
climate 159
Clivo di Rocca Savella 60
clubs 78–9
coda alla vaccinara 77
CO.IN 167
Coin (department store) 130
Colle Oppio 63
Colli Albani 77
Colline Emiliane 137
Colors 176
Colosseum 22, 40, 128
Colosseum & Imperial Fora 7,
  22–3, 119
Column of Marcus Aurelius 40,
  92, 93
communications 168
Condotti 172
coniglio 162
Dei Consoli 174
Constantine I, the Great 38, 41,
  44, 126, 127
Conversion of St Paul
  (Caravaggio) 32
Il Convivio 89
Cordonata 24
Coriolano (Porta Pia) 155
cornetto 162

Coronari Chapel 133
Coronet (hotel) 173
Correggio, Antonio Allegri da
  Danae 21
Cortona, Pietro da
  Galleria Nazionale d'Arte
    Antica 42
  Palazzo Pamphilj fresco 86
  Rape of the Sabines 27
  Santa Maria della Pace
    façade 84
  Santa Maria in Via Lata
    façade and vestibule 94
  Sant'Ivo altarpiece 83
  SS Ambrogio e Carlo al
    Corso 112
Costantini 143
CO.TRA.L. buses 161
courses 159
cover charges 162
crafts, buying 164
Cravatterie Nazionali 115
credit cards 168
crème caramel 162
Cremeria Monteforte 14, 96
Crucifixion of St Peter
  (Caravaggio) 32
Crypta Balbi 52, 101
Cryptoporticus 18
C.U.C.I.N.A. 115
Cul de Sac 88
Curia 16
La Curia di Bacco 101, 106
currency and currency
  exchange 168
customs restrictions
  exports 164
  imports 158
Cybo Chapel (Fontana) 33

D
Da Augusto 75, 148
Da Cesaretto 75
Da Gino 97
Da Giovanni 148
Da Remo 125
Dagnino 137
Daisy Miller (James) 56
Dal Bolognese 111, 117
Danae (Correggio) 21
David (Bernini) 20
Davide Cenci 95
daytrips from Rome 154, 161
*Decline and Fall of the Roman
  Empire* (Gibbon) 57
De la Ville Inter-Continental
  170
Il Delfino 97

Deposition (Caravaggio) 9, 21, 48
design objects, buying 164
dialling codes 168
digestivo 162
Diocletian 41
Di Pietro 125
disabled travellers 167
Il Discount dell'Alta Moda 115
discount shops 130
discounts 166
dolce 162
La Dolce Vita (Fellini) 58, 109
La Dolce Vita venues 136
Domenichino 45, 83
Domine Quo Vadis? church 153
Domitian's Stadium 46, 86
Domus Aventina 173
Domus Augustana 18
Domus Flavia 18
Domus Septimius Severus 18
Don Juan (Byron) 56
Dott. Cesare Lampronti 113
Dott. Sergio de Sanctis 87
Doublé 137
dress etiquette 158
Drunken Ship 78, 106
Il Duca 148

E

E&R Danon 113
Easter Week 67
eating and drinking tips 162
L'Eau Vive 97
Ecstasy of St Teresa (Bernini) 49, 133
Eden (hotel) 136, 170
Edy 117
El Greco 42
electricity 158
Elephant obelisk (Bernini) 93
emergency numbers 169
ENERGIE 143
Enigma 115
ENIT (Italian national tourist office) 158
Enjoy Rome
  hotel reservations 163
  tours 159
Enoteca al Parlamento 96
Enoteca Cavour 313 131
Enoteca Corsi 97
Enoteca la Torre (Viterbo) 155
Enoteca Trastevere 146
espresso 162
Esquiline and Lateran 126–31
  discount shops 130
  itinerary 129
  map 126

Esquiline and Lateran (cont.)
  places to eat 131
  top 10 sights 126–9
Est! Est! Est! 77
etiquette 158, 162
Les Etoiles 149
EUR 64, 151
Eurostar (ES)/Pendolino bullet train 160
Excelsior Hotel 135
exchanging money 168
excursions from Rome 154, 161
Exotic Foods 130
Explora Museum 64

F

Fahrenheit 451 105
families, travelling with 167
Fancelli, Cosimo 99
Farnese (hotel) 171
Farnese, Alessandro *see* Paul III
Farnese Gardens 18
fashion, buying 164
Fausto Santini 114
Fawlty Towers 176
Feast of Sts Peter and Paul 67
Felice 125
Fellini, Federico 59
Fendi 114
Ferragamo 114
Ferrara 149
Festa dell'Unità 66
festivals 66–7
Fiaschetteria Beltramme (da Cesaretto) 117
Fiddler's Elbow 78
Fiesole, Mino da
  Madonna with Child 33
¡Fiesta! 66
Filetti di Baccalà 107
films 58–9
Firmastock 115
F.I.S.H. 131
Fiumicino (Leonardo da Vinci) Airport 160
Fonclea 147
Fontana delle Tartarughe 47, 101
Fontana, Carlo 33, 47, 112, 121
Fontana, Domenico 46, 110
Fontana Paola 142
Fontanella del Facchino 94
food
  Italian menu 162
  safety 169
  specialities 76–7
Fori Imperiali Cavalieri (hotel) 172

La Fornarina (Romano) 133
Foro Boario 100
Foro Italico and Stadio dei Marmi 152–3
Forum *see* Roman Forum
Forum (hotel) 174
Forum of Augustus 23
Forum of Julius Caesar 23
Forum of Nerva 23
Fountain of the Naiads 47
Four Green Fields 147
Four Rivers Fountain 83
Four XXXX Pub 124
Fra' Angelico
  Chapel of Nicholas V 9
  tomb 91
Fra Diamante 11
Franchi 143
Francis, St 140–41
Frascati 77, 154
Fraterna Domus 89
French Academy 110
Friends 146

G

Galatea (Raphael) 139
Galleria Antiquaria 113
Galleria Augusto Consort 113
Galleria Borghese 6, **20–21**, 42, 109, 110
Galleria Comunale d'Arte Moderna 43, 112
Galleria Doria Pamphilj 42–3, 91, 93
Galleria Il Colibri 87
Galleria Nazionale d'Arte Antica 42, 133
Galleria Nazionale d'Arte Moderna 20, 43, 111, 112
Galleria Spada 43
Galleria Veneziani 113
Gangs of New York (Scorsese) 59
Garibaldi, Giuseppe 39
  statue 141
Gatta, Bartolomeo della 11
  Moses Giving his Rod to Joshua 10
Gaudí 73
gay and lesbian travellers 167
Gea Arte Antica 87
Gelateria della Palma 71, 96
gelaterie see cafés and gelaterie
gelato 162
Gesù 100, 101
getting around Rome 161
getting to Rome 160

Ghirlandaio, Domenico 11
    Calling of Peter and Andrew
    10
Gianicolo 60, 141
    view from 53
Gianni Versace 114
La Giara 137
Gibbon, Edward 56–7
I Giganti della Notte 106
Da Giggetto 107
Gilda 116
Giorgio Armani 114
Giolitti 70, 93, 96
Giulio Cesare (hotel) 170
Gli Indifferenti (Moravia) 56
gnocchi di patate 77, 162
Il Goccetto 105
Goethe, Wolfgang 56
    Casa di Goethe 112
    Italian Journey 56, 110
Gran Caffè Doney 70, 135, 136
Gran Caffè Roma 136
Grand Hotel del Gianicolo 171
Grand Hotel de la Minerve 174
Grand Hotel Flora 170
Grand Hotel Plaza 174
Grande Raccordo Anulare 160
grappa 77
Green Line Tours 159
green spaces 62–3
Gregorian chant
    Santa Maria in Montesanto
    111
Gregory the Great, St 39
Gucci 114
Guercino, Gian-Francesco
    Burial of St Petronilla 26
guided tours 159
Il Guru 131
'Gusto 75, 93, 117
Gypsy Fortune-Teller
    (Caravaggio) 26–7

H
Hadrian 41
Hadrian VI tomb 86
Hadrian's Temple 94
Hadrian's Villa 154
Hard Rock Café 136
Harry's Bar 71, 136
Hassler 170
Hawthorne, Nathaniel 56
Head of Medusa (Bernini) 27
health tips 169
Helena, St 127, 128
hidden Rome 54–5
high season 158
history 38–9

Holbein, Hans 42
Holiday Care Service 167
Homs 173
Hostel Alessandro 176
hostels 163
Hostel Sandy 176
hotel categories 163
Hotel Ottaviano 176
Hotel Piranesi 171
hotels and other places to stay
    172–9
    accommodation tips 163
    apartments 177
    bastions of luxury 170
    budget gems 175
    business hotels 174
    comfort, style and value
    hotels 172
    hidden charges 163
    hostels and religious
    institutions 176
    reservation services 163
    residences and apartments
    177
    romantic charmers 171
    rooms with a view 173
House of the Knights of
    Rhodes 23
House of the Vestal Virgins 16

I
Imperial Fora 22–3, 40
information, tourist 158
Inghilterra (hotel) 170
Innocent III 39
Innocent X bust (Bernini) 91
The Innocents Abroad (Twain)
    57
Inn at the Spanish Steps 173
Inn Sport 105
Insalata Ricca 148
Insalata Ricca 2 89
insurance 161, 169
international calls 168
International Horse Show 67
International Trade Corp 130
Internet access 168
Isa (hotel) 172
ISIC card 167
Istituto Italian Arte Artigianato e
    Restauro 159
Italiaidea courses and tours
    159
Italian Hours (James) 56
Italian Journey (Goethe) 110
Italian lessons 159
IVA (sales tax) 164
IYH hostel 163

J
Jackie O' 136
James, Henry 56
jazz festival 67
Jews in Rome 100
John Paul II
Jonathan's Angels 78, 88
Judgment of Paris (Vidal) 57
Judith and Holofernes
    (Caravaggio) 133
Julian (Vidal) 57
Julius II 39
Julius III 51
Julius Caesar 38, 57, 98
Juvenal 57

K
Keats, John 56
    grave 121
Keats-Shelley Memorial 108,
    109
Klimt, Gustav 43
Knights of Malta Keyhole 53

L
Lacrime di Cristo 77
Lago di Albano 154
Landini, Taddeo 101
language courses 159
Laocoön 9
Largo del Pollaro 53
Largo di Torre Argentina 41, 99
Last Judgment (Cavallini) 140,
    141
Lateran see Esquiline and
    Lateran
latte portugese 162
Laura Biagiotti 114
Libreria delle Donne 167
Little India 131
Leam 130
Leo the Great, St 39
Leo X 85, 91
Leonardo da Vinci
    St Jerome 9, 49
Leonardo da Vinci Airport
    160
Leone, Sergio 59
lesbian travellers 167
Lettere Café 147
Libreria Babele 105
Libreria Rinascita 105
Life is Beautiful (Begnini) 59
Life of the Virgin mosaics
    (Cavallini) 139
Lilli 89
Lippi, Filippino
    chapel frescoes 91

Lippi, Filippo 42
  Madonna and Child 133
liqueurs 77
Livia's House 18
Locarno (hotel) 171
Longhi, Martino 84
Lord Byron (hotel) 171
Loyola, Ignatius, tomb of 100
Lunapark 64

M
M Simotti Rocchi 95
M & J Place Hostel 176
Macallé 143
Maccheroni 97
Mad Jack's 106
Maderno, Carlo 51
  statue of St Cecilia 140
Madonna and Child (Filippo Lippi) 133
Madonna della Clemenza 139
Madonna del Loreto (Caravaggio) 84
Madonna del Parto (Sansovino) 84
Madonna della Neve festival 67
Madonna of the Serpent (Caravaggio) 20
maiale 162
mail services 168
Majestic (hotel) 170
Mamertine Prison 22, 23, 52
manzo 162
maps 161
Maratta, Carlo
  Immaculate Conception 33
Marble and Tile Bottega 105
The Marble Faun (Hawthorne) 56
Marcillat, Guillaume de
  Santa Maria del Popolo stained glass 33
Marcus Aurelius 41
  column of 92, 93
  statue of 27
Margutta 175
Maria Teresa Nitti Valentini 95
Mariano 137
markets 69
  haggling 164
Martyrdom of St Matthew (Caravaggio) 83
Mary Magdalene (Caravaggio) 91
MAS 130
Massimo Maria Melis 87
Il Matriciano 149
Maurizio Grossi 113

Maxentius 23
May Day concert 67
Mecenate Palace (hotel) 174
Meier, Richard 91
Mercato dell'Antiquariato 95
Messaggerie Musicali 115
metro, travelling by 161
Michelangelo 11, 42, 50
  Baths of Diocletian cloister 40
  Cordonata 24
  Dome of St Peter's 12
  Moses 49, 127
  Pietà 12, 48
  Palazzo Farnese 104
  Porta del Popolo 112
  Risen Christ 44, 91
  Santa Maria degli Angeli 133
  Sistine Chapel 8, 10–11, 48, 139
midnight mass 67
minestrone 162
Mithraeum (San Clemente) 35
Mithraeum (San Stefano Rotondo) 53
Modigliani, Amedeo 43
Monet, Claude 43
Monte Cavallo 135
Monte Testaccio 118
Montemarini Art Centre 152
Monti D.O.C. 131
Morandi 43
Moravia, Alberto 56
Morelli, Cosimo 86
Moretti, Nanni 59
Moses (Michelangelo) 49
Moses Giving his Rod to Joshua (Signorelli, della Gatta) 10
Mount Gay 124
Mr Brown 146
Musei Capitolini 7, **24–7**, 42, 53, 119
Museo Barracco 53, 104
Museo della Casina della Civette 54
Museo della Civiltà Romana 151
Museo delle Anime del Purgatorio 54
Museo delle Mura 55, 153
Museo di Roma in Trastevere 141, 142
Museo Napoleonico 86
Museo Nazionale delle Paste Alimentari 54
Museo Nazionale Romano 7, **28–31**, 42, 84, 127
museums & galleries 42–3
music clubs 78–9, 147

Mussolini, Benito 39, 47
  EUR 150, 151

N
Nag's Head 116
Napul'è 148
Nardecchia 87
Nativity of the Virgin (del Piombo) 33
Nazca 124
Nazionale a Montecitorio 174
Né Arte ne Parte 125
Nero 38, 41
Nero's Golden House 22, 23, 41, 52, 63, 128
Nervi, Pier Luigi
  audience hall, Vatican Gardens 140
New Fashion 143
newspapers 158
nightspots
  Ancient Rome 124
  Campo de' Fiori to the Capitoline 106
La Noia (Moravia) 56
Nomades 113

O
Obikà 97
Odeon of Domitian 85
Old Bear 88
Ombre Rosse 146
opening hours 158
opera festivals 66
orata 162
Oriental Art Museum 129
Orologeria Mazzella 105
Orto Botanico 62, 141, 142
Orvieto Classico 77
Osteria ar Galletto 107
Osteria dell'Angelo 148
Osteria dell'Ingegno 97
Osteria St Ana 117
Ostia Antica 7, **36–7**, 151
Ovid 57
Oviesse 130

P
package holidays 159
pajata 77
palaces and villas 50–51
Palatine Hill 18, 40, 119
Palatine Museum and Antiquarium 18
Palazzo Altemps 30–31, 84, 85
Palazzo & Galleria Spada 43

Palazzo Barberini 51, 133
Palazzo Borghese 50, 93, 94
Palazzo Braschi 86
Palazzo Chigi 154
Palazzo Colonna 112
Palazzo Corsini 62, 142
Palazzo dei Conservatori 26–7, 99, 119
Palazzo della Cancelleria 51, 101, 104
Palazzo della Sapienza 83
Palazzo del Quirinale 132, 134, 135
Palazzo di Montecitorio 94
Palazzo Farnese 50, 51, 101, 104
Palazzo Madama 85
Palazzo Massimo alle Colonne 50, 82, 85
Palazzo Massimo alle Terme 28–9, 127
Palazzo Nuovo 24–5, 50
Palazzo Pamphilj 86
Palazzo Senatorio 50, 98, 99
Palazzo Spada 51, 104
Palazzo Venezia 47, 51, 104
Palazzo Zuccari 55
Palestrina 154
Palimpsest (Vidal) 57
Panattoni "L'Obitorio" 73
Pane & Company: Forno 95
pane e coperto 162
panini 162
panna cotta 162
Pantheon 6, **14–15**, 40, 93
Pantheon and environs 90–97
best of the rest 94
itinerary 93
map 90
shops 95
things to avoid 165
top 10 sights 90–93
Pantheon (hotel) 172
Il Papiro 95
Parcheggio Borghese market 69
Parco dei Principi (hotel) 174
Parco della Resistenza dell'8 Settembre 63, 121
Parco Savello 60, 121
parking 161
Paschal II 44
Pascucci 96
Pasolini, Pier Paolo 59
Pasquino 84
Paul, St 151
Paul III 39, 50
Paul IV 100
Pauline Bonaparte (Canova) 21

payphones 168
Pentecost 67
La Pergola 149
personal security 169
Perugino 11
Giving the Keys to St Peter 10, 11
Peruzzi, Baldassare 15, 50, 84, 85, 86
Villa Farnesina 139
Peter, St 13, 23, 39, 52, 142, 153
Petronius 57
pharmacies 169
Piazza Augusto Imperatore 93
Piazza Barberini 47, 134, 135
Piazza Borghese 93
Piazza Cairoli 63
Piazza della Rotonda 93
Piazza del Popolo 46, 47, 108, 110, 111
Piazza di Montecitorio 94
Piazza di Pietra 93
Piazza di Sant'Ignazio 92–3, 93
Piazza di Spagna 68, 109, 111
Piazza Navona and environs 46, 82–9
antiques shops 87
chic cafés and bars 88
Christmas market 67
itinerary 85
map 82
places to eat 89
things to avoid 165
top 10 sights 82–5
Piazza of the Knights of Malta 120, 121
Piazza Pasquino 84
Piazza San Cosimato market 69
Piazza San Pietro 12, 46
Piazza Santa Maria in Trastevere 47
Piazza Sant'Eustachio 83, 85, 94
Piazza SS Apostoli 111
Piazza Testaccio market 69
Piazza Venezia 47
pickpockets 165, 169
picnicking 166
Pie' di Marmo 94
Pietà (Michelangelo) 12, 48
Pincio 60, 62, 63, 110

Pincio (cont.)
view from 53
Pinocchio (Frascati) 155
Pinturicchio 11
Adoration 33
Borgia Apartments 9
Piombo, Sebastiano del 139
Nativity of the Virgin 33
Piperno 75, 107
Piranesi, Giambattista 120
Piscina delle Rose 65
pizza à taglio 162
pizza rustica 162
PizzaRè 73
Pizzeria da Baffetto 72, 89
Pizzeria da Ivo 72, 148
Pizzeria da Ricci 72
Pizzeria dar Poeta 72, 73, 141, 148
Pizzeria da Vittorio 73, 148
Pizzeria La Montecarlo 73, 89
pizzerias 72–3
The Place 147
Plautus 57
Pliny the Younger 57
polizia (police) 169
pollo 162
Pollock, Jackson 43
Polvere in Tempo 143
Pomarancio, Niccolò 129
Pompeii 154
Pompey's Theatre 53
Ponte Rotto 142
Ponte Palatino 142
Ponte Sant'Angelo 138, 141
Pontelli, Baccio 84
popes 39
Porta, Giacomo della 47, 83, 101, 110
Porta del Popolo 112
Porta Portese market 69
Porta San Sebastiano 153
Portico d'Ottavia 104
Portrait of a Lady (James) 56
postal services 168
poste restante 168
Pozzo, Andrea 92
Prada 114
Prati
see Trastevere and Prati
prosciutto 162
Protestant Cemetery 121
public holidays 158
public telephones 168
pubs see bars and pubs

Punishment of the Rebels (Botticelli) 10
puppet shows 64–5
Pyramid of Caius Cestius 54 121

Q

Quattro Coronati market 69
Quirinal and Via Veneto 132–7
  la dolce vita venues 136
  itinerary 135
  map 132
  places to eat 137
  top 10 sights 132–5

R

R & Co 136
Raconti Romani (Moravia) 56
RADAR 167
Radio Londra 124
Raguzzini, Francesco 92
Rape of Persephone (Bernini) 20
Rape of the Sabines (Cortona) 27
Raphael 42, 50
  Chigi Chapel (Santa Maria del Popolo) 32
  Deposition 21
  Galatea 139
  Raphael Rooms (Vatican City) 8
  School of Athens 8, 48
  Sibyls 84
  tomb 15
  Transfiguration 9, 48
Raphael (hotel) 171
Red Wall (St Peter's) 13
Regina Baglioni 135, 170
religious festivals 67
religious objects, buying 164
Remainders 115
Reni, Guido 94
renting rooms 163, 177
Residence Babuino 177
Residence in Trastevere 177
Residence Palazzo al Velabro 177
Residence Ripetta 177
Residence Vittoria 177
residences 163, 177
La Residenza 171
Residenza Farnese 177
restaurants & other places to eat
  Ancient Rome 125
  around Piazza Navona 89
  around the Pantheon 97
  best cafés and *gelaterie* 70–71

restaurants (cont.)
  best pizzerias 72–3
  best restaurants 74–5
  Beyond the City Walls 155
  Campo de' Fiori to the Capitoline 107
  cheap eats 166
  eating and drinking tips 162
  Esquiline & the Lateran 131
  guide to price ranges 89
  overcharging 169
  Quirinal & Via Veneto 137
  restaurant types 162
  Roman-Jewish restaurants 107
  Spanish Steps and Villa Borghese 117
  things to avoid 165
  Trastevere and Prati 148, 149
Rest on the Flight into Egypt (Caravaggio) 91
La Rinascente 68
riposo 158
risotto 162
Risen Christ (Michelangelo) 44
Ristorante l'Archeologia (Appian Way) 153, 155
Ristorante Boccondivino 97
Ristoro de' Cocci 125
Rock Castle Café 79, 106
Rodin, Auguste 43
Roma (Fellini) 58
Roma Camping 163
Roma Caput Mundi 146
Roma in Scooter 161
Romaeuropa festival 66
Roman emperors 41
Roman Forum 6, **16–17**, 40, 119
Roman Holiday 59
A Roman Holiday (James) 56
La Romana (Moravia) 56
Romano, Giulio 86, 133
romantic spots 60–61
rombo 162
Rome, Open City (Rossellini) 59
Rome's Birthday festival 66
Romulus and Remus 38, 118, 120
Romulus Augustulus 41
Romulus's Iron-Age Huts 18
Rosselli 11
Rossellini, Roberto 59
Royal Association for Disability and Rehabilitation (RADAR) 167
Rubens, Peter Paul 42, 43, 82, 86

De Russie 170
Rutelli, Francesco 47
Rutelli, Mario 47

S

Sabatini 74, 149
Sabine women 38
sack of Rome 39
Sacred and Profane Love (Titian) 21
Sacro Cuore del Suffragio 54
Salome with the Head of John the Baptist (Titian) 91
saltimbocca 76
Salvi, Nicola 46, 109
San Carlo (hotel) 175
San Carlo alle Quattro Fontane 135
San Clemente 7, **34–5**, 44, 52, 127, 129
San Crisogno 141, 142
San Crispino 70, 111
San Domitilla catacombs 65
San Filippo Neri 62
San Francesco a Ripa 140–41
Sangallo, Antonio da, the Younger 50, 91
San Giovanni in Laterano 44, 126, 127, 129
  May Day concert 67
San Lorenzo in Lucina 94
San Luigi dei Francesi 45, 83, 85
San Marco (Tarquinia) 155
San Paolo fuori le Mura 45, 151
San Pietro in Montorio 141, 142
San Pietro in Vincoli 127–8
San Saba 120, 121
San Salvatore in Lauro 86
Sanctis, Francesco De 109
Sangallo, Francesco da
  tomb of Cardinal Cristoforo 32
Sansovino, Andrea
  Santa Maria del Popolo tombs 33
Sansovino, Jacopo 84
  Madonna del Parto 84
Sant'Agnese fuori le Mura 150, 153
Sant'Agnese in Agone 86
Sant'Agostino 84, 85
Santa Cecilia in Trastevere 139, 140, 141
Santa Chiara 172, 177
Santa Costanza 153
Santa Maria (hotel) 174
Santa Maria degli Angeli 133

Santa Maria dei Miracoli 112
Santa Maria del Popolo 7, **32–3**,
108, 109, 111
Santa Maria dell'Anima 86
Santa Maria della Pace 84
Santa Maria della Scala 142
Santa Maria della Vittoria 133
Santa Maria in Aracoeli 100
Santa Maria in Campitelli 101, 104
Santa Maria in Cosmedin
99–100
Santa Maria in Montesanto
111, 112
Santa Maria in Trastevere 45,
138, 139, 141
Santa Maria in Via Lata 93, 94
Santa Maria Maddalena 94
Santa Maria Maggiore 44, 127,
129
Madonna della Neve festival
67
Santa Maria sopra Minerva 44,
91, 93
Sant'Andrea al Quirinale 134–5
Sant'Andrea della Valle 45, 99,
101
Sant'Anna (hotel) 175
Sant'Antonio dei Portoghesi 86
Santa Prassede 126, 128, 129
Santa Prisca (hotel) 175
Santa Sabina 119, 121
San Teodoro 121
Santi Giovanni e Paolo 126, 129
Sant'Ignazio di Loyola 92, 93
Sant'Ivo 83, 85
Santi Quattro Coronati 129
Santissimi Apostoli 112
Santo Stefano Rotondo 128–9
Sapienza 85
Sapori del Lord Byron 74
Sardi, Giuseppe 94
Satiricon (Petronius) 57
La Scala 137
Scala Santa 127
Scalinata della Trinità dei Monti
see Spanish Steps
Scalinata di Spagna (hotel) 173
School of Athens (Raphael) 48
Sciam (nightspot) 106
Sciam (shop) 105
scooter rental 161
Scylla (Sperlonga) 155
security, personal 169
self-catering apartments 163
Self-Portrait as a Sick Bacchus
(Caravaggio) 21
Seme e la Foglia 125
senior citizen discounts 167

Septimius Severus 41
Septizonium 44
Da Sergio alle Grotte 107
service charges 162
Settimo all'Arancio 97
Seutonius 57
Seven Hills camping 163
Shaki 116
Shanti 106
Shelley, Percy Bysshe 57
grave 112
Keats-Shelley Memorial 109
shopping
around the Pantheon 95
best shopping streets 68–9
Campo de' Fiori to the
Capitoline 105
markets 69
on a budget 166
opening hours 164
Spanish Steps and Villa
Borghese 113–115
tips 164
Trastevere and Prati 143
La Sibilla (Tivoli) 155
Sica, Vittorio de 59
Signorelli, Luca 11
*Moses Giving his Rod to
Joshua* 10
Sistine Chapel 8, 10–11, 48, 139
Sixtus IV 11, 24, 84
Sixtus V 46, 127
Smeraldo 175
Sodoma, Giovanni Antonio
Bazzi
*Wedding Night of Alexander
the Great* 139
sogliola 162
Sole al Pantheon (hotel) 173
Sora Lella 149
Sora Margherita 107
spaghetti alla carbonara 76,
162
Spanish Steps 109, 111
view from 53
Spanish Steps & Villa Borghese
108–117
art and antiques shops 113
best of the rest 112
discount and specialist
shops 115
high fashion boutiques 114
itinerary 111
map 108
places to eat 117
pubs, cafés and bars 116
top 10 sights 108–111
speed limits 161

Sperlonga 154
Spring Festival 67
Square Colosseum (EUR) 150,
151
squares and fountains 46–7
SS Ambrogio e Carlo al Corso
112
Stadio dei Marmi 152–3
Stadium (Palatine Hill) 18
Stairs Club 147
Standa 68
Stardust 79, 147
statue parlante 84
St Anselmo and Villa San Pio
(hotel) 171
St Catherine of Siena 44, 91
St Jerome (Leonardo da Vinci)
49
stock houses 164
Stock Market 143
St Peter's Basilica **12–13**, 44,
53, 65, 139
straciatella 162
St Regis Grand (hotel) 170
student discounts 167
study holidays 159
Synagogue 104

T
Taberna de' Gracchi 149
Tacitus 57
talking statues 84
La Tana dei Noantri 148
tartufo 162
Taverna del Campo 106
La Taverna del Ghetto 107
tavola calda 162
taxes, sales 164
taxi, travelling by 161, 169
La Tazza d'Oro 14, 71, 96
Teatro Argentina 99
Teatro di Pompeo (hotel) 173
Teatropace 33 (hotel) 172
Tebro 115
telephones 168
television 158
Temple of Antoninus and
Faustina 17
Temple of Castor and Pollux 17
Temple of Cybele 18
Temple of Karnak 55
Temple of Saturn 17
Temple of Vespasian 17
Temple of Vesta 16
Termini station 160
Terra di Siena 89

Testaccio see Ancient Rome
Testaccio Village festival 66
Theatre of Marcellus 41, 101
Theatre of Pompey 99, 101
Thé Verde 116
things to avoid 165
Three Coins in a Fountain 109
Tiber Island 142
tipping 161, 162
tiramisù 162
Titian 42
    Sacred and Profane Love
    21
    Salome with the Head of the
    Baptist 91
Titus, Emperor 22
Tivoli 154
Torre della Scimmia 86
Tosca (Puccini) 45
tours 159
train travel 160
Trajan 41
Trajan's Column 23
Trajan's Forum 23
Trajan's Markets 22
Transfiguration (Raphael) 9,
48
Trastevere (hotel/apartments)
175, 177
Trastevere and Prati 138–49
    best of the rest 142
    cheap eats 148
    fine dining 149
    live music venues 147
    locals' favourite shops 143
    map 138
    top 10 sights 138–41
Trattoria Monti 131
travel and transport 160–61
    discounts 166
travellers' cheques 168
Tre Archi 89
Tre Scalini 28, 61, 70, 85, 88
Treno e Scooter 161
Trevi Fountain 61, 46, 109,
111
Tridente 108
Trimani 137
Trinità dei Monti 110
Trinity College 78, 96
Triton Fountain 47
Tritone 172
Torre Ercolana 77
tourist information offices
158
tours and package holidays
159
Twain, Mark 57

U
Umberto I, tomb of 15
underground sights 52–3
UPIM 130
Urban VIII 47, 51
"Urbi et Orbi" Christmas
blessing 67

V
Valadier, Giuseppe 46, 60, 110,
111
Valentino 114
van Dyck 42
van Gogh, Vincent 43
Vasari, Giorgio 51
VAT 164
Vatican City 6, 8–13, 139
Vatican Gardens 140
Vatican Grottoes 52
Vatican Museums 9, 42
    free admission 166
    things to avoid 165
Vecchia Roma 107
Velázquez 42
Vercingetorix 52
Vertecchi 115
Vespasian 41
Via Appia Antica see Appian
    Way
Via Bocca di Leone 69
Via Borgognona 68
Via Cavour 16
Via Cola di Rienzo 68, 138
Via dei Condotti 68, 111
Via dei Coronari 68, 82, 85
Via dei Giubbonari 69
Via dei Santi Quattro Coronati
    market 129
Via del Babuino 68
Via del Corso 68
Via della Pace 82
Via Giulia 104
Via Mamiani market 69, 130
Via Margutta 69
Via Nazionale 69
Via Sacra 17
Via Sannio market 69, 130
Via Trionfale market 69
Via Veneto 132, 134, 135 see
    also Quirinal and Via Veneto
Viale delle Milizie 138
Viale Giulio Cesare 138
Victoria (hotel) 173
The Victoria House Pub 116
Vidal, Gore 57
Vignola, Giacomo 51
Villa Ada 63
Villa Aldobrandini 154

Villa Borghese 20, 60, 62, 64,
110
Villa Celimontana Jazz 67
Villa d'Este 154
Villa Doria Pamphilj 62, 142
Villa Farnesina 50, 139, 141
Villa Giulia 42, 43, 50, 110, 112
Villa Medici 110
Villa Mellini, view from 53
Villa Sciarra 62, 65
Villa Torlonia 54
Villaggio Globale 124
villas and palaces 50–51
La Villetta dal 1940 (Piramide)
155
La Vineria 79, 106
Virgin and Child (d'Arpino) 142
visa requirements 158
Visconti, Luchino 59
Visit of the Seven Churches 62
Vistas 53
vitello 162
Viterbo 154
Il Vittoriano 53, 104
Vittorio Bagagli 95
Vittorio Emanuele II 15, 39, 104
Vittorio Emanuele III 63
Virgil 57
Volpetti 121, 125

W
walking in the city 161
    walking tours 159
water 162, 169
weather 158
websites 158
Wedding Night of Alexander
    the Great (Sodoma) 139
Westin Excelsior 170
what to pack 158
when to go 158
White Night Festival 67
wine 77, 162, 164
women travellers 167
writers in Rome 56–7

Y
Yotvata 107
Young St John the Baptist
    (Caravaggio) 26, 91
youth hostels 163

Z
Zi Fenizia 107
Zio Ciro 89
Zoo (Bioparco) 64
Zuccari, Federico and Taddeo
55

Acknowledgments

Main Contributors

Reid Bramblett is an American writer who has lived in Rome, on and off, since childhood. He has contributed to more than half a dozen guidebooks on Italy, and is also the author of *Eyewitness Top 10 Travel Guide to Tuscany*.

Jeffrey Kennedy is American by birth, but has lived in Rome for almost 18 years. A graduate of Stanford University, he divides his time between producing, writing and acting. Most recently he has been scripting and producing museum guides in Italy and has featured on the Discovery Channel's *Must See Rome* programme.

Produced by Sargasso Media Ltd, London

Project Editor Zoë Ross
Designer Stephen Woosnam-Savage
Picture Research Monica Allende
Proofreader Stewart J Wild
Editorial Assistance Mark Livesey

Main Photographer Demetrio Carrasco

Additional Photography Max Alexander, Foto Carfagna & Associati, Guiseppe Carfagna, John Heseltine, Mike Dunning, Kim Sayer
Illustrator Chris Orr & Associates

For Dorling Kindersley
Senior Art Editor Marisa Renzullo
Senior Publishing Manager Louise Lang
Publishing Managers Kate Poole, Helen Townsend
Art Director Gillian Allan

Cartography Co-ordinator Casper Morris
DTP Jason Little
Production Joanna Bull, Marie Ingledew
Revisions Editors Michelle Crane, Anna Freiberger, Gerard Hutching, Ellie Smith
Design & Editorial Assistance Beverley Ager, Rachel Barber, Nicola Erdpresser, Leonie Loudon, Marianne Petrou, Pete Quinlan, Ellen Root

Maps Dominic Beddow, Simonetta Giori (Draughtsman Ltd)

Special Assistance

The authors would like to thank the following for their assistance: Rob Allyn, Giulia Bernardini, Gianluca Borghese, Jeff Burden, Jolie Chain, Diletta Donati, Elizabeth Geoghegan, Suzanne Hartley, Hanja Kochansky, Clark Lawrence, Adrian McCourt, Roberta Mencucci, Odile Morin, Ruth Morss, Maria Giovanna Musso, Frances Nacman, Claudio Nigro, Elaine O'Reilly, Rachel Potts, Aloma Valentini, Lila Yawn

Picture Credits

t-top; tc-top centre; tr-top right; cla-centre left above; ca-centre above; cra-centre right above; cl-centre left; c-centre; cr-centre right; clb-centre left below; cb-centre below; crb-centre right below; bl-below left; bc-below centre; br-below right.

Every effort has been made to trace the copyright holders, and we apologize in advance for any unintentional omissions. We would be pleased to insert the appropriate acknowledgements in any subsequent edition of this publication.

The publishers would like to thank the following individuals, companies, and picture libraries for permission to reproduce their photographs:

AFP, London: 66b; AISA, Barcelona: 6tr, 8-9c, 9t; AKG, London: 28b, 38tl, 38tr, 39t, 41r, 48tl, 56c, 57r, 58tl, 58tr, 112tl, "*The Creation of Adam*" by Michelangelo Buonarroti 10tl, "*Ezekiel*" by Michelangelo Buonarroti 10tr, "*The Fall from Grace*" by Michelangelo Buonarroti 11c, "*The Life of Moses*" by Sandro Botticelli 11b, "*The School of Athens*" by Raphael 48b, Hilbich 7br, 36-37c, Erich Lessing 19ca, 30b, 31c, 38b, 39r, "*Appointment of St Matthew*" by Caravaggio 49t, Jean-Louis Nou 31b; ALEX-ANDERPLATZ 147tr; THE ART ARCHIVE: Museo Capitolino Rome/Dagli Orti 24c.

BABINGTON'S ENGLISH TEA ROOM: 116tl, 116tr; BRIDGEMAN ART LIBRARY: 56tl, Galleria Borghese "*Sacred and Profane Love*" 1515 6b, 21b, "*Apollo and Daphne*" by Bernini 20b, Pinacoteca Capitolina Palazzo Conservatori "*The Fortune Teller*"

by Caravaggio 27t, Library of Congress 56tr, Keats-Shelley Memorial House Rome 57bl, Palazzo Massimo alle Terme 29cr, 30tr, Santa Maria del Popolo "*The Crucifixion of St Peter*" by Caravaggio 32b, Spirito Santo Prato 67r.

CORBIS: 25ca, 89-81c.

IL DAGHERROTIPO, Rome: Giovanni Rinaldi 66tl, 67c; 165tr; Marco Ravasini 130tl.

JACKIE GORDON: 169tl.

HEMISPHERE IMAGES: Jean du Boisberranger 68tl; HOSTELS ALESSANDRO 176tr.

MARKA, Milan: Roberto Benzi 168tc.

LIBRERIA BABELE: Gioris Guerrini 105tl; LIBRERIA RINASCITA: 105tr.

PA PHOTOS: Epa/Ansa/Luciano del Castillo 66tr.

SCALA: 7ca, 19b, 20ca, 21t, 21c, 28c, 28-29c, 29t, 29ca, 29b, 30tl, 36t, 36cl, 36b, 37t.

All other images are © DK. For further information see www.dkimages.com

Special Editions of DK Travel Guides

DK Travel Guides can be purchased in bulk quantities at discounted prices for use in promotions or as premiums. We are also able to offer special editions and personalized jackets, corporate imprints, and excerpts from all of our books, tailored specifically to meet your own needs.

To find out more, please contact:

(in the United States)

SpecialSales@dk.com

(in the UK) **Sarah.Burgess@dk.com**

(in Canada) DK Special Sales at **general@tourmaline.ca**

(in Australia) **business.development @pearson.com.au**

Phrase Book

In an Emergency

Help!	**Aiuto!**	eye-yoo-toh
Stop!	**Fermate!**	fair-mah-teh
Call a doctor.	**Chiama un medico**	kee-ah-mah oon meh-dee-koh
Call an ambulance.	**Chiama un' ambulanza**	kee-ah-mah oon am-boo-lan-tsa
Call the police.	**Chiama la polizia**	kee-ah-mah lah pol-ee-tsee-ah
Call the fire brigade.	**Chiama i pompieri**	kee-ah-mah ee pom-pee-air-ee

Communication Essentials

Yes/No	**Sì/No**	see/noh
Please	**Per favore**	pair fah-vor-eh
Thank you	**Grazie**	grah-tsee-eh
Excuse me	**Mi scusi**	mee skoo-zee
Hello	**Buon giorno**	bwon jor-noh
Goodbye	**Arrivederci**	ah-ree-veh-dair-chee
Good evening	**Buona sera**	bwon-ah sair-ah
What?	**Quale?**	kwah-leh?
When?	**Quando?**	kwan-doh?
Why?	**Perchè?**	pair-keh?
Where?	**Dove?**	doh-veh?

Useful Phrases

How are you?	**Come sta?**	koh-meh stah?
Very well, thank you.	**Molto bene, grazie.**	moll-toh beh-neh grah-tsee-eh
Pleased to meet you.	**Piacere di conoscerla.**	pee-ah-chair-eh dee-coh-noh-shair-lah
That's fine.	**Va bene.**	va beh-neh
Where is/are...?	**Dov'è/ Dove sono...?**	dov-eh/doveh soh-noh?
How do I get to...?	**Come faccio per arrivare a...?**	koh-meh fah-choh pair arri-var-eh ah...?
Do you speak English?	**Parla inglese?**	par-lah een-gleh-zeh?
I don't understand.	**Non capisco.**	non ka-pee-skoh
I'm sorry.	**Mi dispiace.**	mee dee-spee-ah-cheh

Shopping

How much does this cost?	**Quant'è, per favore?**	kwan-teh pair fah-vor-eh?
I would like...	**Vorrei...**	vor-ray
Do you have...?	**Avete...?**	ah-veh-teh... ?
Do you take credit cards?	**Accettate carte di credito?**	ah-chet-tah-teh kar-teh dee creh-dee-toh?
What time do you open/close?	**A che ora apre/ chiude?**	ah keh or-ah ah-preh/ oo-deh?
this one	**questo**	kweh-stoh
that one	**quello**	kwell-oh
expensive	**caro**	kar-oh
cheap	**a buon prezzo**	ah bwon pret-soh
size, clothes	**la taglia**	lah tah-lee-ah
size, shoes	**il numero**	eel noo-mair-oh
white	**bianco**	bee-ang-koh
black	**nero**	neh-roh
red	**rosso**	ross-oh
yellow	**giallo**	jal-loh
green	**verde**	vair-deh
blue	**blu**	bloo

Types of Shop

bakery	**il forno /il panificio**	eel forn-oh /eel pan-ee-fee-choh
bank	**la banca**	lah bang-kah
bookshop	**la libreria**	lah lee-breh-ree-ah
cake shop	**la pasticceria**	lah pas-tee-chair-ee-ah
chemist	**la farmacia**	lah far-mah-chee-ah
delicatessen	**la salumeria**	lah sah-loo-meh-ree-ah
department store	**il grande magazzino**	eel gran-deh mag-gad-zee-noh
grocery	**alimentari**	ah-lee-men-tah-ree
hairdresser	**il parrucchiere**	eel par-oo-kee-air-eh
ice cream parlour	**la gelateria**	lah jel-lah-tair-ree-ah
market	**il mercato**	eel mair-kah-toh
newsstand	**l'edicola**	leh-dee-koh-lah
post office	**l'ufficio postale**	loo-fee-choh pos-tah-leh
supermarket	**il supermercato**	eel su-pair-mair-kah-toh
tobacconist	**il tabaccaio**	eel tah-bak-eye-oh
travel agency	**l'agenzia di viaggi**	lah-jen-tsee-ah dee vee-ad-jee

Sightseeing

art gallery	**la pinacoteca**	lah peena-koh-teh-kah
bus stop	**la fermata dell'autobus**	lah fair-mah-tah dell ow-toh-booss
church	**la chiesa la basilica**	lah kee-eh-zahy lah bah-seel-i-kah
closed for holidays	**chiuso per le ferie**	kee-oo-zoh pair leh fair-ee-eh
garden	**il giardino**	eel jar-dee-no
museum	**il museo**	eel moo-zeh-oh
railway station	**la stazione**	lah stah-tsee-oh-neh
tourist information	**l'ufficio di turismo**	loo-fee-choh dee too-ree-smoh

Staying in a Hotel

Do you have any vacant rooms?	**Avete camere libere?**	ah-veh-teh kah-mair-eh lee-bair-eh?
double room	**una camera doppia**	oona kah-mair-ah doh-pee-ah
with double bed	**con letto matrimoniale**	kon let-toh mah-tree-moh-nee-ah-leh
twin room	**una camera con due letti**	oona kah-mair-ah kon doo-eh let-tee
single room	**una camera singola**	oona kah-mair-ah sing-goh-lah
room with a bath, shower	**una camera con bagno, con doccia**	oona kah-mair-ah kon ban-yoh, kon dot-chah
I have a reservation.	**Ho fatto una prenotazione.**	oh fat-toh oona preh-noh-tah-tsee-oh-neh

Eating Out

Have you got a table for...?	**Avete una tavola per...?**	ah-veh-teh oona tah-voh-lah pair...?
I'd like to reserve a table.	**Vorrei riservare una tavola.**	vor-ray ree-sair-vah-reh oona tah-voh-lah
breakfast	**colazione**	koh-lah-tsee-oh-neh
lunch	**pranzo**	pran-tsoh
dinner	**cena**	cheh-nah
the bill	**il conto**	eel kon-toh
waitress	**cameriera**	kah-mair-ee-air-ah
waiter	**cameriere**	kah-mair-ee-air-eh
fixed price	**il menù a**	eel meh-noo ah
menu	**prezzo fisso**	pret-soh fee-soh
dish of the day	**piatto del giorno**	pee-ah-toh dell jor-no
starter	**antipasto**	an-tee-pass-toh
first course	**il primo**	eel pree-moh
main course	**il secondo**	eel seh-kon-doh
vegetables	**contorni**	eel kon-tor-noh
dessert	**il dolce**	eel doll-cheh
cover charge	**il coperto**	eel koh-pair-toh
wine list	**la lista dei vini**	lah lee-stah day vee-nee
glass	**il bicchiere**	eel bee-kee-air-eh
bottle	**la bottiglia**	lah bot-teel-yah
knife	**il coltello**	eel kol-tell-oh
fork	**la forchetta**	lah for-ket-tah
spoon	**il cucchiaio**	eel koo-kee-eye-oh

Menu Decoder

l'acqua minerale gassata/ naturale	lah-kwah mee-nair-ah-leh gah-zah-tah/ nah-too-rah-leh	mineral water fizzy/still
agnello	ah-niell-oh	lamb
aglio	al-ee-oh	garlic
al forno	al for-noh	baked
alla griglia	ah-lah greel-yah	grilled
la birra	lah beer-rah	beer
la bistecca	lah bee-stek-keh	steak
il burro	eel boor-oh	butter
il caffè	eel kah-feh	coffee
la carne	la kar-neh	meat
carne di maiale	kar-neh dee mah-yah-leh	pork
la cipolla	la chip-oh-lah	onion
i fagioli	ee fah-joh-lee	beans
il formaggio	eel for-mad-joh	cheese
le fragole	leh frah-goh-leh	strawberries
il fritto misto	eel free-toh mees-toh	mixed fried dish
la frutta	la froot-tah	fruit
frutti di mare	froo-tee dee mah-reh	seafood
i funghi	ee foon-ghee	mushrooms
i gamberi	ee gam-bair-ee	prawns
il gelato	eel jel-lah-toh	ice cream
l'insalata	leen-sah-lah-tah	salad
il latte	eel laht-teh	milk
il manzo	eel man-tsoh	beef
l'olio	loh-lee-oh	oil
il pane	eel pah-neh	bread
le patate	leh pah-tah-teh	potatoes
le patatine	leh pah-tah-teen-eh	chips

fritte	free-teh	chips
il pepe	eel peh-peh	pepper
il pesce	eel pesh-eh	fish
il pollo	eel poll-oh	chicken
il pomodoro	eel poh-moh-dor-oh	tomato
il prosciutto cotto/crudo	eel pro-shoo-toh kot-toh/kroo-doh	ham cooked/cured
il riso	eel ree-zoh	rice
il sale	eel sah-leh	salt
la salsiccia	lah sal-see-chah	sausage
succo d'arancia/ di limone	soo-koh dah-ran-chah/ dee lee-moh-neh	orange/lemon juice
il tè	eel teh	tea
la torta	lah tor-tah	cake/tart
l'uovo	loo-oh-voh	egg
vino bianco	vee-noh bee-ang-koh	white wine
vino rosso	vee-noh ross-oh	red wine
le vongole	leh von-goh-leh	clams
lo zucchero	loh zoo-kair-oh	sugar
la zuppa	lah tsoo-pah	soup

Numbers

1	**uno**	oo-noh
2	**due**	doo-eh
3	**tre**	treh
4	**quattro**	kwat-roh
5	**cinque**	ching-kweh
6	**sei**	say-ee
7	**sette**	set-teh
8	**otto**	ot-toh
9	**nove**	noh-veh
10	**dieci**	dee-eh-chee
11	**undici**	oon-dee-chee
12	**dodici**	doh-dee-chee
13	**tredici**	tray-dee-chee
14	**quattordici**	kwat-tor-dee-chee
15	**quindici**	kwin-dee-chee
16	**sedici**	say-dee-chee
17	**diciassette**	dee-chah-set-teh
18	**diciotto**	dee-chot-toh
19	**diciannove**	dee-chah-noh-veh
20	**venti**	ven-tee
30	**trenta**	tren-tah
40	**quaranta**	kwah-ran-tah
50	**cinquanta**	ching-kwan-tah
60	**sessanta**	sess-an-tah
70	**settanta**	set-tan-tah
80	**ottanta**	ot-tan-tah
90	**novanta**	noh-van-tah
100	**cento**	chen-toh
1,000	**mille**	mee-leh
2,000	**duemila**	doo-eh mee-lah
1,000,000	**un milione**	oon meel-yoh-neh

Time

one minute	**un minuto**	oon mee-noo-toh
one hour	**un'ora**	oon or-ah
a day	**un giorno**	oon jor-noh
Monday	**lunedì**	loo-neh-dee
Tuesday	**martedì**	mar-teh-dee
Wednesday	**mercoledì**	mair-koh-leh-dee
Thursday	**giovedì**	joh-veh-dee
Friday	**venerdì**	ven-air-dee
Saturday	**sabato**	sah-bah-toh
Sunday	**domenica**	doh-meh-nee-kah

Street Index

Alberto, Via Carlo F3
Alessandrina, Via P4
Angelico, Viale B1
Appia Nuova, Via G5
Arenula, Largo M4
Arenula, Via L5
Arnaldo da Brescia, Lungot. C1
Augusta, Lungotevere in D2
Aurelia Antica, Via A4
Aurelia, Via A3
Aventino, Lungotevere D5
Aventino, Via E5
Babuino, Via del D2
Banchi Nuovi, Via dei J2
Banchi Vecchi, Via dei J3
Banco Santo Spirito, Via del J2
Barberini, Piazza Q1
Barberini, Via Q1
Barletta, Via B2
Belle Arti, Viale delle D1
Biscione, Piazza del L4
Bocca della Verità, Piazza N6
Bologna, Vicolo del K6
Borghese, Piazza M1
Botteghe Oscure, Via delle M4
Britannia, Via G6
Cairoli, Piazza Benedetto L5
Campidoglio, Piazza del P5
Campitelli, Piazza N5
Campo Marzio, Via di M2
Cancelleria, Piazza della L4
Capo di Ferro, Via L4
Cappellari, Via dei K4
Capranica, Piazza M2
Castello, Lungotevere K1
Cavalieri di Malta, Piazza dei D5
Cavour, Piazza C2
Cavour, Via R4
Cenci, Lungotevere dei M5
Cenci, Piazza M5
Cerchi, Via dei D5
Cernaia, Via F2
Cesare, Viale Giulio B2
Cestari, Via dei M3
Chiavari, Via L4
Chiesa Nuova, Piazza della K3
Cinque Lune, Piazza delle L2
Cinque, Vicolo del K6
Circo Massimo, Via del D5
Claudia, Via E5
Clementino, Via di M1
Cola di Rienzo, Via C2
Collegio Romano, Via del N3
Colonna, Piazza N2
Colosseo, Piazza del R6
Conciliazione, Via della B3
Condotti, Via dei D2
Consolazione, Piazza della N6
Coppelle, Piazza M2
Coppelle, Via M2
Coronari, Via dei K2
Corso, Via del N3
Crescenzi, Salita de M3
Crescenzio, Via C2
Crispi, Via Francesco P1
Croce, Via della D2
Depretis, Via Agostino E3
Doria, Via Andrea A2
Due Macelli, Via P1
Farnese, Piazza K4
Farnesi, Via dei K4
Farnesina, Lungotevere della J4
Filiberto, Via Emanuele F4

Fiori, Campo de' L4
Firenze, Piazza M1
Flaminia, Via C1
Florida, Via M4
Fontanella Borghese, Via M1
Fori Imperiali, Via dei P4
Fossa, Via della K3
Galvani, Via D6
Gambero, Via del N1
Garibaldi, Piazza Giuseppe B4
Garibaldi, Via Giuseppe C4
Gesù, Piazza del M4
Gesù, Via del M3
Giolitti, Via Giovanni F3
Giubbonari, Via dei L4
Giulia, Via J3
Governo Vecchio, Via del K3
Grotte, Vicolo delle L4
Italia, Corso d' E2
IV Novembre, Via P3
Lanza, Via Giovanni E4
Leone IV, Via B2
Librari, Largo dei L4
Luce, Via della M6
Lungara, Via della J5
Lungaretta, Via della K6
Maddalena, Via della M2
Magnanapoli, Largo Q4
Manara, Luciano Via C5
Margutta, Via D2
Mario de' Fiori, Via D2
Marmorata, Via D5
Marzio, Lungotevere L1
Mattei, Piazza M5
Mazzini, Viale Giuseppe C1
Merulana, Via F4
Minerva, Piazza della M3
Monserrato, Via K4
Monte Brianzo, Via di L1
Monte dei Cenci, Via M5
Monte di Pietà, Piazza del L4
Monte Testaccio, Via D6
Montecitorio, Piazza di M2
Moro, Via del K6
Muratte, Via delle N2
Muro Torto, Viale del D2
Navicella, Via della E5
Navona, Piazza L2
Nazionale, Via Q3
Nicola, Viale E. de F3
Oratorio, Piazza d' N2
Orfani, Via d' M2
Orlando, Via V. Emanuele E3
Ostiense, Via D6
Ottaviano, Via B2
Pace, Via della K3
Panetteria, Via della P2
Panisperna, Via Q4
Paradiso, Piazza del L4
Parlamento, Piazza del M1
Parlamento, Via del M1
Pastini, Via dei M2
Pellegrino, Via del K3
Piave, Via F2
Piemonte, Via E2
Pigna, Piazza della M3
Pilotta, Piazza della P3
Pilotta, Via della P3
Pinciana, Via E1
Pio XII, Piazza B3
Pio, Borgo B3
Piramide Cestia, Via della D6
Plebiscito, Via del N4

Polo, Viale Marco D6
Popolo, Piazza del D2
Porta Angelica, Via di B2
Porta Cavalleggeri, Via B3
Porta Maggiore, Via G4
Portico d'Ottavia, Via M5
Portuense, Via C6
Prati, Lungotevere L1
Pretorio, Viale Castro F2
Quattro Fontane, Via delle Q1
Quirinale, Piazza del P2
Quirinale, Via del Q2
Renzi, Piazza de' K6
Repubblica, Piazza della E3
Rinascimento, Corso del L3
Ripa, Lungotevere D5
Ripetta, Via di D2
Risorgimento, Piazza del B2
Rotonda, Piazza della M3
Rotonda, Via delle M3
San Cosimato, Piazza C5
San Francesco a Ripa, Via C5
San G. in Laterano, Via di F5
San Gregorio, Via di E5
San Lorenzo in Lucina, Pza. M1
San Marco, Piazza N4
San Pancrazio, Via di B5
San Pietro in Vincoli, Piazza R5
San Pietro, Piazza B3
San Salvatore in Lauro, Pza. K2
San Silvestro, Piazza N1
Sangallo, Lungotevere del J3
Sannio, Via F5
Sant' Apollinare, Piazza L2
Sant' Agostino, Via di L2
Sant' Eustachio, Piazza M3
Sant' Ignazio, Piazza di N3
Sant' Ignazio, Via N3
Santa Dorotea, Via di K5
Santa Maria dell' Anima, V. di L3
Santa Maria in Trastevere, Pza. K6
Santa Sabina, Via di D5
Santi Apostoli, Via N3
Santo Spirito, Borgo B3
Sanzio, Lungotevere Raffaello L6
Savoia, Via Ludovico di D2
Scala, Via della K6
Scrofa, Via della L1
Sistina, Via Q1
Solferino, Via F3
Spagna, Piazza di D2
Spezia, Via la G5
Stamperia, Via della P2
Teatro di Marcello, Via del N4
Terme di Caracalla, Via delle E5
Testaccio, Lungotevere C6
Tiburtina, Via G3
Tor di Nona, Lungotevere K2
Tor Sanguigna, Piazza di L2
Torre Argentina, Largo di M4
Torre Argentina, Via di M3
Trastevere, Viale di C5
Trevi, Piazza di P2
Tritone, Via del P1
Vaticano, Lungotevere J1
Veneto, Via Vittorio E2
Venezia, Piazza N4
Vidoni, Piazza L4
Villa Pamphilj, Viale di B5
Vittorio Emanuele II, Corso J2
XX Settembre, Via R1
XXIV Maggio, Via Q3
Zanardelli, Via L2